ADVANCE PRAISE FOR

Learning Relations

"Alexander M. Sidorkin has given us an innovative and interesting approach to relational pedagogy. This book is important, useful, and fun to read."

Nel Noddings, Lee Jacks Professor of Education Emerita,
Stanford University

"With a richness of palette reminiscent of John Dewey, Alexander M. Sidorkin presents a refreshingly accessible, grounded picture of why and how human relations (student-student, as well as teacher-student) must be taken seriously in schools and beyond. Arguing that notions of school reform need themselves to be reformed, Sidorkin helps us understand the importance of restoring adult authority in schools without reinstating cruel, exclusionary practices. Sidorkin's proposal calls for courage: we need no less than to confront the evil in others *and in ourselves*. *Learning Relations*, a seminal work, is a must-read for teachers, scholars, policymakers, and others who care deeply about schools, society, and human formation."

Donna H. Kerr, Professor and Chair in Educational Leadership & Policy Studies,
College of Education, University of Washington

Learning Relations

Studies in the
Postmodern Theory of Education

Joe L. Kincheloe and Shirley R. Steinberg
General Editors

Vol. 173

PETER LANG
New York • Washington, D.C./Baltimore • Bern
Frankfurt am Main • Berlin • Brussels • Vienna • Oxford

Alexander M. Sidorkin

Learning Relations

Impure Education, Deschooled Schools,
& Dialogue with Evil

PETER LANG
New York • Washington, D.C./Baltimore • Bern
Frankfurt am Main • Berlin • Brussels • Vienna • Oxford

Library of Congress Cataloging-in-Publication Data

Sidorkin, Alexander M.
Learning relations: impure education, deschooled schools,
and dialogue with evil / Alexander M. Sidorkin.
p. cm. — (Counterpoints; v. 173)
Includes bibliographical references and index.
1. Education—Philosophy. 2. Postmodernism
and education. 3. Teacher-student relationship. I. Title.
II. Counterpoints (New York, N.Y.); v. 173.
LB14.7 .S535 370'.1—dc21   2002023804
ISBN 0-8204-5179-7
ISSN 1058-1634

Die Deutsche Bibliothek-CIP-Einheitsaufnahme

Sidorkin, Alexander M.:
Learning relations: impure education, deschooled schools,
and dialogue with evil / Alexander M. Sidorkin.
—New York; Washington, D.C./Baltimore; Bern;
Frankfurt am Main; Berlin; Brussels; Vienna; Oxford: Lang.
(Counterpoints; Vol. 173)
ISBN 0-8204-5179-7

Cover art by Svetlana Sidorkina
Cover design by Lisa Dillon

The paper in this book meets the guidelines for permanence and durability
of the Committee on Production Guidelines for Book Longevity
of the Council of Library Resources.

© 2002 Peter Lang Publishing, Inc., New York

All rights reserved.
Reprint or reproduction, even partially, in all forms such as microfilm,
xerography, microfiche, microcard, and offset strictly prohibited.

Printed in the United States of America

To Maria and Gleb

TABLE OF CONTENTS

Acknowledgments ix
Pedagogy of Relation: An Introduction 1
Part I. Critique of Pure Education 9

    Chapter 1.   The God of Useless Things: A Definition of Education 11
    Chapter 2.   Labor of Learning 26
    Chapter 3.   Learning to Be 42
    Chapter 4.   Crisis of Authority 53
    Chapter 5.   Education and Violence 62

Part II. The Educational Relation 77

    Chapter 6.   A Case for the Pedagogy of Relation 79
    Chapter 7.   Ontology, Anthropology, and Epistemology of Relation 91
    Chapter 8.   Between Eros and Athena: The Economy of Relations 103
    Chapter 9.   Relational Fields 116
    Chapter 10.   Deschooling Schools 127

Part III. Polyphony 137

    Chapter 11.   The Problem of Educational Authority 139
    Chapter 12.   On the Value of Double Messages 151
    Chapter 13.   Lyotard vs. Bakhtin 162
    Chapter 14.   Multiculturalism, Postmodernism, and Critical Theory 173
    Chapter 15.   Dialogue with Evil 185

Relation and Praxis: A Conclusion 197
Bibliography 199
Index 207

ACKNOWLEDGMENTS

The completion of this book was possible because of the generous support of the Spencer Foundation and the National Academy of Education. I am grateful to Nel Noddings for her encouragement, criticism, and generous help.

Parts of this book appeared in the following journals, whose editors, reviewers, and staff I thank for helping to develop my ideas:

Educational Theory, The Interchange, The Journal of Thought, Studies in Philosophy and Education, East/West Education, Philosophical Studies in Education, Journal of Philosophy of Education, Education and Society.*

---

*Alexander Sidorkin, "Toward a Pedagogy of Relation," *Philosophical Studies in Education* 32 (2000): 9-14. "Aesthetics and the Paradox of Educational Relation" (with Charles Bingham), *Journal of Philosophy of Education* 35, Issue 1 (2001): 21-30. "Labor of Learning," *Educational Theory* 51 (2001): 91-108. "Lyotard and Bakhtin: Engaged Diversity in Education," *The Interchange*, 33/1 (2002); 85-97. "Authoritarianism and Democracy in Soviet Schools: A Tale of John Dewey's Ideas and the Woman Who Brought Down the Berlin Wall," *East/West Education* 19 (1998-2000): 121-130. "Dialogue with Evil," *Journal of Thought* 34 (1999): 9-19. "The Fine Art of Sitting on Two Stools: Multicultural Education between Postmodernism and Critical Theory," *Studies in Philosophy and Education* 18 (1999): 143-155. "Redefinition of Plurality: On the Value of Double Messages," *Education and Society* 16 (1998): 99-104.

PEDAGOGY OF RELATION: AN INTRODUCTION

When I started to teach, one of my first unpleasant discoveries was that I could not model other teachers. Some instructional methods and tricks I could copy, but when it came to what some call "classroom management," nothing seemed to allow replication. Students seemed to conspire to treat their teachers differently—some were allowed to yell but not others; some could be sarcastic but not others. Some teachers were treated with contempt and provoked rebellion regardless of what they did, while others inspired respect and deference without any apparent connection to their actions. What exactly one did as a teacher did not appear that important.

A little later, I understood that this rule equally applies to instruction. Some teachers use the most outdated methods of teaching and still achieve great results, while others failed with the most advanced novelties we had learned in college. Of course, in many cases, great teaching methods produced great learning results, but the exceptions bothered me. One teacher would lecture the whole time, and students not only succeeded but also could not get enough of him. Another tried active learning, problem solving, visuals, etc. but students did not learn, would not behave, and disliked the teacher.

Three sixth-grade History classes I taught in 1983-1984 in Novosibirsk school #110 helped me to make another discovery: what worked in one of them (both in instruction and classroom management) did not necessarily work in another. My fourth period was energetic and argumentative; they loved a good discussion and enjoyed a good story. The fifth period was just as smart but did not particularly like what I had to offer. Of course, every teacher knows that there is no such thing as one prep; you always have to adjust for each class, but I did not know that at the time.

On top of all these uncertainties, it became apparent that what works on Tuesday did not work on Wednesday with the same group of kids. In short, nothing seemed to work consistently in teaching. The sense of reality was slowly slipping from under my feet. Most of the advice I received from experienced teachers and college professors suddenly looked irrelevant. "Set the limits at the start." "Do not smile till Christmas." "Reinforce positive behavior." "Keep them busy." "Present a problem, not a simple question." What good is advice if it only works half of the time? After many errors, I finally learned how to be a decent teacher, which involves a lot of improvisation, paying attention to my own intuition, listening to the kids, and trying to take it easy. Having learned to do something is not the same as understanding why it works.

Much later, in graduate school, another important discovery came to me: the best of the best in our profession—both teachers and administrators, some of whom I had a chance to observe and interview—do not understand why they are successful. These wonderful people had many great ideas that explained their own success, but the successful educators tend to concentrate on what they *do,* assuming that everyone else who would do the same will achieve similar results. Of course, such an assumption has been repeatedly proven wrong. One of the very few clearly established facts in educational theory is that good teaching practices as well as good organizational structures are remarkably difficult to transfer from one setting to another. This fact was at the root of all my small discoveries. Thinking about education in terms of doing is frustratingly unproductive; it causes one to lose the sense of reality, because everything seems so relative. Amidst these small personal discoveries, the individual human beings and their actions started to fade away for me, and relations came into focus.

In this book, I argue that an underlying reality of human relations constitutes the crucial context of education. What teachers, administrators, and students do and say could only have meaning and be understood against this invisible but very real matrix of intersecting relations. This is an attempt at a theoretical reconstruction of the relational reality in education.

Learning is a function of relation; therefore, educators should pay close attention to it. Relations shape everything teachers do and say to such an extent that very "wrong" actions and words would be okay or even beneficial when a relationship is good. At the same time, the best practices and most effective words would become meaningless or harmful against the background of an unhealthy relationship. Therefore, educators should really concentrate on establishing effective educational relations and only then worry about what to do.

About the genre: A travel TV channel host described how Westminster Abbey looked when it was new, plush with gold and excessive decorations: "It must have been awfully gaudy then, but time makes everything beautiful." This must also be true for the way of thinking developed by great European philosophers. There is something both frightening and exhilarating in steady Hegelian ascent from the abstract to the concrete, from an elemental cell of something, from a fact taken in its most simple, directly observable form, to the splendid concreteness of a fully developed phenomenon. This book, especially the first part, is an exercise in dialectics, where dialectics is an old, rusty, but charming mechanism, still working, even though in need of constant repair. I tried to understand the essence of education although there is little certainty that such an essence could exist or could be plausibly invented. Here is my report on the exercise: chasing the non-existent is a deeply satisfying and productive activity; I recommend it highly. Writing an essentialist book in the early years of the twenty-first century is a pleasure, simply because no one will take the essentialism very seriously—an indulgence the thinkers of modernity were denied.

It is like rebuilding an antique bureau: in the end, it should not look old but rather retro. One would fix and polish it just enough to let the buyer know that the drawers will not get stuck and hinges will not fall off, and yet it contains enough old wood to have character. The essentialism of this book is of that sort. When I give a definition of education, no one with any sense will believe it to be *the* definition. Still, I hope for more—that no one will think that I think it is the one true definition. One can trust the readers to understand that the author is not entirely serious in the choice of his theoretical tools. I find it increasingly difficult to remain serious about any theoretical tool, including the tool of irony.

Postmodernity is akin to recycling, and philosophy has produced a lot of recyclable material to play with. Some of it I quote, some I mention, and some I steal. It would be foolish and presumptuous to identify all recycled parts as such; that would defy the whole purpose of recycling. The essentialist critique of education was not easy to position with respect to existing debates in educational theory. This is not surprising, because in the English-speaking world, the conversation on aims of education, essence of education, etc. died out a long time ago without producing many tangible results. Yet I find such a conversation very interesting and worth reviving.

If the genre is not entirely serious, the content is a different story altogether. I am very serious and very worried about the fate of education, especially in the K-12 public schools. What worries me especially is the way many good people worry about it. It never ceases to amaze me how little the public knows about schools. What I have in mind here is the most basic understanding, an understanding on a level of a primal myth, of a basic story. In one of the graduate classes for in-service teachers I taught, we learned about what most academics think is the philosophy of education: mainly issues of equity, class, race, and gender in education. After several classes, an elementary school teacher suddenly blurted out: "But you don't understand, I come every day to the classroom, and I teach all these kids to read and write, day after day, after day..." and then she stopped as if short of words. She was upset because she did not find herself in all these books. Her voice was not heard, her experiences were not reflected upon, and her story was not told. It was not as if the teachers resisted the class-race-gender analysis of education as such; they liked to discuss the hot political issues around education, too. All they wanted was for a more basic layer of school life to be shown first and then the very important issues of politics and justice against that background. When she spoke, I decided that if there were a book worth writing about schools, it should somehow explain how different schools are from the rest of the social world.

Without such basic understanding, state and federal legislative bodies are condemned to repeat the vicious circle of school reforming for accountability of the unknown. People are trying to outdo each other in changing something they do not understand; moreover, they insist on measuring that change. Like all complex non-deterministic systems, education will avenge ignorance. Brain surgery cannot be done with a butcher knife, whatever the intention, schools cannot be improved by testing, whatever the frequency. What worries me the most is the pervasive assumption that anything could be done in education. Politicians treat education as a political problem, an issue of will and of choice. Conservatives believe that high expectations will produce higher achievement. Liberals (at least some of them) believe that addressing the problem of inequality will automatically make education better. Interestingly, both of these beliefs treat education as a black box, without thinking about what education is, what its limits are, and what can and cannot be done about it. This way of thinking is strikingly different from how the same politicians think about the economy. No one believes that the government can increase productivity or change prices at will. When the market took a dip in September 2001, no one called it an outrage; the government developed stimulus packages but avoided direct intervention. After failed Communist experiments, no one is willing to try anything crazy or to legislate economic development. The healthy respect for complexity of market mechanisms implicitly acknowledges a certain mystery, some limits of our knowledge. At the same time, most people acknowledge that the market economy has its own intrinsic laws and regularities to be understood and taken into consideration. Only recently, with the advent of environmental movement, a similar type of thinking extended onto the natural environment. My wish is that people, especially policy makers, would learn to think about education in similar terms.

Fundamentally, education is different from the rest of the social world, and nothing can be done to improve it unless we have at least some idea about its specifics. The evasive character of effective educational relations could only be discovered through understanding the specifics of the educational world. An intuition about the distinctive nature of education has been haunting me for a long time, probably some 15 years. Yet, there was always a more focused project to be completed—my Russian dissertation on school development, then the American one on dialogue, then papers that would count toward tenure. This book is much riskier and thus much more enjoyable to write.

Here is the book's logic: Part I presents problems, Part II offers an outline of a solution, and Part III addresses further problems with the solution offered. First, I attempt to understand education as a form of division of labor. Total human labor, I argue, always includes wasteful labor, when laborers are not skilled enough to make anything truly useful. Eventually, this wasteful, but necessary, labor is separated from the rest of labor, thus creating the educational sphere. Learning can be described as production of useless things, and education as a social sphere where learning occurs systematically. A perfectly reasonable development, it had unexpected side effects—simply speaking, it is not much fun to be producing useless things, which is what learning is mostly about. I go to great length to show that the activity of learning only *appears* to be useless when, in fact, it creates tangible economic value. Therefore, learning is not only badly motivated but also may very well be exploitative of children. However, for my overall argument, it is very important to establish that learning is very difficult to motivate—not because the teaching is bad but because learning has certain intrinsic limits. There is a flaw in the whole of the educational enterprise that goes beyond poor funding, bad administration, and unimaginative teaching. In historical terms, this flaw just began to show up because of the "massification" of schooling, and loss of traditional authoritarian means of control over students. If unattended, this crisis of authority will only get worse and may increase the level of school violence. A contemporary model of schooling with its emphasis on academic achievement becomes theoretically and practically impossible.

My proposal in Part II of this book is to establish a theory and a practice of relational pedagogy. Educational theory must find its way out of the dead end, where teaching and learning are too closely linked with specific behaviors or activities. On a more practical level, educators must find an alternative source of learning motivation, and I must try to demonstrate that human relations can provide such motivation. In other words, teaching today can only be successful if based on a solid foundation of interhuman relations. Teaching and learning in the context of a school depend on a specific mutual transformation of relations that I call erotic and athenaic. Educational relations are almost impossible to cultivate without much greater variety of activities and situations than a typical school allows. Therefore, "pure education" on which our schools are oriented is too strong of a drink for them to stomach. Schools would be more viable as hybrid institutions that combine functions of school proper with those of a volunteer youth association and a neighborhood club.

Part III deals with certain theoretical problems that the pedagogy of relation brings. First is the problem of teacher's authority, which has to be reconciled with mutuality in any student-teacher relationship. I use Bakhtin's notion of polyphony to address this issue, but polyphony itself may harbor difficulties. One is that the plurality of voices seems to dissolve consistency of educational message. I then attempt to show that, in fact, a true educational message cannot be consistent. Another problem of relational pedagogy is the possibility of relation across difference. Chapters 13 and 14 deal with the problem so that difference is examined in terms of relation, not in terms of separation. One logical extension of the same problem of difference concerns the extent to which one would consider relationship with the other when the other is evil. In other words, I wanted to see if there are limits to relationality.

This book is a result of realization that educational theory cannot go any further if based on telling educators what to do. A teacher who heard my presentation once asked, "What seems to be working in education?" My answer was, "Nothing does." I did not mean it in a pessimistic way; on the contrary, I am very optimistic about how education can change. However, the language of action applies no more. We cannot tell teachers which actions to take so that their students will fall in love with learning and achieve great results. We cannot tell this not because we do not know, but because the question is formulated incorrectly, it is impossible to answer.

Educational thought of the twentieth century was puzzled by many challenges. One of them could be described as follows: if one moves away from universal claims, then education should become highly contextual. How can one understand and describe something as elusive and as indefinable as context? This is, of course, another incarnation of the postmodern challenge; however, it has special significance in our field. As an applied discipline, educational theory cannot exist without being prescriptive. We cannot simply tell educators: "Oh, just pay attention to the context; it all depends on context." If this were all we can say, it would be better not to say anything at all. We have to provide a theory that can be helpful. The concept of relations, if properly developed, can serve as a more useful description of contextuality. What I offer is not simply "It depends on context" but "It depends on relations." The notion of context is, in fact, a negative one—we bring it up when we do not know or cannot know all circumstances of human actions. Relation is a positive interpretation of context.

This book is about the pedagogy of relation—an approach to educational theory centered on the notion of relation. In addition to this author, a group of theorists in the United States and beyond agreed to work on a theoretical framework for the pedagogy of relations. Only time will show how successful we are in developing it into a real theory. This book is only a part of this larger collective effort, in which I invite everyone to participate.

PART I. CRITIQUE OF PURE EDUCATION

CHAPTER 1.
THE GOD OF USELESS THINGS:
A DEFINITION OF EDUCATION

Imagine living in a strange country, very much unlike all others. All its inhabitants work, but no one uses any products of their labor. No one sits on chairs they build; no one wears clothes they sew. An editor of a local journal reads a paper submitted by a reporter, corrects mistakes, and sends it back without publishing it. In fact, he has never published anything written by the locals. The country imports absolutely everything and exports nothing. It does not sell anything to the outside but still offers comfortable standards of living. All the material and immaterial things, such as houses, cars, clothes, works of literature, music, scientific knowledge, and all services are brought in from elsewhere. Yet everyone in this country is expected to work every day. Local culture and ideology exert enormous pressure on people to keep working, regardless of what is happening to the results of their work. People dutifully cook food that no one eats. Domestically built aircraft are stored somewhere while people fly on those imported, better airplanes. Writers spend countless hours writing novels and essays that no one reads. Scientists do research that no one publishes, because it always turns out that the scientists from other countries have already made all the discoveries.

Imagine yourself working for a software company in this strange country. You spend a few weeks writing a good piece of software. Your supervisor checks it and says, "What a marvelous job you've done! I am so proud of you." Then he promptly deletes all the files without even waiting for you to leave the room. It does not matter how much money you are making at this company. You will hate the job; you will be puzzled and confused by the whole country. Imagine building cars that go directly under press, and building houses that are demolished immediately after you shine your last brass door handle. Would you not feel awful when your creations are destroyed? Would you want to show up for work tomorrow?

The picture I just painted is a world of Kafkaesque absurdity. With all the postmodern tolerance for the absurd, it does feel fictional—an allegory for something real but not a direct description of the reality. What sort of story could take place in such a world? We would expect our hero to survive, of course, but also to rebel against the meaningless work. The hero must first awaken to the absurdity of her existence, find out what is behind all this, and what compels all these people to keep producing junk in enormous quantities. This can make an interesting fantasy fiction story with an inevitable end to the mystery. Perhaps our hero discovers that there is some meaning to all this, that someone behind the scene somehow benefits. Alternatively, perhaps, a lunatic created this world following his own strange logic. However, let me spare you the suspense and go straight to the end of the story. The strange country is education, and the absurd world is the everyday reality of millions of school-aged children all over this world. Education is but an enterprise dedicated to production of useless things.

To clarify this claim, allow me another thought experiment—the Little Green People experiment. Now imagine an alien ship landing on a school rooftop and a crew of invisible alien anthropologists bursting out to study the "new" type of social units called "schools." Having researched a great many other social units on Earth, the aliens understood that all the offices, plants, warehouses, theaters, stadiums, barbershops, farms, firms, factories, all these units are actually a part of one large network called "the economy." Humans seem to make their society work by constantly exchanging useful goods and services among each other through money or directly. However, this particular unit is something else entirely. On one hand, it appears that earthlings here also produce things. They are busy several hours each day, working individually or in groups, under supervision of slightly larger humans, producing, producing, and producing. One detail-oriented alien anthropologist gives an incomplete list of things produced in "school": Literary essays; stories; and whole books; statistical reports; mathematical calculations, including graphs, tables, and separate problem solutions; choral and instrumental musical performances; oral presentations, scientific research (in the form of experimental studies and analytical scientific papers in chemistry, physics, biology, and other disciplines); theater shows; and political analysis papers.

They also fix cars, paint, and draw; make ceramic pots, newspapers, and exhibitions. This seems to be a remarkably versatile corporation.

It is highly peculiar that the overwhelming majority of goods and services produced in "school" are not offered to the outside world either as items for sale or as gifts. To be exact, all these things end up in wastebaskets and then in dumpsters. The humans in school appear to be receiving all the needed goods and services from humans of other social units but not giving anything useful in return.

The report ends with a record of mystery for future generations of alien anthropologists to solve: "I can understand that one part of human society can get things they need for free from other parts. What I don't understand is what motivates all these people to produce absolutely useless things. To work for the wastebasket continuously for many years must be an awful experience. To force others to do so seems impossible, so the managers here are even more mysterious than the workers."

Of course, we are not as naïve as the alien anthropologist. The Little Green People have no concept of education, for they come into the world fully formed. In our world, students produce all these useless things because they need to learn. That is, in order to be able to produce a great many useful things in the future, they have to develop needed skills and knowledge. Nevertheless, this background knowledge does not annul the alien anthropologist's observation; indeed, education appears to be the production of many things that no one needs. We may have a different or better explanation for this fact, but it is an observable fact nonetheless. In my opinion, the anthropologist is right in one more respect—it is very hard to stay enthusiastic about producing things that go straight to the wastebasket. This is why, as a rule, students do not really want to do the schoolwork. This is why we have compulsory school attendance laws and a whole ideology of school justification and glorification.

The most important fact about learning is so obvious that it goes little noticed in theoretical work on education: because children are asked to make things that no one really needs, they do not want to make these things. Now, the fact of *not wanting* is fairly well established.[1] What is almost totally ignored is the simple explanation of *why* students do not want to learn: because learning involves massive production of useless things. Students can be as unaware of this fact as the rest of us are. It took me a while, for instance, to explain to my fifteen-year-old son what I mean by the wastebasket economy of schooling and why, in my opinion, it impedes his motivation for learning. He finally agreed that this may be true, but immediately shrugged off my conclusion. Why worry about things you cannot change? Yet, the absurd does not become reasonable when it is generally accepted or goes unnoticed.

My attention here is focused on the things students produce, which is not a commonly accepted point of interest in educational theory and therefore requires some elaboration. Traditionally, education has been almost always viewed as a certain process that occurs between students and teachers. There is no agreement on what exactly this process is, but its location did not generate much controversy. My aim is to look for education elsewhere, namely, in the space between students and things they make while learning.

The products of students' work lead a rather shadowy and invisible existence in educational theory and common educational discourse. A teacher friend of mine jokes that whenever it is time to throw away his students' drawings, he feels guilty, as if the god of children were watching him and shaking his head disapprovingly. Every teacher can probably share this sentiment. It is a sad moment in teaching when the cute and awkward things children produce end their short lives. Teachers usually try to burden parents with such an unpleasant responsibility. "Take your work home, show it to your parents, hang it on the wall." Pieces of art are especially hard to let go, but so are student essays, stories, posters, models, and even worksheets. Perhaps because we feel guilty about throwing children's work away, we also tend to ignore these things in theory. The teacher guilt here shows that we often sense the unfairness of such destruction. It goes against one of the basic ethical tenets of our species since we began systematic work—anything that contains human work may not be needlessly destroyed. We can be described as a race of creators; even when we destroy, we imagine it to be for the sake of some imagined future creations (like in war). The fate of things produced by students in the process of learning clearly falls out of this pattern, because we systematically destroy what our children make.

We can unlock some mysteries of the educational world if we pay attention to the products of students' work. Consider a paper airplane and a Boeing 777: there is something in common between these two things besides the name and the ability to fly. Both are results of human work; someone spent time, energy, creativity; someone spent a portion of one's life *creating* these things. These are both objects of transformed nature. Therefore, there is much in common between making the real airplane and making a paper airplane while learning about flight. Learning is largely a function of making things; it is a function and a consequence of making something. The kinship of learning to making things or to the world of utilitarian production is definitely not new and is commonly assumed in

Marxist literature and also in the work of such Progressives as Dewey, Kilpatrick, and others and in the Vygotsky and Leontiev traditions in Russian psychology.[2] However, one may point at instances when students learn without leaving any material trace simply by listening and observing.[3] I will return later to this important special case. For now, let us assume that learning at school more often than not involves the production of numerous tangible and intangible objects, some of which were listed for us by the Little Green alien anthropologist.

Learning belongs to the family of human activities associated with production of certain artifacts and intangibles. If this is a characteristic of a genus, what then is the characteristic of learning as a species within the genus? Unlike most other human enterprises, learning is an utterly unproductive activity. The things that students *produce* while learning are never being consumed; no one needs them. In contrast to utilitarian production, learning can be defined as wasteful work. Indeed, if the things children produce become useful directly to them or to someone else, if they are sold, exchanged, or simply used, then education loses its point, and schools become factories, firms, and research labs. In order to call something "school," we have to make sure it produces junk. Education is a world with relatively cleanly drawn boundaries. In a very physical sense, education occurs only when materials are turned into waste.

A potter must make a number of faulty pots in order to learn how to make good ones. As long as he is making faulty pots, he is a student; as soon as he starts turning out good ones, learning is over, and real production begins. A student must write essays no one wants to publish; as soon as she has paying readers or just readers who read her work for pleasure, she stops being a student and becomes a writer. Now, an adult writer can also write for years with no real readers. However, consider the difference in meaning between the student's writing and the writer's writing. The latter intends her work to be read by an audience; the former does not have such illusions. Her teacher is her only fan, and the essay is doomed to be forgotten in a few days.

Modern education as a social sphere appears as a particular form of division of labor. It is important to understand the genesis of organized education in light of the concept of division of labor, because the concept clarifies the importance of the uselessness in my definition. One can imagine a master potter, tired of all the apprentices taking too much time from the regular potters. The master decides to build another shop just for the apprentices to learn some basics of pottery-making first. Economically, such a move would make much sense. Mass manufacturing requires breaking up the work process into simpler operations. So if learning to make pots was (and still is) a necessary part of the production, it could be safely separated from the main production and moved into another shop. This is done by the same logic as mixing clay, turning tables, and firing could be separated into different operations, done by different workers in different shops. A separate shop for apprentices, established so they can practice, generally outlines the concept of a school. The genius of our ancestors is apparent here: schools are efficient because they minimize damage to the productive sphere of the economy.

Of course, historically, the young scribes and the future clerics were the first ones to be moved from the regular workplace to separate facilities. The pottery example is just much more vivid. The broken pots provide a better imagery for the sort of things an educational institution produces. The historically inaccurate choice of the example does not change the nature of the student activity, which is to produce many useless writings before they can be allowed to write for real. The young scribes and the clerics could, in theory, work alongside with real scribes and clerics and learn their trade by watching and performing simple tasks. Yet the nature of literacy and importance of writing as a channel of communication made it impossible to tolerate a high percentage of faulty production. In occupations that require literacy, the division of labor between students and adult workers started very early, probably almost simultaneously with the invention of writing.

Moreover, predecessors of organized schooling go back well beyond the age of literacy, when ancient hunters and gatherers put together groups of children to play and practice skills necessary for survival. Shooting arrows into a practice target is also education—it is completely unproductive, but at least kids do not spook the game and do learn how to aim. One can also trace education into the animal kingdom. I am not trying to make an historical claim. The important concept here is that schooling is a case of division of labor. Any kind of labor, if taken in its totality throughout the society, includes production of useless things. The world of education was gradually created when the complexity of most kinds of labor began to require division between production of useful and useless things. As with any other form of division of labor, this made great economic sense but produced its own problems. One is the problem of motivation. The blessed instincts of play and curiosity with which evolution had supplied us eventually run out of capacity to satisfy the demands of our civilization. At one point, the average resource of curiosity found in a human being could no longer provide motivation for learning what an average human being needed to know. Now we either must find a better motivation for learning or reduce the amount of skill and knowledge required of most of us.

Since the beginning of schooling, teachers have realized how hard it is to motivate all children to learn. This is due to the fact that the products of student work have *no utility*. Of course, it is possible to motivate children to learn—well, sometimes. Teachers tend to remember bright eyes, bushy tails, engaged discussions, and the delightful buzz of children who work in school and enjoy it. These moments make teaching the great profession it is. Yet this is possible only for a few moments, when children forget where the results of their work are going. As a rule, the following condition always prevails: One can make some children enthusiastic about learning all the time, or one can make all children enthusiastic about learning some of the time, but one cannot make all children enthusiastic about learning all the time.

I take this condition to be a natural law, like the law of preservation of energy, not pessimistic but pragmatic. This seems to be an inevitable consequence of modern civilization with its hugely expanded knowledge base—we need children to spend many years producing useless things against their will in order for them to be ready to lead productive lives. This is not exactly an optimistic endorsement of schooling but a more accurate reflection of its limits. Okay, the perpetual motion is impossible— this does not mean we need not produce energy. Another analogy—we are all mortal, which does not mean we have to give up living right away. The lack of motivation in learning is a limit of similar nature—one has to come to terms with rather than overcome it.

The lack of motivation is a direct consequence of the fact that things produced by students are useless. When the apprentice potter was still in the main shop, he could very clearly see the connection between his efforts, the broken pots, and the good ones. The connection was direct, obvious, and non-problematic. As soon as he was moved to a separate building, this connection was interrupted. For the sake of efficiency, all pots from the apprentice building went into the dumpster, even the good ones. One would be foolish to organize quality control, storage, delivery, etc., for a facility that is supposed to produce mainly broken pots. This would defy the benefits created by the division of labor. If this makes the apprentices less motivated; fine, such is the price of efficiency. Students can produce many useful things, but economic considerations prevent schools from making those things available to the market.

The fact that all of the things produced by students have no obvious utility creates a strange microeconomy of the wastebasket, which, in turn, affects the students' motivation, the character of social relations in schools, and the nature of schools as organizations. The whole range of the wastebasket economy's consequences will be examined later in this book. The most important for me is to reverse the assumption that making useless things is a byproduct of learning. To the contrary, learning is a byproduct of making useless things. I also want to emphasize that this is not an accident of history but a rational and necessary consequence of the division of labor. Now, the question I need to consider next is that learning also still occurs as a byproduct of making *useful* things. I will examine this argument with respect to labor, although it generally applies to all forms of purposeful human activity such as play, creative arts, communications, etc.

It is easy to notice that *any* labor, indeed any activity, has two sides to it: one side is increasing the value of the object of labor; another side is increasing the value of the labor power of the worker. In other words, any labor is a production of something external to the worker, and at the same time, it is a process of changing the worker herself. Even an experienced potter learns something every time she makes a pot; this is why work experience is valued so much on the labor market. Marx never had a chance to develop the anthropology of labor, but he was certainly aware of the fact that a laborer, besides changing the material world around her also changes herself: "By thus acting on the external world and changing it, he at the same time changes his own nature. He develops his slumbering powers and compels them to act in obedience to his sway."[4] On the margins of *The German Ideology*, Marx scribbled about two sides to every activity: transformation (*Bearbeitung*) of nature by people and transformation of people by people.[5]

Let us note that Marx is referring to that second side of activity as "transformation of people by people." What he means is that the change that occurs in the laborer because of the labor process is significantly social in its nature. What we "learn" by doing something is a specifically human or social way of doing it. The very notions of skill and knowledge refer to the social knowledge of better ways of doing things. I will need to abstract from this fact, however, so that the main point remains more visible: anything we do has two sides to it—the productive side, which refers to the immediate goal of the person's activity, and the "learning" side, a sum of all gainful changes that occur in the person who is the subject of such activity. The mere fact that a person is learning something does not make his or her activity a learning activity (the production of useless things), and it does not make the social institution in which it takes place educational.

A distinction between learning activity and learning as an effect of any activity may help clarify the duality of human activity. Learning as an effect is present whenever we do something, whether we are active for pleasure, for utilitarian purposes, or specifically for learning. However, only when we do something primarily for learning, do we engage in the learning activity. For instance, reading a book for pleasure may result in some learning, but it is not a learning activity. Reading a book primarily for school is a learning activity.

The *only* difference between the learning activity and the productive labor is that in the learning activity, the first, productive side of labor is missing or greatly overshadowed by the second, "learning" side. Learning activity is therefore defined here not by what it has but by what it lacks. I will call these sides the object-transforming and the subject-transforming. In the "real," adult labor, the productive (object-transforming) side of labor clearly dominates. Learning activity is simply the sort of labor with the oversized, hypertrophied subject-transforming side that Marx called "transformation of people by people." This difference defines learning activity and demarcates the boundaries of the educational world, not only of learning in schools. For the purposes of my further argument, I want to emphasize that despite different relations between the two sides of activity, learning activity still has both sides. Learning activity still aims at transforming some object, although this does not constitute its primary goal.

Of course, there exists a great variety of human activities with different ratios of the two sides; some are closer to learning activity, some to the productive labor. Some, like on-the-job training, are in between, which means that workers produce real commodities or services to be sold but not as efficiently or with lesser quality. Yet things being thrown away in large quantities usually clearly indicate an educational institution. One can tell a school from a manufacturing plant by their respective dumpsters. A school can be defined as a building where delivery trucks unload but never load. Every morning school buses bring as many children as they take away in the afternoon. Totally invisibly for drivers and for the passengers, the afternoon buses carry more valuable cargo than the morning buses because of the value accumulated during the day in the minds and bodies of future laborers.

Let me return to the special case of learning that occurs seemingly without producing any object, tangible or intangible, by simple listening, reading, and observing. Academic learning activity in a sense of "gaining knowledge" is a case of knowledge production. A distinction between knowledge production and knowledge consumption may be helpful in understanding this special case of learning. One can produce knowledge without consuming it, and one can consume knowledge without producing it. Of course, one can also produce and consume knowledge at the same time. To *produce* knowledge is to record certain meaningful information using any mechanical, electronic, or biological medium, including the human brain. To *consume* knowledge is to retrieve and use it for any number of practical and not-so-practical purposes, from impressing a cocktail party acquaintance to developing a new scientific instrument.

Generally, people want to produce knowledge for at least four distinctive purposes, which correspond with four types of knowledge consumption. The first one is for immediate personal consumption. We open the phone book to produce some knowledge that is immediately useful for some practical task. The second is for pure pleasure and without any practical goal in mind. In this case, knowledge production and knowledge consumption are very closely intertwined, but the type of consumption (pleasure) is different from type one. Such pleasurable consumption of knowledge is not without practical consequences (we never know what will become useful in the future—this applies equally to theoretical physics and to watching "Jeopardy"), but its primary motivation is pleasure. The third is to produce knowledge for others, knowledge to be sold or exchanged just like any other commodity. Most of the research and much of the information technology related work falls into this category. Finally, the fourth type of knowledge production is one specifically designed as the learning activity. As such, it is no different from producing faulty clay pots. Students *produce* knowledge that is not new, is as useless as broken pots or paper airplanes. It is obviously not the knowledge production of type three, since no one else consumes it. However, it is also rarely of types one and two; students almost never need it for personal use, nor do they often derive pleasure from its consumption.

The big hope of Progressive education was to change academic learning activity in a way that its components would fall into either type one, two, or three of knowledge production. Variations of the same hope still inspire many teachers and curriculum developers. Admittedly, some serious progress has been made in this direction, and I would be the last to underestimate the importance of hands-on, project-oriented, student-centered, or constructivist learning. Yet it is very unlikely that such attempts can be ultimately successful. We cannot make all the knowledge production needed for contemporary education pleasurable or personally useful or socially needed. The hope that all kids will learn quadratic equations and the names of amino acids out of sheer curiosity is simply unrealistic. Nel Noddings comments on such unreasonable expectations: "Many teachers believe their own propaganda—that is, they believe something is wrong with either students or teachers if students do not evince an interest in a given subject."[6] Noddings's own solution is to work with students' existing motives, with which I agree. The next step is to find out how.

Of course, there is always a question as to whether the kids should know all these things. Yet, however you may want to revamp the curriculum in today's knowledge-saturated society, one has to produce enormous amounts of useless knowledge to be able to produce some useful knowledge. Noddings believes that curriculum can be changed to accommodate the variety of motives students may or may not have; I doubt such a possibility. The real benefit of academic learning is not the knowledge that students produce (it is mostly useless); rather, it is the enhanced ability to produce knowledge of types one, two, and three.

The Progressives and their constructivist heirs have trouble realizing that to achieve their goal of completely motivated learning they have to eliminate education itself. A school where kids learn out of curiosity only is really an entertainment establishment. A school where they make real discoveries and produce valuable information is a research firm. A school where kids learn only what they really need right now is a street corner. A real school is where students produce useless knowledge to learn to produce useful knowledge.

Dewey saw the contradiction between the two sides of learning activity, which I called the object-transforming and the subject-transforming sides. However, he perceived the contradiction as neither fundamental nor irredeemable. On the contrary, much of *The Child and the Curriculum* is an attempt to bridge the two by psychologizing the learning. It is not my intention to give a critique of Dewey's educational theory here. The general thrust of his argument, in my scheme of things, is to give a boost of the object-transforming aspect of learning activity; it is to make learning a lot closer to non-educational productive activity (labor). Dewey wanted boys and girls to do real things with their hands and brains, so that motivation similar to that present in the adult world would kick in, and at the same time to stay away from narrow utilitarian aspects of adult occupations. In short, this does not work because while we can tilt the balance between the object-transforming and the subject-transforming components of learning activity, we cannot really alter that balance. The subject-transforming side must always come first unless we want to turn school into a regular company producing real products to be sold on the market.

In *The Child and the Curriculum,* Dewey developed an intriguing argument, starting basically with the same assumption about the two sides of learning activity. "Every study of subject thus has two aspects: one for the scientist as a scientist; the other for the teacher as teacher. These two aspects are in no sense opposed or conflicting. But neither are they immediately identical."[7] A closet Hegelian, he then goes on to claim that the failure to take into consideration the double aspect of subject matter causes the three evils associated with setting the child and the curriculum against each other. First is that "the lack of any organic connection with what the child has already seen and felt and loved makes material purely formal and symbolic (202)." The second evil is the lack of motivation connected to the lack of connection between child's present needs and the material to be mastered. The third evil is that by the time it gets to the child, the scientific side of material drops out.ABewey finds the contradiction but hopes it will somehow go away; the thesis and antithesis will disappear in a puff of synthesis.

Over the years, many creative attempts to redeem the essential lack of motivation in learning have been undertaken. The use of play in learning introduces intrinsic motivation disassociated from any direct products of activity. The use of problem-solving learning enlists curiosity and fascination with mind games as additional motives. Behaviorists attempted to introduce fake economies of points and tokens that supposedly make one's learning directly tied to the world of goods and services (regular grading systems are, in fact, versions of same token economy systems). Here is an example by a classroom teacher of how such a pseudo-economy fails:

> Scholar dollar was a reward program for good work or behavior. Teachers were given a certain number of scholar dollars to pass out to deserving students—30 scholar dollars got you a pencil; 100 got you pizza for lunch. In the beginning, it worked like a charm. But the whole thing slowly became perverted. First, some teachers were extremely generous and others stingy, leading to cries among students that it wasn't fair. Second, it was impossible to get a new supply, so teachers started to run them off on the copy machine. Once the children realized that, they started to counterfeit their own. The scholar dollars' value cheapened dramatically. End of program.[8]

All these attempts, just like the Deweyan Progressive approach, were only partially successful. They took large bites of the enormous problem of learning motivation without ever getting close to its core. Schools are wastebasket-oriented economies and will remain such for the foreseeable future just because they are schools. This basic fact only became more apparent with the introduction of mass education. In the past, the very threat of expulsion from school created a forceful social pressure on children to keep learning. With this threat largely gone, it becomes increasingly difficult to convince children to produce more essays, reports, calculations, and experiments. I will explore this development further in Chapter 5.

For the purposes of my argument, learning activity can be defined as an activity, an immediate product of which is not as important as changes that occur in the person—the subject of the activity. Education, in turn, is a social sphere where learning activity plays a central role.[9] Education is a sum of social institutions and practices that are specifically designed and focused on the practices of learning activity as defined above.

Notice that a relation between a teacher and a student does not create education; rather, it is a special relation between a subject and an object of a student's activity. The subject in this equation is a student; the object is that toward which student activity is directed. Generally, having a teacher is not a necessary condition to learning activity; doing something is. Learning is a special way of doing. This is not to say that learning can occur outside of social relations. This only means that the teacher must not be there physically for every act of learning; this also means that the phenomenon of "teacher" may not necessarily be traced to one particular human individual. When a teacher directly participates, the only difference he or she makes is that the subject of learning activity becomes a complex one. Learning is still a function of doing things, but now the one who is doing is a group of people rather than one individual. However, from the student's point of view, this activity, even shared with a teacher or with peers, remains useless, whereas, for the teacher, it is not.

One important consequence of the production of useless things is that schools are excluded from economic cycle of commodity exchange. Nothing they produce has any economic value. Of course, schools exist within the economy, provided for out of taxpayer money or tuition payments. However, this money has no relation whatsoever to the vast majority of goods and services students produce. Dewey describes the bright side of such a unique position of schools in *The School and Society*: "But in the school the typical occupations followed are freed from all economic stress. The aim is not the economic value of the products, but the development of social power and insight. It is this liberation from narrow utilities, this openness to the possibilities of human spirit that makes these practical activities in the school allies of art and centers of science and history."[10] I would only add that this freedom from economic stress is characteristic of not only what Dewey calls "active occupations" but of any learning activity in any school, including the traditional schooling Dewey criticizes. The not-so-bright side of this extra-economical status of schools is the fundamental, unavoidable, essential lack of motivation for learning.

When I link effective motivation to exchange of commodities, I am not trying to idealize the capitalist economy. As Marx has convincingly shown, the commodity exchange will be a way of exploiting the hired labor as long as means of production remain alienated from the worker. However, Marxist analysis takes the act of exchange of goods way beyond the narrowly constructed capitalist way of doing it. Marx criticized not the exchange of values but a particular alienating way of performing such an exchange. When people exchange goods they produce, they also materialize their relations. The act of exchange of useful things between individuals constitutes a fundamental fact of human condition, whether it is done through money-mediated market economy, or through communal exchanges of non-capitalist cultures, or as an immediate act of gift giving. When you and I exchange products of our work, we also exchange our individual beings while creating the fabric of social life that really defines us as humans.

Despite existence of enormously different ways of product exchange, from thoroughly immoral to most noble and uplifting, they all share one feature—an exchange makes sense only when products and services have use-value. Accordingly, much of what we do is motivated by orientation toward the possibility of an exchange. This is one of the most important engines of social life, and it is missing in the world of education. It is missing not because of someone's fault, or lack of ideas and effort; the lack of motivation seems to be an essential feature of education. This fact has a whole range of implications, some of which I will explore.

This claim of lack of learning motivation puts me in a rather precarious position with respect to extensive literature on the subject.[11] I do not wish to appear dismissive toward the major theories of learning motivation, nor do I believe a systematic critique of such theories can significantly benefit this book. Simply put, my interest for learning motivation lies mainly outside of the field of psychology. I am interested in political economy and anthropology of learning, not in psychological mechanisms of it.

I began by examining the things students produce and concluded that education is a troublesome project mainly because these things are not exchangeable. My hope is to show that we can take the peculiarities of education into consideration and find social forms of exchange in education. The problem of motivation is solvable if we allow ourselves to go beyond the limits of education.

NOTES

[1] See, for example, Nel Noddings, "Must We Motivate?," in *Teaching and Its Predicaments*, eds. Nicholas G. Burbules and David T. Hansen (Boulder, CO: Westview Press, 1997), 29-44.

[2] Vygotsky simply assumes that learning occurs when a student cooperates with an adult or with a more advanced student; he does not attempt to prove this self-evident truth. Cooperation, of course, is doing something together, so that the student and the teacher act as one complex subject of an activity.

[3] For empirical evidence of observational learning, see Albert Bandura, *Social Foundations of Thought and Actions: A Social-Cognitive Theory* (Englewood Cliffs, NJ: Prentice-Hall, 1986).

[4] Karl Marx, *Capital* (Chicago: Encyclopaedia Britannica, 1957), 85.

[5] "Bisher haben wir hauptsächlich nur die eine Seite der menschlichen Tätigkeit, die *Bearbeitung der Natur* durch die Menschen betrachtet. Die andere Seite, die *Bearbeitung der* Menschen durch *die Menschen...*" Karl Marx, *Die Deutsche Ideologie* (http://www.mlwerke.de/me/me03/me03_anm.htm#M1).

[6] Nel Noddings, "Must We Motivate?" 30.

[7] John Dewey, *The School and Society. The Child and the Curriculum* (Chicago and London: The University of Chicago Press, 1990), 200.

[8] Jacqueline G. Kingon, "A View from the Trenches," *The New York Times Education Life*, April 8, 2001, 37.

[9] I use the word "sphere" as Michael Walzer uses it in *Spheres of Justice: A Defense of Pluralism and Equality* (New York: Basic Books, 1983).

[10] John Dewey, *The School and Society. The Child and the Curriculum*, 18.

[11] For a good overview of psychological theories of motivation, see Deborah Stipek, *Motivation to Learn*, Second Edition (Boston, MA: Allyn and Bacon, 1988, 1993). However, even an overview like this one barely scratches the surface of research on learning motivation. To a request for "learning motivation," ERIC database answers with a staggering: "2708 records match your search."

CHAPTER 2.
LABOR OF LEARNING

One paradox of education is that in one sense it produces nothing, while in another sense it generates great economic value. Learning activity may appear useless to an individual, but socially it is indispensable. The strangest thing is that such a deceitful appearance is not an accident and not a result of ignorance. The world of education is indeed deeply ambivalent. The false appearance of useless work is essential to the success of the whole enterprise.

This chapter is an attempt to understand learning activity as labor—not metaphorically or psychologically, but from the point of view of the political economy of education. Where does learning activity fit in the great scheme of things in the contemporary economy? How does this affect the theoretical view of schooling? In schools, students are asked to produce numerous things, and I will try to understand them in economic terms of value and use-value. My analysis suggests that learning activity—any school learning activity, even within a free school, democratic school, or a school of human development—remains essentially an exploitative economic enterprise.

First, something needs to be said about the human capital theory and its Marxist critique. A comprehensive review of literature related to the subject is not among my objectives. What follows is only a brief outline of some existing theoretical context. In *Human Capital,* Gary Becker clearly demonstrates the increasing role of education in the economy as a whole as well as for the individual income of workers.[1] Indeed, one can view the investment in education as the creation of a special form of capital, one with a rather high rate of return. Marxist critics point out that the human capital theory totally ignores the social aspects of capitalist production and schooling and has no theory of reproduction.[2] In other words, Becker is not really interested in why working class kids get working class jobs and whether this is a problem at all.[3] Bowles and Gintis accuse Becker of treating school as a black box, but, curiously, their own account of schooling, in turn, treats learning activity—the central process—as a black box, too. Learning activity for them is disconnected from labor, and it is certainly not a form of labor. It is the periphery of school life (supplying credentials, getting used to supervisory authority, forming motivational patterns, segmentation of workers) that produces the economic result capitalist employers desire. I use "periphery" without implying unimportance, but simply to point out that this is not learning activity itself. In other words, all the objectives of a capitalist school according to Bowles and Gintis can be equally achieved if schools would not be centered on learning. Their critique aims at processes that could be easily found outside of the world of schooling; the critique lacks educational specificity. Functions of schooling that worry Bowles and Gintis are not directly connected to learning.

In my opinion, the critique of human capital theory by Bowles and Gintis is quite convincing, but it does not tell the whole story. Learning itself is not innocent and benign, and it certainly cannot be understood as an investment. Learning activity is a form of labor, and the only thing that human capital theorists demonstrate is that some of it actually gets paid much later. However, to suggest that the belated and partial payment is a return on capital investment is the same as to say that a factory worker invests in herself by working, and her paycheck is her profit.

Suppose I have a piggy bank, into which I put a penny a day for ten years. Of course, I should have $36.52 or $36.53 when I break it, depending on how many leap years will be during the decade. However, when I actually break the bank, it produces $65. The mystery could have two solutions: first is that I somehow invested this money into a new form of capital, human capital, and hence the return. Little gnomes took my money at night, built a company, bought equipment, hired workers, sold their product, and then returned the money into the piggy bank with interest. The second solution is that some days I forgot that I put a penny in, and put in two or three, or that my family wanted to get rid of loose change and dumped it into my piggy bank. Why human capital theorists subscribe to the first type of solution is beyond me. They assume there must be some magic within the piggy bank rather than assuming something more mundane. Indeed, people who invest in education get more money than they put in, but maybe this is just because we overlook some of the contributions. Much of the contributions into the educational piggy bank may be coming not in the form of money but in the form of labor.

Human capital theory is not new, but it quietly continues to inform educational policies and educational rhetoric on various levels. One only has to look at the U.S. Department of Education documents to see the rhetoric directly or indirectly informed by the human capital theory. My argument can be viewed as an extension of a Marxist critique of human capital theory, which attempts to show on a theoretical level from where the extra pennies might be coming. However, my conclusions can hardly be considered Marxist and have to do with a vision of school reform within the existing economic relations.

To all products of student work, the following Karl Marx account may apply: "Nothing can have value, without being an object of utility. If the thing is useless, so is the labour contained in it: the labour does not count as labour, and therefore creates no value."[4] The things produced by students obviously do not have characteristics of commodities. They are neither sold nor exchanged; they are neither gifts, nor are they produced for personal consumption. Therefore, students perceive their work as zero-value production. Such is the appearance available to students, but as Marx himself has convincingly demonstrated, appearances can be very deceiving in economic relations. Moreover, the *appearance* of learning activity as non-labor has very serious economic implications. If not deliberately calculated, such appearance is certainly useful to those benefiting from the capitalist mode of production. Learning activity *is* a form of productive labor although it creates a very special form of value.

According to Marx, the value of a commodity is nothing but a mere congelation of homogeneous human labor.[5] Marx viewed labor power as a unique form of commodity that is "*a source not only of value, but of more value than it has itself.*"[6] The value of labor power is, in turn, determined by the labor that went into the creation and re-creation of labor power. In other words, the value of labor power is the labor of all other workers that went into the production of food, clothing, and shelter for the worker. Note that accumulating or "storing" value in either material objects or human beings is not the same thing as capital investment as human capital theorists may sometimes lead us to believe. Storing value does not produce more value than was originally stored. Marx considered education to be one of these components of labor that goes into the creation of labor power:

> In order to modify the human organism, so that it may acquire skills and handiness in a given branch of industry, and become labour power of a special kind, a special education or training is requisite, and this, on its part, costs an

equivalent in commodities of a greater or less amount. [...] The expenses of this education (excessively small in the case of ordinary labour power) enter *pro tanto*[7] into the total value spent in its production.[8]

Two points are to be made here. First, things have changed dramatically since Marx was writing *das Kapital*. The portion of labor power value associated with training and education has grown tremendously as postindustrial society becomes a reality. According to the U.S. Census Bureau, a college graduate earns, roughly, 1.7 times more than a high school graduate per lifetime, and a person with a Ph.D. earns 2.6 times more money.[9] The very fact that the U.S. economy is functioning and thriving shows that even though the value of labor power really increases dramatically with the input of more education, workers still are able to create much more value than their labor power contains. In other words, it makes good economic sense for capitalists to hire educated workers, despite the cost differential. Again, I would like to refer to the human capital theorists who extensively demonstrated this point and effectively repudiated Marx's and other classical economists' simplistic assumption about the homogeneity of labor.

Second, Marx was no educational theorist; he simply did not know much about education. Had he more opportunity or desire to look closely into the processes that make up education, he could have noticed that the labor that goes into education is only partially the labor of a teacher and other school staff. *Students themselves* do the lion's share of work, which the human capital theory also largely overlooks. At any given time, about thirty students work in a classroom with one teacher. We may argue that a teacher's work is more intensive or more complex or that for each classroom teacher there is at least one administrator or school support staff working, but still one has to agree that students do most of the work that produces learning.

Dewey made clear the connection between the student's own activity and learning. A child cannot learn unless she *does* something, unless she expends her muscle, brain, and imagination. The work a student puts into writing a paper, solving a problem, or making a paper airplane is a necessary and major component of the educational process. Dewey made such an argument in the context of supporting his ideas of new Progressive education; he did not see the same connection between students' work and learning applied to the old, traditional academic learning activity. Indeed, from a psychological point of view, there is a huge difference between traditional academic learning and the active learning Dewey had in mind. However, from an economic standpoint, this difference does not exist; all learning involves student activity of some sort. Even passive listening to a teacher's lecture is work, a purposeful expenditure of an individual's strength. I am afraid the 100-year-old debate between Progressive and traditional education did nothing to illuminate the economic meaning of schooling. Importantly, learning activity is students' work—but is it labor?

When we pay a doctor's bill, we cover not only the value of services rendered but also the value of a, say, one-paragraph story about a princess in the far-away land that our doctor wrote when she was a second grader. In order to be able to make a diagnosis and write a prescription, it is necessary for her to write the princess story (just as necessary as her hospital internship training). As a customer, you and I purchase a fraction of that story when we receive medical services even though we have never read it and do not know about its existence. In a similar way, when purchasing a ceramic pot we also pay for the production of all broken ones on which the potter practiced. Student labor is unique in that it deposits value not in its immediate product (the princess story or a broken pot), but in the doctor, the worker herself, or, more precisely, in her labor power. The princess story has no utility; it is a non-commodity, which *does not mean* that the little girl's labor is a non-labor. She creates real value by writing the story, but this value is transferred only much later from her onto an entirely different product, the medical service. The value created by students is a Sleeping Beauty who appears to be dead only to be resurrected under different circumstances in another form.

The things produced by students are, in essence, means of production, like machines or materials in an industrial process. Here is how Marx describes the process of value transfer from the means of production to a new product:

> While productive labour is changing the means of production into constituent elements of a new product, their value undergoes a metempsychosis. It deserts the consumed body, to occupy the newly created one. ... The property therefore which labour-power in action, living labour, possesses of preserving value, at the same time that it adds it, is a gift of Nature which costs the labourer nothing, but which is very advantageous to the capitalist inasmuch as it preserves the existing value of his capital.[10]

The specifics of learning activity as labor are that its material products are short lived. As soon as they are ready, they are already consumed, and the value created in them deserts them so quickly that no one even notices they had value. Producing the princess story *is* consuming it; by the time the story is ready, it is consumed, and what remains is a valueless corpse of a thing. Yet the value created does not just disappear into thin air; it is now a part of the future doctor's labor power and is only awaiting the right circumstances to show up in medical services she provides. The doctor then not only creates new value but also preserves (transfers) the value created by her as a student—largely as a gift to her employer.

Let us get back to the value created by learning activity. The total labor that goes into the value of each commodity we see on the market consists of two parts: the immediately productive labor and the labor of learning activity. The economic shadow of the little princess story, as intangible as it is, remains in the doctor's mind and body and quietly trickles down to the prescription slip. As I have pointed out earlier, the portion of learning labor tends to increase as society moves toward a more education-driven economy. A contemporary American worker spends at least 13 years in the classroom, which means that for every three years of employment, we spend one year in the classroom. Every hour of productive work now requires almost 20 minutes of learning activity. Every 8-hour workday is in reality a 10-hour day, if we add years of formal education to it.

Critics of schooling long observed that most of the learning activity that takes place in schools is irrelevant to work experience, yet it makes no difference that much of the learning activity is irrelevant or has little to do with future productive labor. Some proponents of traditional academic schooling, of course, say that learning activity is meant to be largely irrelevant to the future labor, and I will address this criticism later. In part, this is only a *perceived* irrelevancy, resulting from the difficulty with which we can link the princess story with the medical service directly. Each particular story our doctor wrote may indeed have very little to do with the prescription she wrote for us. However, the sum of all the school activities and the tons of garbage the doctor produced while in school has definitely everything to do with what she has become. Let us still assume that a significant part of the learning activity is a complete waste of time or is even detrimental to the value of labor power. Just as it is with any labor, the socially necessary waste and labor associated with that waste should be taken into consideration when determining the value of the final product. In other words, even a skilled potter breaks a pot or two now and then—we pay for the wasted materials and wasted labor anyway. The opinion that modern education is especially wasteful or harmful may or may not be true, but it makes little difference with respect to the economic meaning of learning activity. Here is another useful if not very graceful quote from Marx that can illustrate this point:

> Suppose that in spinning cotton, the waste for every 115 lbs. used amounts to 15 lbs., which is converted, not into yarn, but into "devil's dust." Now, although this 15 lbs. of cotton never becomes a constituent element of the yarn, yet assuming this amount of waste to be normal and inevitable under average conditions of

spinning, its value is just as surely transferred to the value of the yarn, as is the value of the 100 lbs. that form the substance of the yarn. The use-value of 15 lbs. of cotton must vanish into dust, before 100 lbs. of yarn can be made.[11]

As long as more "efficient" forms of education are not a reality, the waste in education is a normal part of the economic process. I am using the term "efficient" only to indicate an idealized form of learning activity, where all student activities would significantly contribute to increasing students' skills and knowledge. As will become apparent, I believe such education is neither possible nor desirable. The efficiency models a la Taylor in education, which all but killed the Progressive education experiments, stem from the assumption that such efficiency is possible.

As the labor of learning is hidden and removed from the actual production of commodities, contemporary capitalism uses it as an additional form of surplus value extraction. Even poorly motivated, students work for free for many years, and as a result their labor power accumulates enormous value. However, when the time comes for workers to sell their labor power on the market, what they sell is their actual labor power, that is, their capacity for work, *not their past labor as students.* The labor of learning and the value created by it do not count when labor power is sold. There are lots and lots of extra pennies when it is time to break the piggy bank of contemporary labor power.

One may object by suggesting that the value accumulated from learning activity results in higher wages of a more qualified worker. In other words, one can argue that learning activity is well paid as labor. According to the U.S. Census Bureau, a bachelor's degree increases one's lifetime income by $600,000. Following this logic, a college student makes $150,000 (in future earnings) per year just by being a student. Even considering the skyrocketing cost of higher education, this is not a bad investment. I am not denying that more educated labor power has more value and therefore costs more to employers, yet the student's own labor during the years of primary and secondary education is not taken into consideration when labor power is purchased. In other words, educated labor power has much more value than uneducated labor power, the difference is larger than the income figures may suggest. Economically speaking, an employer purchases the actual ability to work, not the past labor.

Let us assume for a moment that the "Learn now—get paid later" theory that the U.S. federal government assumes to be true is valid. Even then, education may not benefit students that much, if at all. A high school graduate makes $821,000 during her lifetime (the Census Bureau assumes an average 40 years of work between the ages of 25 and 65). The 13 years of schooling can then be directly factored in. We should really spread the amount over 53 years of work life. Just by doing that we can see that the real average yearly income of a high school graduate is $15,490. Even the Statistic Brief tells us that the income of high school graduates actually *dropped* during the 20 years from 1974 to 1994 if adjusted for inflation. One needs a college education now to maintain the same standard of living that one's parents could afford with a high school diploma. In 1973, only 30 percent of high school graduates enrolled in college, but by 1993, 41 percent did.[12] In other words, people need to *work longer* to earn the same amount of money if we assume that learning activity is real, value-producing work. Americans have some of the longest workweeks in the industrialized world,[13] but on top of that, consider two facts.

First, women who entered the paid work force in previous decades dramatically increased the total workweek of an American family.[14] A two-income family works twice as much as a one-income family of the 1950s. Let us not forget that the domestic labor women are providing is also a form of unpaid labor, which has very real use-value, and greatly contributes to the economy. What really changed is that one part of their domestic labor has become automated, and thus more efficient, and another part was taken over by schools (inadequately, as Jane R. Martin amply demonstrated[15]), and yet another part simply moved to the second shift.

Second, by shifting toward universal 13-year education, Americans now put significantly more hidden school hours into their total working time. It would take massive statistical research to illustrate these trends, and I must limit myself to pointing them out. The unprecedented economic growth of the 1990s is not only a result of new technologies, it is also a result of the unprecedented exploitation of an unusually educated labor force.

I must acknowledge that these statistical manipulations make sense if and only if one spreads the lifetime income over the years of learning. In reality, however, students are not paid at all during their years of learning. The essential elements of selling and purchasing of labor power are obviously missing here. The specific form of labor—learning activity—never figures on the balance sheets of employers, it is never compensated, and is never thought of as labor. For all practical purposes, learning activity is work gratis. Students spend 13 years of their lives just to get to ground zero, where they become barely employable. Employers, in turn, accept much of these 13 years of value-creating labor as a free gift from the public and the workers. Most of this labor is unpaid; moreover, it is compulsory.

If we assume learning activity to be labor, then the compulsory character of education comes to a new grim light. It is one thing to justify compulsory learning, if it is something a student does for his own good, but it is much more difficult to justify compulsory labor. Here is how the U.S. Department of Labor describes the history of the child labor laws to kids:

> From the mid 1800s to the early part of this century, many young children were employed in what we now call "sweatshop conditions." These children spent many hours working hard at dangerous jobs instead of going to school and getting a good education. Many factories and other firms hired kids because they could be paid less than adults. Many children were overworked and underpaid, often working 16 hours a day, six days a week, and earning only pennies an hour. Kids often were injured or killed while working under these brutal conditions. The child labor laws came into being to stop these abuses and help young people obtain schooling. These laws were passed to protect the health, safety, and well being of young workers while at the same time affording them an opportunity to obtain an education.[16]

The introduction of universal compulsory education is linked to the abolition of child labor. In 1827, Massachusetts adopted the nation's first compulsory education law, mandating tax-supported schools in every Massachusetts community with 500 families or more.[17] In 1836, Massachusetts Legislature adopted a law prohibiting the employment of any child under 15 years of age who had received less than 3 months of schooling in the previous year.[18] As years passed, child labor became more and more obsolete, but schooling became more and more compulsory, sometimes absurdly so. Detroit parents today, for instance, might spend 90 days in jail if their children skip schools.[19] It looks bad enough if you think of schools as forced baby-sitting; this looks even worse if they are, in fact, forced sweatshops. Let me mention again, that if I ignore the social aspect of schooling (the imposing of work ethics, reproduction of class structure, etc.) that Marxist theorists described, it is not because I think of it as unimportant, but simply because from the point of view of social justice the "core" of schooling—learning activity—is as worrisome as the social aspect of schooling.

The abolition of child labor in industrialized nations was, in fact, a shift to a different, more efficient, and unpaid form of child labor that is called school learning. Let us notice that the nineteenth-century child labor was still paid at a higher rate than the labor of learning in the twenty-first century. As terrible as working conditions were, the child factory laborer of the nineteenth century could still support herself; a contemporary youngster is completely dependent on her parents or on public support. In other words, more people are forced to work for more years and lesser pay as students.

The invisible labor army of schoolchildren is not unlike the army of women who helped build modern economies with their unpaid domestic labor. From the economic point of view, the labor of schoolchildren and domestic labor of women are no different from the unpaid labor of slaves or Gulag prisoners. The differences are in political forms of organizing the unpaid labor. However, I need to stay closer to the theme of this book. The huge accumulated invisible value from the child labor of learning becomes a major source of wealth. The new knowledge-based economy simply could not be possible without mass schooling and mass labor of students. Unprecedented gains in work productivity are only possible with the more educated labor force. To do well in today's economy, a capitalist needs to convince workers to spend many long years in school preparing themselves for the workplace of the future. A theory such as human capital or the version of it the U.S. Census Bureau subscribes to are quite suitable tools for it. Unfortunately, a large portion of educational theory implicitly supports such a theory by searching for better forms of learning without thinking about who really benefits from it.

One can certainly object to the gloomy picture I paint by suggesting that the purpose of learning is much larger than creating labor power; that we learn for ourselves, not for our future employer. The cultural archetype of education goes hand in hand with ideals of personal emancipation, liberty, and democracy. Many educators think of education as the essential noble endeavor, which, despite all of its shortcomings, contains a promise of human freedom and happiness. As an educator, I have a stake in promoting such an understanding, too. Even the most far-reaching critics of education such as Paulo Freire and critical theorists almost without exception target the real-life oppressive education and offer another version of good, democratic, or free education.[20] Not many question education, *any organized education*, as such. It does not take extensive historical study to trace such faith in education to the Enlightenment and then to German Idealism. Kant went as far as to suggest that a person becomes fully human only through education; education for Kant is a major precondition of emancipation.[21] He meant, of course, a liberal arts education, not so much *Buildung* as *Erziehung*.

Similarly, Dewey professed almost religious faith in education. Robert Westbrook, for instance, believes that for Dewey, the school replaced the church as the key institution in the saving of souls for democracy.[22] Characteristically, President Clinton used the language of faith and revolution in his last State of the Union Address:

> First and foremost, we need a 21st century revolution in education, guided by our faith that every child can learn. Because education is more than ever the key to our children's future, we must make sure all our children have that key.[23]

Before the War on Terrorism, George W. Bush made education a key feature of his agenda: "My focus will be on making sure every child is educated.... I've seen how real education reform can lift up scores in schools and effectively change lives."[24] Yet his educational program is barely distinguishable from that of the previous president.

A sober look into what schools actually teach will inevitably reveal that *Erziehung*, or social and character education in connection with liberal arts curriculum, has all but disappeared from educational horizon. Here is the list of *President's & Secretary's Priorities,* as supplied by the U.S. Department of Education:

- All students will read independently and well by the end of 3rd grade.
- All students will master challenging mathematics, including the foundations of algebra and geometry, by the end of 8th grade.
- By 18 years of age, all students will be prepared for and able to afford college.
- All states and schools will have challenging and clear standards of achievement and accountability for all children, and effective strategies for reaching those standards.
- There will be a talented, dedicated and well-prepared teacher in every classroom.
- Every classroom will be connected to the Internet by the year 2000 and all students will be technologically literate.
- Every school will be strong, safe, drug-free and disciplined.[25]

Of course, these were Clinton's educational priorities. The Bush administration came up with its own set of seven priorities:

- Improving the academic performance of disadvantaged students
- Boosting teacher quality
- Moving limited English proficient students to English fluency
- Promoting informed parental choice and innovative programs
- Encouraging safe schools for the 21st Century
- Increasing funding for Impact Aid
- Encouraging freedom and accountability[26]

In both sets of priorities, there is not a trace of *Erziehung*, nothing about liberation, or emancipation; it is all about training workers. In the

Bush plan, freedom refers to freeing states, districts, and schools from regulations in exchange for higher testing scores; it has nothing to do with pursuing freedom as an educational aim. Kant surely had something entirely different in mind. We may believe that Johnny and Jenny will use their reading skills attained by the end of 3rd grade to read great novels for their own pleasure and spiritual growth, but as adults they are more likely to read instruction manuals, technical literature, or finance reports. Their prospects of reading presidential election pamphlets are also limited, so the argument that democracy somehow requires 13 years of schooling does not strike as true. Johnny and Jenny will learn to connect to the Internet so they can become the uniquely resourceful and enormously productive working machines of "the American middle class." I invite the reader to guess how much knowledge content and how many skills learned at school she or he uses for private and public life outside of work for the sort of things associated with emancipation, personal freedom, and self-realization. What we now call education does make our financial prospects brighter but hardly liberates us.

I will set aside the discussion of whether the Enlightenment project of education as emancipation had any chance to succeed. For now, let us establish that it has not yet succeeded. The next question is whether it can truly work in the future. A multitude of critical theorists argues that education controls, disciplines, and oppresses. In my opinion, it is also a form of labor, and as such, it constitutes *economically* exploitative relations. At least, we must recognize the exploitative economic nature of learning activity as labor. Learning needs to be understood not as a personal liberation but as a form of forced labor.

"And what exactly do we do then?" the reader will certainly ask. Theorists like Paul Goodman and Ivan Illich suggested that we get rid of organized schooling altogether.[27] The contemporary proponents of home schooling make similar suggestions.[28] Their critique of schooling is very convincing, but their conclusions are less than satisfactory. If organized education is indeed an essentially flawed project, what else is there to do? Here is where I depart from Marxism as a theoretical guide.

Capitalism is certainly an exploitative economic system, but I would be the last to suggest abandoning it in favor of a socialist economy of any kind. Consider this the personal bias of a person who grew up in the Soviet Union. I just find it extremely hard to believe that humane or even reasonably democratic socialism is possible. In a certain sense, a socialist society feels like one big school where people are students and the Party is faculty. The ideals of economic equality provide little incentive for anyone to work. Therefore, the Party has no choice but to introduce extra-economic means of coercion, which is political terror. The link between utopianism, lack of motivation to work, and political repression has been investigated extensively in Russian press and academic writing of the past 15 years, but I do not think even Russians see the close resemblance of their Communist experiments to practices of schooling. Both entail some sort of repression because both are based on unrealistic expectations and lack of motivation. In other words, my economic critique of capitalist schooling is not a critique of capitalism as a system; it is a critique of capitalist schooling only.

Granted, capitalism inevitably produces social inequality, poverty, and unemployment, but it is the best working economic principle we have. Like a powerful but hazardous and dangerous technology, the capitalist economic system should be tolerated but amended, regulated, contained to be more suitable for human society. As it is the case with any other powerful technology, attempts to abandon it and go back to non-economic principles of social organization ultimately fail. Unregulated capitalism creates tremendous inequality and human suffering; capitalism that is regulated and limited by political democracy can work for the interest of the public. Certain fundamental changes of schooling that I am trying to outline in this book should be viewed in the context of many historical attempts to tame the social technology of capitalism but not to destroy it.

I do not believe schooling can be completely freed of the economic exploitation. As an integral part of the capitalist economic machine, schooling must continue despite its exploitative nature. Organized education should be classified as one of society's unavoidable ills. We should tolerate education, restrain it, regulate it, and try to make it more humane but never admire or idealize it. Of course, no one idealizes the *existing* schooling, but I would argue that one must not fall into piety about any *ideal* model of schooling as well. We must abandon the great metanarrative of education in favor of a much more critical understanding of its limits and its enormous human cost. In general, it is much better to see, tolerate, and amend evil than to believe it to be good.

There are two implications of the learning activity as labor theory: one economical and one pedagogical. The economical implication has to do with recognition of who benefits from education and who pays for it. Corporations of the industrialized world must contribute to public education to a much greater extent than they do now but without exercising undue influence on the content and the process of schooling. Currently, the indicators of industrial productivity are largely skewed because the unpaid labor of learning activity is made possible only by massive public subsidies and economic support of one group of workers (parents) to another group of workers (students). The contemporary capitalism has learned to make a profit from parental love. Unfortunately, the universities are happy to perpetuate the myth of education as emancipation and to cash in on the ever-increasing number of students forced to go to college for purely economic reasons.

The pedagogical implication is to reduce the level of coercion in education. One of the main problems is that a compulsory educational institution is often a place that has to rely on extra-economical means of coercion to motivate its workers. One can argue that, in a certain sense, schools are feudal remnants within the capitalist economies. They can also be called socialist institutions, because real-life socialism has to rely heavily on extra-economical stimuli (read violence) as well. The level of coercion in public schooling is unacceptable and contradicts the doctrine of universal human rights. Article 4 of the *Universal Declaration of Human Rights* states: "No one shall be held in slavery or servitude." Paradoxically, the same declaration, in Article 26, says: "Elementary education shall be compulsory." I see an obvious contradiction here, for compulsory education if it is a form of labor is also servitude.[29] In addition, forced labor of students is very inefficient, which became abundantly clear since the introduction of truly mass schooling. Again, the fact that it is inefficient has little to do with the economic value created by that labor, and with its exploitative nature.

To reduce the level of extra-economic coercion we need to move schools closer to the regular economic form of motivation that capitalism developed. Simply paying students money for their labor is probably out of the question, at least for the foreseeable future. Yet students need some compensation for learning activity. They need *something else* besides learning from school. This book is an attempt to solve the problem of learning activity motivation with the help of what I call the pedagogy of relation. However, before I move on to explication of the pedagogy of relation, let us consider some other consequences of the wastebasket economy of schooling.

NOTES

[1] G.S.Becker, *Human Capital: A Theoretical and Empirical Analysis, with Special Reference to Education* (Chicago: The University of Chicago Press, 1993).

[2] Samuel Bowles and Herbert Gintis, "The Problem with Human Capital Theory—A Marxian Critique, " *The American Economic Review* 65, 2 (1975), 74-82.

[3] This, of course, is a reference to Paul Willis' book *Learning to Labor: How Working Class Kids Get Working Class Jobs* (New York: Columbia University Press, 1981, 1977). The title of this chapter is another reference to the same book. A fascinating cultural account that illustrates the reproduction theory, the book assumes that learning and labor are two different things—an assumption I question.

[4] Marx, *Capital*, 16.

[5] Marx, *Capital*, 15.

[6] Marx, *Capital*, 93.

[7] To that extent.

[8] Marx, *Capital*, 81.

[9] U.S. Census Bureau Statistical Brief, *More Education Means Higher Career Earnings* (http://www.census.gov/apsd/www/statbrief/sb94_17.pdf, 1994).

[10] Marx, *Capital*, 100.

[11] Marx, *Capital*, 99.

[12] *More Education Means Higher Career Earnings*, U.S.Bureau of Census, 1994 (http://www.census.gov/apsd/www/statbrief/sb94_25.pdf).

[13] In 1997, about 30 percent of men and 15 percent of women usually worked more than 44 hours per week (http://www.bls.gov/opub/ted/1998/dec/wk4/art03.htm).

[14] In 1991, there were 1.6 million "latchkey kids" in the United States between the ages of 5 and 14. See *Child Labor*. Wage and Hour Division of U.S. Department of Labor (http://www.census.gov/apsd/www/statbrief/sb94_5.pdf).

[15] Jane R. Martin *The Schoolhome: Rethinking Schools for Changing Families* (Cambridge: Harvard University Press, 1995).

[16] *Child Labor* (http://www.dol.gov/dol/esa/public/youth/cltour1.htm).

[17] *The Encarta® 99 New World Timeline* (CD ROM: Helicon Publishing, 1998).

[18] "Child Labor," *Microsoft® Encarta® 97 Encyclopedia*. 1993-1996 Microsoft Corporation.

[19] Brian Harmon, "Truants' Parents May Be Charged," *The Detroit News*, November 29, 1999 (http://www.detnews.com).

[20] Paulo Freire, *Pedagogy of the Oppressed* (New York: Continuum, 1993).

[21] "Der Mensch kann nur Mensch werden durch Erziehung. Er ist nichts, als was die Erziehung aus ihm macht." Immanuel Kant, *Ueber Padagogic*, In Kant, *Schriften zur Antropologie, Geschichtsphilosophie. Politik und Padagogik* (http://www-user.uni-bremen.de/~kr538/kantpaed.html).

[22] Robert Westbrook, *John Dewey and American Democracy* (Ithaca and London: Cornell University Press, 1992), 184. Westbrook agrees with Robert Crunden on this point.

[23] William Clinton, "The State of the Union," *New York Times*, January 28, 2000.

[24] "Excerpt from Bush Statement Announcing Start of His Education Initiative." *The New York Times on the Web*, January 24, 2001 (http://www.nytimes.com/).

[25] *President's & Secretary's Priorities*, U.S. Department of Education 2000 (http://www.ed.gov/inits.html), Retrieved in January, 2000 (no longer available on-line).

[26] *No Child Left Behind*, Executive summary, U.S. Department of Education (http://www.ed.gov/inits/nclb/part2.html).

[27] Ivan Illich, *De-Schooling Society* (New York: Harper and Row, 1971). Paul Goodman, *Compulsory Mis-education* (New York: Horizon Press, 1964).

[28] Grace Llewellyn, The Teenage Liberation Handbook: How to Quit School and Get a Real Life and Education (Eugene, OR: Lowry House, 1991).

[29] *Universal Declaration of Human Rights*. U.N. Office of the High Commissioner for Human Rights (http://www.unhchr.ch/udhr/lang/eng.htm).

CHAPTER 3.
LEARNING TO BE

Another consequence of the wastebasket economy is existential. The existential status of schooling is not trivial. For students, the quality of being is different from everyone else's. "A student" is a mode of existence and so is "a teacher." These are not simply social roles one could easily enter and leave without such a role sticking to one's skin. I will now examine the existential aspect of "student" in relation to the institution of compulsory schooling.

Our coming to this world is gradual. Neither conception, nor birth, nor some point in between represents a sudden leap from non-being into being. Childhood is a crucial experience that shapes how it is to be human. One of the first things a person learns upon arriving into this world is that she is not quite here. To be, among other things, means to be an adult. David Kennedy points out the inseparability of the concepts of adulthood and childhood: "To say what a child is is also to say how one becomes an adult; and to say what an adult is is to say what relationship one is in to one's childhood."[1] Childhood is thus an experience of becoming rather than that of being. We really come to existence through the experience of childhood, which is an experience of not quite being, of half-existing, and of movement toward full-existence. Acquiring an identity of a child means understanding that you do not quite exist yet. It is an identity oriented toward the future, and therefore an identity that undervalues the present. Being a child is overcoming partial existence and acquiring full-existence. This is both the drive and the teleology of childhood.

The lesson of half-being includes experiences of one-sided dependency, when one takes from others much more than one contributes. It is also a lesson that the real existence only comes forth when one begins to contribute and therefore acquires some influence over others and becomes present for them. Children discover very early that they are not contributors, at least not in a sense that truly matters. In modern times, children came to matter a lot to their parents and to the society in general, but I would argue that this situation does not cancel or resolve the essential quality of childhood existence, which boils down to not-quite-existence and movement toward full-existence. A child is a person with a huge potentiality that greatly overshadows her actuality. In this regard, her being is an advance given by the others, which only emphasizes the not-quite-here quality of her existence.

Nel Noddings provides a detailed analysis of unequal relationships, relying on Buberian framework.[2] Her main point is to show that unequal relationships can be mutual. Relationship of care requires the cared-for to reciprocate, to be aware and respond to care received from the one-caring: "the recognition of caring by one-cared is necessary to the caring relation."[3] Indeed, to receive care, one has to be there. Yes, kids are very much alive and very much involved in their relationships with adults, especially those who care deeply about them. Yet the existential aspect of unequal relationship is unequal, regardless of the psychological aspect. Even the very act of conscious acceptance of care is also an act of recognizing one's need and one's inability to enter the relationship as equal. Like any relationship, it is a two-way street, but the traffic on the two sides of the street is very different: it is mostly needs moving on one side, and mostly gifts on the other.

If human existence can be meaningfully described as a being with others, that is, if one accepts sociality as constitutive of human existence, then it becomes apparent that the quality of the sociality and the quality of being are different for children. Our biology and our culture conspire to prevent children from full-existence for some time. Human existence is a project rather than a state; it is something to be achieved. Some may refer to Rousseau and other romantic interpreters of childhood to show that childhood is a fuller mode of being than adulthood. There is a whole tradition of such interpretation of childhood, along with the opposite tradition of seeing childhood as a deficiency.[4] However, even romantics would agree that the one unalienable quality of childhood is knowing that one will grow up. Adult existence is followed by death and is therefore intent on making some meaning of itself. Children's existence is followed by another mode of existence; this is why children are not compelled to give it an independent, separate meaning. An intelligent chrysalis would not be preoccupied with the dilemma of life and death; it would ponder the meaning of metamorphosis. The Peter Pan syndrome is just that, a syndrome, an aberration, an avoidance of full being and retreat into the safety of half-existence.

Someone can also question that human existence has degrees or levels rather than simply different kinds. Isn't being a child just different from being an adult? Don't children have the same degree of presence (if not the sort of presence) in the world as their parents? If one can speak of Dasein or some other non-Heideggerian but specifically human kind of existence (and I see no way to have any sort of anthropology without such a device), then one has to admit that children do not yet possess the qualities making such an existence possible. If this were not true, the drama of human life as a process would make no sense. What separates us from a rock is that the rock just is, and we need to figure out how to be. The process of figuring out in large part occurs in childhood.

The extended period of dependency is what sets us apart from our animal cousins. We became an intelligent species thanks to a biological defect of a sort. Any reasonable mammal would point out to us that human babies are born immature. Our response is that immaturity allows us to have large and complex brains without killing our mothers at birth with our huge heads. Human babies remain dependent and pliable for a very long time, which allows them to learn much more than any other species has managed to pass from generation to generation. The partial existence of a child makes it possible for us to be human. The enormous productivity of an adult human directly depends on her unproductivity as a child. Humans can be defined as animals that produce mountains of useless things and engage in many useless activities for a very long time. One can easily view the mass compulsory education in evolutionary terms; it is nothing but further extension of the period of dependency, which allows our kids to learn even more before they become independent, fully existent, and unteachable. We are simply capitalizing on our existing biological advantages/deficiencies. Educators always hope to make learning more intensive, so we can teach kids more during the same period of time. However, it remains unclear whether such a strategy can be effective. I wonder also if a notion of intensive childhood is an oxymoron and if the whole point of childhood is to *not be* intensive.

Meanwhile, childhood has definitely changed. As Michel Foucault had demonstrated, institutions alter our existence. Following his way of thinking somewhat, I want to find out what happens to childhood when schooling becomes universal? Mass schooling became a reality only relatively recently, and I will examine some other implications of this development in Chapter 4. Schools have been significantly altered and enhanced in the redefined childhood.[5] Childhood has become a public affair, the affair of state and a matter of close public scrutiny. It has now been stretched over many years, institutionalized, turned over to mass production, defined and supported by the modern society. Childhood is not a private matter any more; it is a matter of a huge public industry called schooling. The mode of existence previously known as childhood thus took very specific cultural forms. Being a child became equivalent to being a student, and experience of childhood and adolescence became confluent with experience of schooling. A schoolbag and a grade report card have become inevitable attributes of growing up as breaking voices and menarche.

What does it mean to institutionalize a particular mode of being? What do institutions have to do with human existence? Here is one particular example. The violence and subjugation have always existed in human history and human societies. When the institution of slavery was developed, it took a specific cultural form, legitimizing and normalizing violence. The institution of slavery legitimized violence and limited it, channeled it to a specific group of human beings with specific status given to them by the society. Slavery made violence part of economy, gave it a productive function, and reduced its destructive function. The mode of existence associated with violation of one's person had been legitimized and made unquestionable. The institution comes between a person and his or her being as an intermediary and as an authority. The same process works for other social institutions and cultural norms such as marriage. The specific mode of existence that people associated with sexual love and economic cooperation becomes unquestionable (or rather questionable with only specific questions) when the institution of marriage comes into the picture.[6]

As a contrast to these two examples, let me bring up some modes of existence that are not institutionalized, and as such, they can become questioned and questionable. The desperation or angst until very recently were uninstitutionalized features of existence. Of course, there were always cultural scenarios for people who are desperate or for people who are uneasy about the world and themselves in it. There is always something to do for people in specific situations. However, when the modern institution with its structure, its hierarchy, its blanks and forms, and its procedures comes into full force, it erodes and ultimately destroys the existential aspect of human experience. The notion of clinical depression makes angst much more explainable, to the point of not becoming problematic.

Angst is not about how to be in the world anymore; it is about which pills to take. It is not as if angst ceased to be a part of human condition; rather it becomes a legitimate and explained part of human condition.

Institutions are social machines for solving human problems on a mass scale. "Solving a problem" does not necessarily mean reduction in suffering or increase of pleasure; it only indicates that certain things become non-problematic. Each solved problem, however, eliminates or hides a particular aspect of human existence that was there before the problem was solved. The institution of criminal justice solves the problem of personal revenge, but it also eliminates the existential aspect of revenge, it narrows the scope of human existence to exclude experiences of revenge as a duty and as an emotion. The institution dissociates Hamlet's question of whether to avenge his father's murder from his other question about whether to be at all. Generally, institutions eat away at the existential questionability of our lives. The institution makes revenge a procedure, a legitimate part of social life. Revenge becomes an industry and thus makes it inaccessible for an individual.

When the modern mass schools became reality, they replaced the reality of the childhood as an existential *problem*; the existential aspect of childhood vanished, and its institutionalized aspect began. Schools solved the problem of childhood. Childhood is not an individual challenge; it is merely a common stage of development. Most importantly, schools are institutions that put the experience of half-being on the scale of industrial production. The half-being is no more a question to be answered by an individual; it is a question to be answered by an institution on behalf of the individual. Slavery makes violence both legitimate and invisible; marriage makes love both legitimate and invisible; criminal justice legitimizes and eliminates revenge. In the same way, schools make childhood both legitimate and strangely invisible.

Let me go back to the phenomenon of the wastebasket economy. Being a student, by definition, means not producing anything useful. Students are excluded from the normal processes of economic and non-economic exchanges that create the fabric of human society. As adults, we do not realize how much of our true existence is owed to the fact that we make something useful that is actually needed by other people. I am not talking only about material production of services or other gainful employment. On another level, family relations, friendship, and political and civic involvement—all include producing something useful to someone else, whether tangible goods, intangible products, or services. Now, students by the very definition are excluded from the cycle of human connection. The problem here is not that they are excluded; the problem is that it is no longer a problem.

As one can see, this is just another side of the same essential problem of childhood, but the problem really changed. Traditional childhood is learning how to exist; schooling is learning how not to exist. Childhood was about how to overcome half-existence; studenthood is about how to accept half-existence and how to play by its rules. Children used to learn how to become adults; now they must first learn how to become students. Schooling is such a well-established institution, with its own life, its own forms of human existence, that one has to spend one's time learning how to be a student. From something that is transitory and highly problematic, childhood became something that is semi-permanent, a life of its own. Schooling solved some of the anxieties of childhood by legitimizing them and making them invisible. One can define a student as a child whose partial being is no longer a problem. A student is a child whose non-being is both legitimized and made invisible.

A school looks like real life, feels like real life, but, of course, it isn't real life. School is an artificially produced version of human existence, where everything looks as if it mattered, when in fact nothing in schools does matter to a larger world. What is produced in schools has to be destroyed; only bits of knowledge and useful skills in individual students' brains and bodies are salvaged and reused in the future. This goes against every other human enterprise, where accumulation of individual efforts produces results. In school, a common result, whenever it is achieved, has to be ransacked by individual students. Schools are very strange social entities without a mutual compelling interest to sustain social bonds.

Schools are ghost towns whose inhabitants do not realize they are ghosts, but all have a vague suspicion that they might be. Nothing they do truly matters, as if there were a certain space ripple that separates them from the world of true existence. The only ones they can really hurt or help are other ghosts. Teachers are guardians of the town, whose job consists mainly of proving to students that this *is* the real existence. Teaching involves a thankless task of convincing ghosts that they really exist. The main way of doing this is organization of large-scale public works that look a lot like work in the real world with plans, materials, supervisors, procedures, and products, fake money and fake rewards, fake failures and fake successes. Phoney is what schools are, not by neglect but by necessity. Only dumpster truck drivers who come at night and pick up large containers from the school yard are fully aware of the truth, but who is listening to the dumpster truck drivers?

I cannot emphasize enough that the unreality, the disconnectedness of school life is not as much an economical as an existential phenomenon. Being a student is the most inconsequential position in the world. Whatever you do or do not do does not affect the rest of the world in one way or the other. The experience of schooling does not necessarily feel negative; it can be quite elating, for detachment indicates freedom from responsibility. The half-existence does not have to be bad. We all remember the moments of freedom in the carefree world of school pranks, mischief, and curiosity. If one believes the movies, ghosts can have fun, and the fun derives exactly from their detachment. Yet, as any movie eventually shows, if one cannot make an impact on what one observes, this will cause anguish and suffering.

Unlike Foucault, I do not believe the development of institutions such as schools is a result of progressive development of power techniques and aims at better control over people. Mass schooling is a more or less natural consequence of social evolution that is hard to explain plausibly with the concept of power. Prolonged compulsory schooling must exist for a variety of economical and political reasons. There are just too many things to learn and too many people need to know them for schooling to go away. The idea of education has been visibly penetrating all age groups along with youth culture, thus increasing infantilism of the entire society. The period of inconsequential half-existence tends to become longer and longer, and the period of full-existence shortens (but, hopefully, deepens). Quite naturally, we are gradually becoming *Homo Lentus,* the lingering human. One can imagine us turning into a species that will spend most of life lingering and learning in preparation of a short burst of a very demanding and complex productive activity and then slipping back into a semi-childhood of early retirement. As I count the years of my own education, a suspicion crawls in that we are almost there.

Whichever its *raison d'être*, mass schooling has altered the picture of human existence and brought new problems with it. What does schooling do to our children? What does the ghost life do to a person? Children need to master the art of half-existence first and then, presumably, learn how to achieve full-existence. Of course, the question is whether learning how to not exist makes learning how to exist more difficult. My guess is that it does. Long schooling decreases our ability to be responsible and responsive. Our civilization's vitality may be in danger because people learn too well how to not quite exist. The fabric of human existence is eroding because of the growth of schooling. It is clear that schooling cannot proliferate indefinitely, neither extensively (increasing years of schooling) nor intensively (further reducing schooling to pure academic education). I acknowledge that mass schooling may be unavoidable, but turning more and more of human life into more and more intensive studenthood is a potentially dangerous prospect. Learning is to be somehow mutated into learning how not to be; schooling starts defying its purpose.

I am not in a position to explore these larger cultural implications, because this book is about education. What I do know is that the existential peculiarities of schooling certainly affect school life itself. It is very difficult to make a strong impact on a ghost, because the disengagement from the world cuts both ways. As much as students do not matter to the world, the world becomes less important to students. Alienation from the world penetrates the internal universe of a school and makes relating to each other difficult.

Schools may have a much deeper problem than inadequate funding, poor management, and lack of imagination. There is something very peculiar and very threatening about the project itself. Because of the existential rift, schools are very different from comparable social institutions. The logic of business management, government, or family may not apply there. Whatever we use to motivate adults to work, to make them manageable, to help them live fuller lives may not work in schools. Educational theorists need to understand what is unique about the world of education. One of the first things I have learned in my American graduate school is that education is not really a discipline; it is simply a field where other disciplines such as psychology, cognitive science, sociology, etc., are applied. This may be a true description of the current state of affairs in American academia,[7] but what an unfortunate idea. There is no lack of specificity in the educational world, but there is a lack of appreciation for such specificity.

The specifics of the educational world have something to do with its limits. Mine is just one among many possible attempts to search for limits of education. Comprehending the limits of any human condition provides an important key to understanding it. I will borrow an illustration and part of the discussion from Martha Nussbaum's *Love's Knowledge*.

Calypso offers Odysseus the opportunity to stay with her on the island, to avoid all future struggles, to become immortal and ageless.

> He is choosing, quite simply, what is his: his own history, the form of a human life and the possibilities of excellence, love and achievement that inhabit that form. [...] We don't quite know what it would be for this hero, known for his courage, craft, resourcefulness, and loyal love to enter into life in which courage would atrophy, in which cunning and resourcefulness would have little point, since the risks with which they grapple would be removed, and in which love, insofar as it appears at all, would be very different in shape from the love that

> connects man to wife and child in the human world of the poem. The very possibility makes one uneasy: for where, and who, in such a life, would our hero actually be? Do we wish for him a good result that involves a transformation so total that he might not remain himself?
>
> For surely one reason why the choice for transcendence seems unappealing to the reader is that it would, quite clearly, bring the story to an end. [...] What story would be left, if he made the other choice? Plato saw the answer clearly: no story at all, but only praises of the goodness of the good gods and heroes.[8]

Well, this does not seem so obvious to me. Such a radical transformation is an enormous challenge itself. I would really love to know whether Odysseus could survive mentally on Calypso's island. Of course, the actions-driven myth of journey would end. But perhaps a *Bildungsroman* could develop instead? Odysseus would struggle for his sanity and his identity, seek his position in the new world, and somehow redefine his relationship with Calypso. He may regret his decision, seek return, and not find it. He might suffer and make Calypso suffer. And she is capable of suffering, because she is capable of love and does not want her lover to go away. He might finally find a fulfilling life of some sort. Isn't such a story fascinating? This would be an existentialist's Sartre-style novel; something ancient Greeks might not like, but modern people would surely be interested in.

"Human limits structure the human excellencies, and give excellent actions its significance" as Nussbaum suggests.[9] But our limits are within as much as outside. If we do not die, we find something else with which to struggle. Death constructs our universe just because we have chosen to pay so much attention to it. Solzhenitsyn said once that modern man, by putting himself at the center of the world, fears death because death thus becomes the end of all things.[10] The limits Nussbaum is talking about are not external objective things, they are the meanings attached to those things. So, some do not see any point in struggling with enemies, disasters, injustice, and their own death. Others would find limits to be pushed even after becoming immortal and isolated from the real world. Nussbaum is right in one regard, though: we do not know what kind of limits immortals encounter, so the story might not be as convincing and too far off the ground.

As long as we do not know what kind of limits education presents, the story of teaching and learning remains uninteresting. With corrections, I will accept Nussbaum's concept of limits. In educational theory and in educational practice, educators need to find or invent limits that would make our choices meaningful. We may as well accept the fact that academic learning can never be interesting to all students. The school-proper part of schooling may always lack motivation. There may be no way to directly link human desire to learning algebra and science. Learning in schools may always be a form of exploitation. Students may always be condemned to the half-existence of the ghost-like life. I will not insist that these are the definite limits of education; my suggestion is merely that limits *like these* ought to be found if we were to understand education.

Schools are Calypso islands, utopian and irrelevant. Odysseus had a semi-real half-existence on Calypso Island just as students lead semi-real half-existence lives in schools. Again, this is not a lack of limits as Nussbaum fears and as Dewey hopes. Calypso Island represents another set of limits to be understood, challenged, and used as stepping stones to excellence. Human excellence in schools should be measured against the limits of schools. Schools should organize themselves with full awareness of the limits of schooling. Schools should make the half-existence of students as humane and as human as possible.

I want to question one cultural assumption—that education, despite all of its shortcoming, ideally is an innocent, noble endeavor. This is the same as saying that education has no limits to it. This assumption takes roots in the ideology of European Enlightenment. Since then education is framed in the narrative of individual and social emancipation which I questioned in the previous chapter. Thus, all theoretical efforts were made in attempts to free education of its problems or to achieve the best, the most effective, and just forms of education. Very little has been done to appraise limitations and shortcomings of the whole project of education. Perhaps the project of education is not that innocent; perhaps some of its shortcomings are intrinsic.

Education (I mean organized education here, i.e., schooling) may be defensible as an economic force or as a cultural reproduction mechanism. This does not mean that education is necessarily defensible from the ethical point of view. Education is one of the last metanarratives of our civilization. It is a great project started by Enlightenment and still going at full speed with some modifications. The compulsory character of contemporary schooling is but one illustration to the postmodernist thesis that a metanarrative always includes some mechanisms of terror. It is extremely difficult for an educator to entertain the thought that she or he is involved into activity that is less than noble and is perhaps dominating and manipulative. Most of us use all sorts of psychological defenses and rationalizations to convince ourselves otherwise. Yet even the constant rhetoric of education as an ultimately virtuous project betrays our deep uneasiness about the project.

NOTES

[1] David Kennedy, "Notes on the Philosophy of Childhood and the Politics of Subjectivity." (http://www.bu.edu/wcp/Papers/Chil/ChilKenn.htm).

[2] Nel Noddings, *Caring: A Feminine Approach to Ethics and Moral Education* (Berkeley, CA: University of California Press, 1986).

[3] Nel Noddings, *Caring*, 71.

[4] For an interesting discussion of the two traditions, see David Kennedy.

[5] I will collapse notions of adolescence into the notion of childhood.

[6] See Michel Foucault, *The Care of the Self. The History of Sexuality*, Volume 3 (New York: Vintage, 1988).

[7] Although educational theory has the status of a true discipline in Russian academia, it has not yet produced major work explaining the specifics of education in comparison to other social spheres.

[8] Martha Nussbaum, *Love's Knowledge* (New York: Oxford University Press, 1990), 366-367.

[9] Nussbaum, *Love's Knowledge*, 378.

[10] Remnick, David."The exile returns," *The New Yorker* Feb.14, 1994, 83.

CHAPTER 4.
CRISIS OF AUTHORITY

During most of the twentieth century, institutions of compulsory education have been steadily losing traditional means of control over students. This would not be a problem in itself if not for the fundamental motivational flaw of schooling I explored in the first three chapters. Certain long-term historical changes brought the problem of motivation to the surface although they did not create that problem. Any learning activity at any historical moment involves the production of useless things. However, the institutional conditions of education have been dramatically changed during the past 100 years. These conditions made the fundamental flaw of education an institutional rather than personal or cultural issue. It is important to understand that what I describe as the crisis of authority in schools is essentially connected to the understanding of education I outlined earlier.

The crisis of authority indicates that schools are slowly transforming into a different type of institution. Our efforts in educational theory can be more effective if we aim to understand the nature of changes in education and abandon the idea that educational theory somehow drives these changes. Instead of asking, "What should be done in education?," we may try to ask "What is going on in education, and how can we understand the changes?" A theorist can admit the existence of some more or less objective tendencies of social evolution without falling into fallacies of great metanarratives. This chapter attempts to show that institutions of compulsory education are evolving into something much less educational and less compulsory whether anyone wants it or not. A theory able to accommodate these changes will have to be built around the notion of relation.

Our alien anthropologist, if you recall, was dismayed not only by the fact that the earthlings produce so much junk in schools but also wondered how such an institution can be run. I am not sure if we could explain it to him. Indeed, how do you run an organization where workers have very little incentive to work, and their supervisors have very little power to force them? Our disadvantage to the alien anthropologist is that we have become excessively accustomed to the realities of schooling to see that schools are becoming impossible organizations.

All my teacher education students really worry about is classroom management. I usually suggest that there is a good reason to worry about it, which makes them even more anxious. If you have kids who are seriously determined to disobey, there is almost nothing you can do about it. Specifically, I say, you can neither hit any of the children nor can you really expel them from school. After that, invariably, some of the students lament this unfortunate situation, and more than one suggest that both of the enforcement measures I mention were not such a bad idea. Then someone brings up an idea that it is the parents' responsibility to control (read "beat into submission") their own children. I know the conversation by heart, know what will come next, but can never get used to how easy it is for the future teachers to slip into the language and imagery of cruelty. It is not their fault, though. They sense the real crisis of authority in schools. They are scared, and fear is the father of all cruelty. How do I explain that a crisis is not always a bad thing?

Authority of traditional teachers was based on these two prerogatives: the power to expel and the power to inflict pain. Two processes have been slowly but fundamentally undermining these prerogatives: "massification" of schooling and gradual abandonment of corporal punishment. Both of these processes continued through many decades, and neither of the two is truly completed. According to the U.S. Census Bureau, in 1960, only 41.1 percent of all persons 25 years and older completed 4 years of high school or more. In 1998, 82.8 percent have done the same.[1] Only relatively recently universal secondary education began to become a reality. As for corporal punishment, it is diminishing but is still a reality. In the 1997–1998 school year, almost half a million American kids, or 1 percent of the entire student population, were subjected to corporal punishment in schools.[2] Only 27 states have bans on corporal punishment. In addition, many teachers still can inflict pain on their students, if not directly, then through parents. The threat of expulsion from school still works in private or otherwise exclusive and postsecondary schools. Yet the large number of educators in regular public schools sorely lack power of enforcement and have yet to find any good substitutes.

It is not among my objectives to examine the causes of the two processes. Mass schooling definitely has something to do with economic need for educated labor; compulsory learning can indeed be understood as a form of forced labor. Late capitalism is somehow reverting to pre-capitalist forms of extra-economic coercion. The abolition of physical punishment may be explained with Foucault's theory of transition from physical punishment to subtler and more efficient technique of discipline, which I will more closely examine in the next chapter.[3] I am not ruling out a possibility of some moral progress actually being made by the human race, although Foucault believes this may not be the case. For whatever reasons, schools have lost or are quickly losing the two most effective instruments of social control. One also needs to remember that usual economic means of behavior control (like the danger of losing one's paycheck) do not apply to students at all. All other public places where authority is exercised have some mechanism of enforcement that is tied to money, revocation of rights, or physical pain. These are all very tangible and effective instruments embodied in tax auditors, policemen, and judges. In public schools, there exists a real vacuum of power to which many teachers and school administrators can testify.

Empirical evidence of the crisis of authority is hard to find, mainly because we deal with a long-range historical process here. Statistical data I found contain so much noise that they are hardly useful. It is impossible to prove empirically that public schools of 150 years ago had more or less difficulty in exercising authority over their students than the schools of today. Teachers have always complained about declining discipline, and I am not sure how much of it is a true reflection of the historical changes. No one keeps statistics on how many times an average teacher asks students to be quiet and how many times students comply. Nobody knows how much time is wasted every day in schools due to disciplinary problems or simply lack of effort on students' parts. Such adjacent indicators as school crime, expulsion numbers, etc., reflect changing reporting practices, demographics, and especially, changing policies rather than changes in the character of the institution of schooling. Someone with more sophistication and interest in statistical analysis and with better knowledge of historical sources may be more effective in establishing the facts of the authority crisis in schools. I will have to rely on a speculative theoretical assertion that when essential tools of authority become unavailable, the authority weakens. It is very difficult to imagine that the "massification" of schooling did *nothing* to undermine adult authority in schools.

Many school administrators and teachers experience a tremendous vacuum of power. Anyone who has ever stood in a classroom facing 35 agitated 7th graders and tried to make them do things they are not inclined to do can attest to this statement. I find that only people who actually are or have been teachers can fully appreciate how impossible the everyday task of a teacher is. A teacher's main challenge is to organize and direct an activity that dramatically lacks intrinsic motivation without the use of direct violence. No other social institution operates this way. How do you make people do something they don't want to do? Writing warning slips, yelling, lunch detention, shaming, cajoling, begging, bribing, threatening, praising—all these and many other tricks of the trade are notoriously unreliable.

The crisis of authority progresses unevenly. The late 60s and early 70s appear to be the peak of the authority crisis in American schools; it seemed to subdue in the 80s and 90s. The popular explanation closely tied the situation in schools with cultural and political trends of the larger society. One would be foolish to deny such influences, but it is dangerous to overestimate them. Schools are a distinct institution and have their own path of evolution. I grew up and started my teaching career in the Soviet Union where cultural and political trends were very dissimilar from those in American society. Moreover, the model of schooling was quite different. Among other things, it was an educational system that the American conservatives like Ravitch, Hirsh, and Damon dream about—very high standards; uniform academic curriculum with strong emphasis on reading, writing, and sciences; clearly defined and exercised authority; generous financial and political support of the state. Despite dissimilarities with the U.S. system, it is fairly obvious that the Soviet schools suffered from the same crisis of authority throughout the second half of the twentieth century before and after the collapse of Communism. One feature the Soviet school shared with their American counterparts was the fact of compulsory mass schooling. Another commonality, corporal punishment in schools, was outlawed immediately after the Russian Revolution of 1917. This example shows that political and cultural influences can slow down or enhance this process but cannot alter its general direction.

In America, urban schools felt the impact of the crisis first, because racism, social injustice, enormous funding inequity, alienation from authorities, and erosion of traditional respect for the school exacerbated the universal crisis of school authority. Critical theorists suggest that these factors *are* the reasons (not secondary components) for the crisis, but I will insist that these enormously important factors could not explain the extent and the timing of the crisis. Minority and poor students are just more likely to challenge (and suffer from the consequences of) the weakened authority of schools because their own subcultures are more likely to confront the injustices and biases of the power structure. The social injustice will not explain some of the most horrifying recent breakdowns of authority in suburban schools. Rather, urban schools are slightly ahead of time, and they show what will happen to more and more schools in the future should we fail to understand the implications of the authority crisis.

Of course, my predictions cannot achieve any measure of accuracy, because the crisis of authority affects schools in different ways and at different speeds depending on the cultural and socioeconomic positioning of each school. Some suburban or rural teachers will not even begin to understand what I am talking about, because they personally are not affected by the crisis of authority. What holds such schools together is the inertia of tradition. An analogy with the institution of family may be helpful here. Forces of tradition kept families stable much longer than the economic need or legalized brutality. Domestic violence is still widespread despite legal protection of women and the degree of economic independence women can achieve. It is only when cultural mechanisms of the new family (discourse of relation, counseling, legal framework for divorce, acceptance of remarriage, etc.) came to full force that the traditional views of the stable family began to fade away. The same thing is happening to schools—millions of kids still obediently come into classrooms and do what they are told under the pressure of tradition. Only a few have realized so far that the emperor is naked, and that there is no real power in their teachers' hands. The traditional component of authority is still strong, but not perpetual; eventually schools will have to find something better than pleas for obedience but less cruel than expulsion and physical violence.

The negative consequences of the crisis of authority are obvious, and the conservatives never fail to point those out. Their solution is to reestablish the old means of social control to whatever extent possible. Of course, it is politically difficult to argue openly for corporal punishment or for throwing students out of schools. Yet the conservative solutions are not far from that. One recent trend is the ever-growing presence of police officers in schools. The main reason for a police officer to be present in school is his or her ability to exercise physical force. The police uniform signifies the threat of legitimate violence. The following data predate the Columbine shooting; one has to project an increase in recent years. Note that the percent of public schools with full-time police officers is probably high in urban schools that have a much larger percent of all students:

6 percent of public schools had police or other law enforcement representatives stationed 30 hours or more at the school, 1 percent of schools had law enforcement officials stationed 10 to 29 hours, 3 percent had officials stationed from 1 to 9 hours, 12 percent of schools did not have officials stationed during a typical week (but were available as needed), and 78 percent of schools did not have any officials stationed at their school during the 1996-1997 school year.[4]

The wave of high-stake testing in schools under the rhetoric of accountability is a de-facto attempt to reverse the "massification" of schools. If students are denied promotion or graduation, it is only another form of hidden expulsion from schools. It is also a tacit admission that we have no other means of motivating students to learn but the threat of full or partial exclusion. I find it very hypocritical when George W. Bush in the same short speech tells us that the standards should be raised but that no child should be left behind. If he would acknowledge that raising standards would inevitably push some students out of schools, his proposal would be at least honest. Just to be fair, Bill Clinton and his administration engaged in the same kind of verbal trickery.

Of course, another conservative remedy is gradual dismantling of public education by vouchers, which will also reintroduce the elitist model based on exclusion. One cannot deny that the conservative ways of dealing with the loss of authority may have some short-time benefits at least for some schools and some students. One cannot deny either that the threat of expulsion and physical force will restore authority and make schools more manageable. What I question is the viability of these choices in the long run and their moral defensibility.

Diane Ravitch reiterates one quite common conservative solution in her recent book *Left Back*.[5] After a devastating critique of Progressive education, her plan is to keep all children in school (no exclusion) but to establish high expectations and a challenging academic curriculum. These would be fine ideas if she could explain how and why children would be willing to be in such a school and follow the rules there. She apparently believes that enthusiastic teachers and forceful administrators can will themselves out of the authority crisis. The belief that education can be changed by enthusiasm is an interesting phenomenon in itself. The belief goes like this: as long as educators have a vision (no matter what kind) and worked consistently on its implementation, anything is possible. This reminds me of the Chinese Great Leap Forward or similar Russian utopian experiments.

The Progressives, whom Ravitch dislikes, at least realized that there is something fundamentally wrong with motivation in the traditional model of schooling and perhaps anticipated the authority crisis schools are experiencing now. Poorly motivated learning is tolerable as long as there is institutionally enforced extrinsic motivation. In other words, one does not have to worry about motivating students to learn as long as one can effectively expel and punish them.

The Progressives worked on the problem of intrinsic motivation for learning, even if most of their solutions turned out to be unrealistic, and some consequences of their reforms undesirable. I will return to the achievements and shortcomings of Progressivism later, but their theoretical intent still makes more sense than ignoring the problem of authority and, most importantly, the tendency for this problem to get worse. In the end, it is very unclear how Ravitch will transplant the traditional academic model of schooling from the exclusionary and elitist schools of the past into the universal compulsory schools of today and tomorrow. She consistently points out that the Progressive experiments worked only in a few exceptional schools. What makes her think that the conservative experiments will work in a regular public school is beyond me. This argument can be valid only if one assumes that mass schooling and elitist schooling are essentially the same.

Ravitch argues that the elitism of nineteenth-century schooling was caused by lack of economic opportunity and not by lack of desire to learn among the lower-class children. This is probably true, but mass schooling is not different from elite schooling because the poor and minority children joined in; it is different because all children joined in. The threat of expulsion worked for affluent students because the millions of unschooled children made schooling a desirable and precious opportunity. The threat of exclusion and physical violence would be equally effective on poor children. "Massification" of school is not the same thing as democratization of access to schools. The exclusionary character of nineteenth-century schools was not accidental; it is constitutive of the whole institution.

Ravitch's views on learning are very reasonable. Indeed, it would be very desirable to educate every student according to high academic standards. I see nothing wrong with her preference of academic subjects to more utilitarian curriculum. In theory, it is possible for nearly every child to succeed in traditional academic curriculum. There are no psychological, cultural, or cognitive obstacles to that. This does not mean, however, that mass schools in their present form can do the job. Someone can both know how and have the ability to work productively at his or her place of employment but choose not to do it. This should be true for education, too. The question is not whether students can learn and not whether we can teach them, but why would they want to learn *in school.*

The conservative solutions will not work in education, because schools have changed irreversibly. The very nature of the mass schooling made it impossible for the traditional school to remain unchanged. I will argue that the crisis of authority in education is essentially a good thing. The glass seems to me half full rather than half empty. Consider the radical transformation of the institution of the family. The old patriarchal family was stable and manageable largely because of the economic dependency and brutal physical suppression of women. The new family that has been slowly evolving over two centuries is much less stable but is free of brutalities of the old one. Is a 50 percent rate of divorce a reasonable price for society to pay for elimination of subjugation and cruelty? It certainly is for me, as it would be for most people should they respond to such a question. We simply cannot have both the unshakeable stability and the humaneness, because the new family is based on such fuzzy things as love and respect, not on solid ties of economic necessity and brutal force.

Something like this is happening to schooling. Social change is often both radical and slow to the point that contemporaries do not notice it at all. As it was 400 years ago, a school is still a large building where kids sit behind their desks and a teacher talks to them about something important. Yet it is a very different social species, one not based on effective means of control but *potentially* much more humane. I want to stress *potentially*, because loss of control can also turn schools into much more brutal institutions than before, which I will show in the next chapter. It may get worse before it gets better.

The crisis of authority requires rethinking the institution of schooling in a way that provides some grounds for adult authority to be reestablished without reverting to traditional methods of exclusion and punishment. Yet before I lay out my proposal, I want to address some of the consequences of the crisis of power.

NOTES

[1] U.S. Census Bureau Statistical Abstract of the United States: 1999. (http://www.census.gov/prod/99pubs/99statab/sec04.pdf), 10.

[2] *Facts About Corporal Punishment*, National Coalition to Abolish Corporal Punishment in Schools (http://www.stophitting.com/NCACPS/NCACPS_facts_about_corporal_punishment.htm#Punishment%20in%20U.S.%20Public.).

[3] Foucault mentions, but does not elaborate on, the connection between economic compulsion that is characteristic to capitalism and the spread of discipline. See Michel Foucault, *Discipline and Punish: The Birth of the Prison* (New York: Vintage Books, 1977).

[4] *Violence and Discipline Problems in U.S. Public Schools: 1996-97*, National Center for Education Statistics (http://nces.ed.gov/pubs98/violence/98030009.html#Presence).

[5] Diane Ravitch, *Left Back: A Century of Failed School Reforms* (New York: Simon & Schuster, 2000).

CHAPTER 5.
EDUCATION AND VIOLENCE

The crisis of authority described in the previous chapter creates a situation conducive to the abuse of power. This may sound paradoxical, but, in fact, such a claim makes sense. Milder, more humane forms of power appear only when authority is firmly in place. Violence is the resort of a weakened authority. In other words, the crisis of authority will not automatically lead to the emergence of a more humane school; this can happen only if we make conscious efforts based on understanding the power dynamics in schools. This chapter is an examination of what is happening and what will happen in schools if we as a society will not react to the transformation of schooling. The "natural" flow of changes is dangerous, because it tends to produce more and more violent schools.

The fundamental lack of motivation in schools makes them essentially utopian enterprises. Students are expected to work for the wastebasket without any real incentives, just for an idea such as "the development of social power and insight," as Dewey puts it. As the mass schooling firmly establishes itself, it also shows the signs of power imbalances. Education is marked with the tragedy of power conflicts, of the need to force students into doing something they do not want to do. Faced with the crisis of authority, educators resort to indirect violence.

Schools are violent institutions. This statement could express at least two different opinions depending on assumptions on how education and violence are connected. One opinion is based on the assumption that violence is an extrinsic, superficial, and certainly unnecessary part of school life; a part that our society can get rid of, if we only learned how to run schools better or if we eliminated certain social ills of injustice, unequal distribution of wealth, and violent elements of popular culture.

Another opinion, which I intend to defend, considers violence to be an intrinsic and necessary part of compulsory education, a part that is extremely hard to eliminate. The reasons for educational violence do not derive exclusively from the forms of social oppression exercised in the larger society. These reasons cannot also be reduced to purely psychological ones. This chapter aims to show that in schools, education has a special connection to violence, depends on violence for its success, and encourages at least some forms of peer violence. The school violence is not only a manifestation of violence that occurs in other social spheres; schools produce their own unique motivation for violence.

How dangerous are schools really? One indication of violence is that being a student is more dangerous than being an average adult employee. Despite the drop in crime rates, including school crime, a school is a relatively more dangerous place than an average workplace. Here are some statistics from the U.S. Department of Education. In 1998, American public schools reported about 1,000 crimes per 100,000 students. This number included about 950 crimes that were not serious or violent (theft, vandalism, fights, or assaults without a weapon) and about 50 serious violent crimes per 100,000 students (rape or sexual battery, robbery, fight with a weapon, suicide).[1]

Let us compare these data with those from another source, the U.S. Bureau of Labor Statistics Survey of Occupational Injuries and Illnesses for 1992 (*before* the recent drop in crime rates). In 1992, there were about 118,000,000 people employed.[2] Remember, 1,000 crimes are reported per 100,000 students but only about 19 crimes per 100,000 working adults. I can anticipate criticism of these comparisons, since the method of reporting is different for the two sets of data. The Bureau only tracks incidents that result in lost days of work, while schools report incidents they consider to be serious. But even if we exclude the so-called non-serious crimes (which curiously include fights or assaults without a weapon), still about 50 serious crimes (rape or sexual battery, robbery, fight with a weapon, suicide) per 100,000 students were committed *in schools* as opposed to 19 per 100,000 workers at their place of employment. Let us not forget that the lion's share of workplace injuries is specific to dangerous character of work. According to the *Workplace Violence* brief by the U.S. Department of Justice,

> Nonfatal assaults were primarily encounters between patients and nursing staff in health care institutions. Other occupations where violence at work produced lost work time included private security guards, truck drivers, and sales workers. Almost two-thirds of nonfatal assaults occurred in service industries, such as nursing homes, hospitals, and establishments providing residential care and other social services.[3]

Of course, schools are safer than the streets, as a recent report by the U.S. Department of Education proudly proclaims.[4] Yet one wonders if such a comparison is fair, since schools are organizations with some structure, supervision, authority, etc. Schools should be compared to similar institutions such as places of employment. Such comparison reveals that schools *are* more dangerous than a comparable adult organization. The absolute majority of school violence is perpetrated by students, which may suggest that the school as an institution has nothing to do with it. After all, teachers do not normally go around beating, shoving, and kicking kids. Yet such a conclusion may be premature.

My analysis of why school violence occurs begins with a real-life situation. Several years ago, I was working as a substitute teacher for a large urban school district on the West Coast. Once I substituted for a high school auto shop teacher. Students were moving around the shop, going about their own business—a rather peaceful afternoon. In one group boys appeared to be horsing around and laughing—nothing to attract special attention. Suddenly one of the boys broke away from the group, came up to me, and demanded to call security because he was being harassed and threatened by other boys. One question was going through my mind while I dealt with the situation: why did I not notice what was going on? Very soon, I realized that I did not want to notice, just as I did not want to call security and hoped the situation would solve itself with the proverbial ring of the school bell.

Much later, I also realized that the problem was not that something in the school system made it a hassle for me to deal with the instance of peer violence. In other words, I was not simply tired, lazy, or indifferent. Rather, there was a strong motivation for me to ignore the harassment.

What would have happened if I detected the harassment pattern (which I surely would have done if the interest had been there), and tried to interfere? To begin with, the perpetrators belonged to the clique in power. Students have a way of showing new teachers and subs the pecking order in the classroom. In this case, these were the tough guys (delinquents), but they as easily have been jocks, "gangsters" or another high school crowd. As a sub, I had only one way to establish a semblance of authority in this classroom—cooperation with students at the top of social hierarchy. It does not take long to figure out what happens if you do not establish your authority. A sub can have an entire classroom leave, furniture broken, books thrown on the floor. If this gets to the school administration, the sub is reprimanded; he or she acquires the reputation of a poor disciplinarian, which makes getting a permanent position in the school district rather problematic. After investing years into obtaining a teacher certificate, such a prospect does not look too appealing. Regular teachers face similar dilemmas, which boil down to finding a way to keep one's classroom in order or to getting into all kinds of trouble with the school administration.

Within a few moments into this auto shop class, we made a silent deal: I acknowledged the power clique, and the clique remained nice to me, thus ensuring other students' acceptance and decent behavior. In exchange for such support, I was to allow more freedom and more privileges to the power clique members. This included instances of threats, harassment, or open violence toward other students. Of course, I allowed it only to a certain extent. Actually, the most I could do for them was to ignore certain things or pretend I didn't see other things. They also cooperated only to a certain extent. Yet in most cases, we were able to find a common ground.

Teachers face peer violence every day, and their reactions are at best ambivalent. Here is the typical reaction as reported by Foyne Mahaffey:

> "Last week," a colleague recently confided, "I saw a boy humping against a girl, right in her face, and he was laughing. He was transferred over here because of a sexual assault on another girl."
>
> "What did you do about it?" I asked.
>
> Painfully and sadly she admitted, "I was tired, tired after a whole day of it. Tired of seeing it, yelling about it. I am tired. I didn't do anything."[5]

Far from trying simply to implicate teachers, I am convinced the reasons for doing nothing are larger than "I am tired" and are worth exploring.

For the purposes of this book, I will distinguish irrational violence from rational violence. These are closely related but differently motivated types of violence although the distinction is quite arbitrary. Nevertheless, let us assume that in some instances, people are violent even though it goes against their own interest. This is irrational violence, which I leave beyond the scope of this analysis. The connection between irrational and rational forms of violence is a fascinating topic, which awaits its exploration in the context of schooling. The only suggestion I can make is that when a social system relies on rational violence, irrational violence finds its way out and flourishes. In other words, when violence is advantageous, human aggression finds a fertile soil. In many instances, people are violent because they have something to gain from it. This is the rational violence, which includes most of the peer violence in schools, especially bullying. Bullies may or may not torment their victims out of some irrational subconscious motivation. However, more often than not a rational motive contributes to the act of violence.

The choice of a victim is motivated by the trends in larger society but, in general, is arbitrary. Gay youth and those not confirming to masculine stereotypes are probably the most likely victims. Violence against girls is another underreported and understudied phenomenon.[6] Yet other distinctions based on gender, class, or race are just as likely to play a role in determining who is to be victimized. While schools have been marginally successful in shifting around the role of victim from one group to another (for instance, from race to sexual orientation), they have shown very little success in eliminating peer violence altogether. What fuels bullying is not only the prejudice children freely absorb from the society at large but also the immediate needs of power relations as they exist in schools.

A power clique such as one I befriended in the auto shop is not necessarily violent in a personal or psychological sort of way. They realize that the leading position based on a threat of violence requires an occasional demonstration. The role of an outcast is to suffer and to discourage other students from crossing paths with the ruling clique. This is nothing personal, just a matter of reputation. Of course, helping adults to maintain some control over the student body is not among primary goals of the ruling clique. In fact, the power clique may perceive its relations with the school authorities as hostile. But even so, control is their currency in gaining some perks and privileges from the school while maintaining their power position. It is hard to imagine a power clique of students in complete opposition to adult authority in school. Such a school would collapse very quickly. More often, the two power centers develop a certain mode of coexistence and reach a tacit understanding based on occasional conflict, occasional cooperation, and general division of spheres of influence.

The existence of a power-sharing compromise between adult authority and student elite has been demonstrated in educational literature a long time ago.[7] Without a doubt, student elites systematically provide certain services to adult authorities in exchange for privileges. What has not been discussed enough is the role of physical violence in this unholy pact. Obviously, student elites show a remarkable variety of ways to maintain control over other students. Philip Cusick, for instance, describes a group of popular girls who run everything in their senior class. The means of enforcement the girls use seem to be strictly non-violent: "They have big parties to which they invite only their friends, you just don't get invited unless you're in with them,"[8] according to a non-elite girl. Yet curiously, Cusick, then a 32-year-old researcher, explains why he did not study the leading group of girls closely in these words: "some of these girls dated athletes and I did not want to get between any of the boys and their girl friends."[9] Even when student hierarchy is not routinely enforced by acts of physical violence, the latter plays at least some role in the hierarchy—if not direct violence, then a threat of violence, if not a direct threat, then a symbolic threat by emphasizing athletic abilities, or access to guns or gang connections. Violence looms large in the background of school life even though it may not be at the forefront of it.

I do not believe many people will want to dispute my description of violence in the school peer culture, aside from the question of how typical such violence is. However, some may doubt the benefits that adult authorities derive from this violence. Even more people will doubt that teachers and administrators have anything to do with supporting peer violence. Educators would rather speak of it as a menace and a destructive force in schools. Most of them will vehemently deny my charge.

Yet adult authorities benefit from peer violence even if no privileges are given to the power clique. Here is how two college juniors involved in the Free Student Press Project describe the ancient wisdom of "divide and conquer" as applied to high schools:

> The isolation and divisions between students really works to the school's advantage. I mean if the students can't get it together they are robbed of the power they could have as a whole. Students fail to see their community as people in an oppressive environment because, by this time, they have taken lessons from the school and blame each other for being the problems. This is to say little of the model of inequality that schools reinforce by sanctioning this type of socialization.[10]

To keep the fragmentation of students going, adults must at least tolerate animosity between cliques, or bullying, or both. In other words, a certain level of peer violence is not only acceptable but also necessary to maintain order in schools.

Alternative explanations attribute peer violence to developmental or cultural peculiarities of school-age youth. These explanations seem plausible, except for one question: why does peer violence, especially bullying, all but stop as soon as students move from high schools to university campuses? College students still fight, but nowhere does a clique run a college campus by way of violence. Both level and character of violence change. Is there any developmental change that universally occurs after the senior prom? Do students become less susceptible to the culture of violence on mass media? Do they suddenly move from one youth subculture to another? Perhaps the key to understanding the rational violence in secondary schools lies with the unique social situation of the school itself, a situation different from that of a college.

In *Discipline and Punish,* Foucault draws a fascinating, almost epic, picture of successive forms of power technologies. The general line of development was from brutal, public, and physical forms of punishment to a less brutal, less visible, but more effective technology of discipline. Foucault begins with descriptions of torture and public execution: "The public execution is to be understood not only as judicial, but also as a political ritual. It belongs, even in minor cases, to the ceremonies by which power is manifested."[11] The public execution was, according to Foucault, an open, ritualized conflict between the power of the prince and the power of the people. As such, it was too dangerous for authorities and had to be abolished by means of penal reform.

The aims of the reform were these: "to make the punishment and repression of illegalities a regular function, coextensive with society; not to punish less, but to punish better; to punish with an attenuated severity perhaps, but in order to punish with more universality and necessity; to insert the power to punish more deeply into the social body."[12] Foucault then goes on to describe the new technology of power, the disciplines, which became the general formulas of domination in the seventeenth and eighteenth centuries.[13] He meticulously documents the elements and forms of discipline technologies as applied in the army, prisons, schools, factories, and hospitals. The discipline is still based on manipulations to the body, on including the body into the machinery of power but not with ancient physical forms of public violence.

Foucault treats schools as yet another example of discipline-based and discipline-producing institutions without attempting to explore their specifics. I would like to point out that in schools, the ancient forms of spectacular forms of violence never disappeared completely. The logic of succession of power techniques does not apply to schools. This is a consequence of the special status of schools that did not move toward economic means of enforcement along with most social institutions. For instance, the phenomenon of bullying frighteningly resembles the liturgy of torture and public execution analyzed by Foucault. Dan Savage writes:

> In high school, I had much more to worry about than tests and papers. Like most students, I lived in fear of the small slights and public humiliations used to reinforce the rigid high school caste system: poor girls were sluts, soft boys were fags. And at each of my schools, there were students who lived in daily fear of physical violence. There was a boy named Marty at my second school, Saint Gregory the Great, who was beaten up daily for four years. Jocks would rip his clothes knowing his parents couldn't afford to buy him a new uniform, and he would piss his pants rather than risk being caught alone in the bathroom. He couldn't walk the halls without being called a fag, and freshmen would beat him up to impress the older kids. Teachers, presumably the caretakers in this so-

called safe environment, knew what was going on—some even witnessed the abuse—and did nothing to stop it.[14]

In this description, one cannot help noticing the visibility and the ritualistic character of violence. A bully tortures his victim similarly to how a medieval prince executed the condemned: as a political ritual, as a demonstration of brutal power, mediated through an individual victim. Granted, modern schools employ a whole range of disciplinary techniques and thus exemplify perhaps the most developed discipline technology available. Ways of ordering bodies, observation, controlling every aspect of life, engaging in unnecessary work as a means of submission—these are all elements of the arts of discipline. Yet schools paradoxically allow and, I argue, benefit from violent forms of punishment from a different epoch.

Teachers and administrators rely on peer hierarchy (and ultimately, peer violence) because they have no other reliable means of control over students, as I have discussed in the previous chapter. Lacking means of direct control, teachers and administrators have to rely on peer hierarchy and peer violence to maintain social order in schools. This happens not because they are individually immoral or corrupt but because no other means of exercising power are available to them. But why do adults need this sort of harsh social control over their students? If what I describe is true, a school's social structure is similar to prison, where gangs of inmates enforce order in exchange for certain concessions from authorities. Why can't school be more like the workplace where managers exercise a great deal of control over employees without resorting to physical violence? Why can't school be more like a family, a social club, or any number of other social structures that do not rely on violence in democratic societies? In other words, why are schools compulsory institutions, which positions them next to prisons and mental hospitals as Philip Jackson rightly pointed out?[15]

Foucault mentions that the development of industrial capitalism and the new forms of power are closely connected.[16] One can plausibly suggest that these two processes are two sides of the same process. The proletarization of the masses (expropriation of means of production from peasants and artisans) made it possible to rely on more efficient techniques of power, simply because capitalism produced the wage slave—a person whose only choice is to work at a capitalist factory or to starve. The art of discipline works only when the threat of expulsion from a particular social organization is great. In the modern capitalist society, the discipline still works very well in the workplace. Schools have never acquired this foundation of economic coercion. Students do not need to go to school in order to survive. Although shaped to produce efficient labor for a capitalist society, schools have never become truly capitalist institutions, because the logic of a wage slave does not apply to them.

The systemic roots of peer violence in schools have little to do with age, culture, or any other demographic characteristic of students. Schools are compulsory institutions because academic learning is an activity that fundamentally lacks motivation. Nothing like a capitalist worker's motivation is available to students. On one hand, they do not get paid for learning. Even if they did, students rely on family for most necessities. On the other hand, after decades of very persistent and intelligent efforts of curriculum theorists, psychologists, and teachers to prove the contrary, it is as obvious as ever that there is no way to make all or even most of learning engaging and thus intrinsically motivating.

John Dewey explored the problem of learning motivation and its implications for the school's social structure. In *The School and Society*, he writes, for instance:

> The radical reason that the present school cannot organize itself as a natural social unit is just because this element of common and productive activity is absent. Upon the playground, in game and sport, social organization takes place spontaneously and inevitably. There is something to do, some activity to be carried on, requiring natural division of labor, selection of leaders and followers, mutual cooperation and emulation. In the schoolroom the motive and the cement of social organization are alike wanting.[17]

This critique strikes me as very accurate. Dewey discovered what amounts to a general principle of social organization: for any given group, the type of predominant shared activity directly affects the type of social relation within the group. His views here are similar to one of the main Marxist heuristics about the dialectical connection between the mode of production and the superstructure (social relations) in society. Dewey analyzed the activity/relation link for a traditional school as a particular case of that principle. Dewey's conclusion was that the regular object-lesson learning as an activity provides a very poor foundation for a "social spirit" or a "social glue" which could hold a school together as a group. Dewey's interpretive tool is very valuable indeed in explaining the many ills of contemporary education. It shows that revising policies, introducing better teaching methods, or investing more resources into schooling cannot significantly affect the fundamental well-being of schools. Following Dewey's idea, schools are organizations that are very hard to manage, which becomes more and more apparent with the passage of time and with the disappearance of some form of extrinsic social control (such as the threat of corporal punishment or expulsion).

What, according to Dewey, was so wrong with the activity of learning that it could not provide the "social spirit" or "the cement of social organization"? His critique of the traditional learning and, especially, his apology for active "occupations" primarily focus on the fact that traditional learning is not like real life; it is not aimed at achieving some real results and therefore is not engaging for students. From Dewey's point of view, the active "occupations" are better because they provide a "genuine motive."

The main problem I see with "occupations" is connected to the very essence of learning. If learning, in whatever active form, becomes too similar to a real "adult" occupation, it simply ceases to be learning. I have already advanced this line of argument in previous chapters. However, let us take, for instance, Dewey's favorite example, "a busy kitchen, in which a group of children is actively engaged in the preparation of food." For such an activity to provide a real motive it should be as "real" as possible, that is, as close as possible to real cooking. However, if children are there mainly to cook food, their activity ceases to be learning and is no different from routine adult cooking. By moving closer to the active occupation, learning loses its meaning as learning. Cooking, as any other learning activity, must remain somewhat unreal and non-utilitarian to preserve its essence.

I have argued that learning in schools more often than not lacks motivation. The second unfortunate characteristic of learning is that it does not serve as a good foundation for an organization. Learning is essentially a very self-centered activity. I would not want to be thought the whole body of literature and practice of cooperative learning.[18] I would only remind the reader that even though the process of learning can be shared, the results of learning remain entirely within each student. There is no real need to cooperate, to divide labor, to work out common solutions. Aside from the problem of motivation, learning does not work well as a social glue. This second characteristic of learning is surely related to the first one (the wastebasket economy, lack of motivation). If kids wanted to be at school in the first place, there would be a reason to cooperate in school. Yet this antisocial nature of learning makes the project of schooling even more questionable.

The emptiness at the core of schools, this absence of social glue, makes them prone to violence. This is why corporal punishment held in schools for hundreds of years longer than in the rest of the society. Let us not be naïve, though; outlawing corporal punishment in schools does not eliminate violence. Any sort of compulsion involves violence at some point. It does not matter who administers the violence—teachers, parents on behalf of teachers, or bullies on behalf of teachers. The bottom line is, unlike other social institutions, schools cannot be run without violence.

Schools pay serious attention to restricting students' bodily movements, as Foucault pointed out. The more violent school is, the more likely one is to find off-limit halls, bans on using lockers at particular hours, no-running halls, detention areas, etc., etc. One of the sacred rights that teachers hold dear is the right to control entering and leaving a classroom. At the very least, a teacher feels it is necessary to be able to send students out to the hall. When some school administrators try to ban this practice to reduce the number of students walking through the halls during classes, teachers get understandably upset.

Another important power tool is control over who may use the restroom and how often. Some teachers are really fixated on the bathroom matters, which, Freudians would believe, is a sign of a larger complex, ultimately connected to obsession with power. To exercise control, a teacher must show that students' bodies do not really belong to them but can be commanded and controlled by the teacher. The power schools try to exercise over their students, is, again, very physical.

Security officers, dressed like police, are very common. Principals love to use walkie-talkies they don't really need because they make them look like cops. In large urban high schools, real police are increasingly becoming more and more common. Granted, all these measures are being taken to cope with peer violence among students. But it would be naïve indeed to think that schools take such measures without an agenda to assert their own power over students. Schools badly need new channels of authority, because, again, there is no intrinsic motivation for students to be there at all, much less to do something, even less to get along with each other and the teachers.

Schools are built in a way that getting into trouble can always lead to another level of trouble, and the highest levels of trouble remain obscure intentionally. Okay, you can refuse to obey your teacher; you can then be sent to a counselor's office. If you are rude with the counselor or get that far too many times, you can be sentenced to seeing the vice-principal. The student may have no idea what seeing a vice-principal can entail; something awful, probably. Then you can even be sent to the principal's office, etc. This is all, of course, one big trick. Many kids go through the levels of trouble only to find that the emperor has no clothes. The principal cannot do anything serious, just like the teacher. Despite all the elaborated schemes, they can't hurt you, as kids realize sooner or later. The key is to keep students in the dark about the next level of trouble as long as possible. Schools work hard to make this hierarchical system of trouble delivery formal and laden with symbols. They print referral slips, initiate formal procedures and policies, appoint discipline committees, and make up elaborate names for various forms of punishment.

One fundamental tool schools use is to delegate violence to parents. Any time a child is hard to control in schools, parents are brought aboard. In theory, parents are called on the phone and summoned to school to discuss the child's needs and problems. In reality, the school tries to annoy and embarrass parents so that the parents will use their greater powers on kids. And parents do, indeed, have greater powers. First, in more families than we would like to think, physical abuse of children continues. Second, parents have the power of the purse, of rationing toys, clothes, privileges, etc.

The great fear of students lies at the heart of teachers' power games. This fear is intimately connected with the essence of learning as an unproductive activity and the ensuing weaknesses of school as a social system. Since there is no common interest and physical violence is difficult to inflict on children, there exists a terrible power void. Every teacher knows that there are very few things that can be done to make these kids behave. It is just teachers and students, and no one else to help. One has to be a teacher to appreciate the depth and intensity of this fear.

As a former teacher, I can testify that tensions between such tasks as keeping order, safety, and cleanliness in a classroom on one side and instructional tasks on the other, are enormous. Then, you still want to keep good relations with the class, do all the paperwork, stretch your energy for 5 hours, be nice to an administrator and not hurt anyone. I can also confirm that in a good school something is done to ease those tensions for a teacher. In a bad school, it is the opposite: administration is interested in keeping teacher under stress, so he will always short one or more task accomplished, so he may be easily kept under control. The idea is this: you never get all the things done, but it is taken lightly as long as you behave.

The main consequence of the crisis of authority is that schools become more and more violent institutions, and this tendency will only grow if left unattended. Reliance on peer violence has its enormous cost. The corrupt alliance between adult authority and school bullies creates a system prone to blow up in form of school shootings. The argument I make in the Part I does not sound too optimistic, but let me summarize it anyway:

a) Schools are organizations where learning is the dominant activity.

b) The type of dominant activity determines the type of social relationship within each organization.

c) Learning lacks motivation AND does not promote cooperation; it is very difficult to run an organization where learning serves as the dominant activity.

d) Schools of today are quickly losing traditional extrinsic means of enforcement.

e) Schools become impossible for adults to control; they have to rely on peer violence.

f) Therefore, schools will create more and more violence.

It is my belief that this argument is correct. I see many bad things happening to our schools in the future unless we do something about them. No one knows whether we have 50 more years, 100 more years, or no time at all. There are only two things that can be done. One is changing (d), that is, reinstating the extrinsic means of authority (the conservative solution). But this is only a temporary solution or no solution at all. Another is changing (a), which seems impossible because (a) sounds like a self-evident truth. But is it really? Perhaps we should revisit the assumption that schools are primarily for learning, and maybe by doing so we can save both the idea of schools and the idea of learning. As long as education remains pure, it may not be salvageable; it may be perfectly viable when mixed with something else.

NOTES

[1] *Violence and Discipline Problems in U.S. Public Schools: 1996-97*, National Center for Educational Statistics (http://nces.ed.gov/pubs98/violence/98030005.html).

[2] *Selected Employment Indicators*, U.S. Bureau of Labor Statistics (http://stats.bls.gov/webapps/legacy/cpsatab4.htm).

[3] *Workplace Violence, 1992-96*, U.S. Department of Justice, Bureau of Justice Statistics (http://www.ojp.usdoj.gov/bjs/pub/pdf/wv96.pdf).

[4] *Indicators of School Crime and Safety 2000*, National Center for Education Statistics (http://nces.ed.gov/pubs2001/2001017a.pdf).

[5] Foyne Mahaffey, "Are We Accepting Too Much?" In *Rethinking Schools: Agenda for Change*, ed. by David Levine (New York: The New Press, 1995), 39.

[6] Foyne Mahaffey, "Are We Accepting Too Much?" 37-39.

[7] C.W. Gordon, *The Social System of the High School* (New York: Free Press, 1957); see also Ralph Larkin, *Suburban Youth in Cultural Crisis* (New York: Oxford University Press, 1979), and Philip Cusick, *Inside High School: The Student's World* (New York: Holt, Rinehart and Winston, 1973).

[8] Cusick, *Inside High School*, 154.

[9] Cusick, *Inside High School*, 155

[10] Lisa O'Keefe and Damon Krane, "The Free Student Press Project" (paper delivered at 1999 Conference of the Institute for Democracy in Education, Athens, Ohio, 10/02/1999).

[11] Michel Foucault, *Discipline and Punish: The Birth of the Prison* (New York: Vintage Books, 1977), 47.

[12] Foucault, *Discipline and Punish*, 82.

[13] Foucault, *Discipline and Punish*, 137.

[14] Dan Savage, "Fear the Geek: Littleton's Silver Lining," *Stranger* (Volume 8, 33, May 5-12, 1999).

[15] Philip Jackson, *Life in Classrooms* (New York: Teachers College Press, 1990).

[16] Foucault, *Discipline and Punish*, 175.

[17] Dewey, *The School and Society. The Child and the Curriculum*, 14-15.

[18] Samuel Totten, *Cooperative Learning: A Guide to Research* (New York: Garland, 1991).

Part II. The Educational Relation

CHAPTER 6.
A CASE FOR THE PEDAGOGY OF RELATION

For the benefit of the reader, as well as for my own, let me restate the limits of education described in Part I. Learning activity is a form of labor that appears to be a production of useless things. Learning in schools is inadequately motivated, partly because of the intrinsic limitations of learning, partly because of the specific shape the institution of schooling took in the late twentieth century. Contemporary schools are a precarious mix of the inescapable problem of learning motivation with a weak institution that does not address the problem. Schools will experience a progressive crisis of authority, and, in a worst-case scenario, an increase in peer violence if left to their own devices. It is my conviction that certain essential limits of schooling may not be overcome, and we will have to learn to live with them. Most importantly, we cannot make most of learning intrinsically motivating. As far ahead as one can see now, schools will retain a massive amount of boring but necessary work. However, the institutional side of the problem can be addressed. My proposal does not include radical change of the core of schooling, which is the learning activity. This book contains no new teaching methods or curriculum improvements. I propose to alter the shape of schooling as an institution so that the adult authority is restored without reinstitution of exclusionary practices. Such a change will require development of an educational theory based on the notion of relation.

Allow me again to draw a parallel between the institutions of family and school. The strong ties of violence and economic dependency gave way to "weak" ties of interhuman relationships, so that the institution of the new family gradually emerged, along with the new concept of relationships. Anthony Giddens gives a very convincing account of this change in *The Transformation of Intimacy*.[1] Of course, the transformation in question is much more complex and controversial than I have the space here to describe. Giddens advances the notion of *pure relationship*, which he defines as "a situation when a social relation is entered for its own sake, for what can be derived by each person from a sustained association with another; and which is continued only insofar as it is thought by both parties to deliver enough satisfactions for each individual to stay within it."[2] Giddens believes that the transformation of intimacy promises the democratization of personal life.

A similar transformation should happen to schools. The old strong mechanisms of authority—corporal punishment and exclusion—should be replaced with the "weak" but ultimately much more reliable forces of pure relationship. The Progressives' solution was to make learning exciting and thus keep students in schools. It seems obvious to me that such solutions failed to a large degree. Teachers cannot compete with MTV and should not be expected to do so. My hope is that students will be attracted to schools because of the quality of human relationship, the quality of communal experiences there. In other words, students will want to go to school not because of what they will do but because of who they will meet. The pedagogy of relation is based on the assumption that most children and adolescents possess an innate social instinct, a drive to relate, and a desire to belong. Millions of kids get up every morning and go to school mainly to see their friends and perhaps a few agreeable adults. The need to socialize that has been relegated to the background of the educational enterprise is the only factor that saves schools from total disintegration. The only compensation kids get for endless hours of demanding schoolwork is the opportunity to be social. Educators have been foolish to let this only real link of kids' interests and school organization wither in recent years. What we need to do now is to restore the power of relations in schools.

The emergence of the new non-compulsory and non-violent family became possible when, in addition to the disappearance of the old strong ties of dependency and violence, the new ties of human relationships took a particular cultural form. A long and painful transition, the birth of the new family, did not occur automatically without extensive theoretical and cultural work. In *The History of Sexuality*, Foucault shows that discourse actually creates the social reality it is supposed to describe. Giddens agrees with this claim, although he cautions that the relation between the discourse and the social organization is not a one-way street.[3] Even with such a correction, Foucault presents a powerful case for the mechanism of shaping social life by talking about it in certain ways. There exists now a huge cultural industry of marital relationships, which, at least partially, creates the institution of marriage. It includes the production of certain ideologies of marital love, conflict resolution, counseling, romance, sexual relations, etc. The list of popular books on marital relationships is enormous and keeps growing. Counseling is an industry in itself and so is the big chunk of mass culture that focuses on romantic and family relationships. From sitcom to .com—there is no escape from it. Our civilization has developed a complex language that deals with human relationships in the context of family. There is nothing of equal or even comparable magnitude about relations in schools. Much work on relations has been done in educational theory, but it is far from becoming a mass culture phenomenon. Literature that does exist tends to be not so much about relations as about skills of interpersonal communications.[4] There are no self-help books for teachers with catchy names like "Eight steps to a great relationship with your students."

Developing a discourse on educational relations will require some serious theoretical work and experimentation. No one has yet developed a more or less comprehensive educational theory centered on the notion of relation. No reform movement or an experimental school explicitly placed its bets on relations. Of course, many good schools and other educational institutions pay close attention to the complex web of peer and student-teacher relationships, and I will show how they do it. For a long time now, a number of de-facto relational approaches to education have been in existence. We need a good theory to make the practical findings available to all.

A strange mix of theories informs the educational practice of today's schools. The ideas about learning itself come from a quite sophisticated discourse established by cognitive-developmental psychology and related educational research. The whole area of classroom management, discipline, school organization, etc., is still largely informed by behaviorist beliefs. In other words, we know quite a bit about how children learn. We have very little knowledge about why they learn at all and even less about why they do it at school. Therefore, the questions of learning motivation and school by default often go to behaviorists. Behaviorism also remains a commanding force in popular educational lore. Politicians and educational policy makers of all persuasions routinely make assumptions that boil down to the S R formula. Far from accusing the policy makers of ignorance, I know that many of them comprehend the complexities of the educational world well. However, the lack of a better theory forces them to fall back on behaviorist frameworks, crude but simple and appealing to the public. Thus, talk of "accountability" and "consequences" permeates popular educational discourse. Yet, both cognitive psychology and behaviorism are ill equipped to address the problem of learning motivation in the institutional context of a compulsory school—the former because it does not understand motivation in general, the latter because it falls apart in complex environments of social life.

It is not among my aims to offer a full-fledged critique of behavioral theories of learning and related classroom management theorizing. Perhaps our future teachers should learn all about Pavlov's dog, Thorndike's law of effect, and Skinner's operant conditioning. Perhaps, they need to appreciate the fine difference between negative reinforcers and punishment. I am not questioning the validity of all these fundamental findings of twentieth-century psychology; however, they are about as useful in teaching as Newtonian physics is in building a computer. A computer still has mass, and if dropped, its potential energy will inevitably convert into kinetic energy. To know this is great, but has little to do with how computers work. In the same way, the generic laws that probably regulate human behavior have little application in a classroom. Here are two randomly chosen pieces of advice from a randomly chosen educational psychology textbook:

> In dealing with misbehavior, the principle of immediacy of consequences can be applied by responding immediately and positively when students are not misbehaving, catching them in the act of being good![5]

> Anything the teacher can delay doing until after a lesson should be delayed. For example, if the teacher has started a lesson and a student walks in late, the teacher should go on with the lesson and deal with the tardiness issue later.[6]

I find recommendations of this sort disturbingly irresponsible. Catching a student being good could mean a thousand different things, depending on the relational context of the classroom. Is the student concerned with appearing to be a teacher's pet? Will she be glad or irritated to receive the praise? Was she "good" or simply tired? Similar questions could be asked about a student being late to class. What does his lateness mean? An accident? A declaration of war? Nothing at all? What was the expression on his face when he walked in? What was the class's reaction? Behaviorists (and cognitivists) simply have no language to address these sorts of questions in a meaningful way.

Constructivism, an intellectual heir of Progressivism, is not much more helpful in explaining the motivational side of learning in schools. For example, APA's *Learner-Centered Psychological Principles* basically state that motivation is very important.

> Curiosity, flexible and insightful thinking, and creativity are major indicators of the learners' intrinsic motivation to learn, which is, in large, part, a function of meeting basic needs to be competent and to exercise personal control. Intrinsic motivation is facilitated on tasks that learners perceive as interesting and personally relevant and meaningful, appropriate in complexity and difficulty to the learners' abilities, and on which they believe they can succeed. Intrinsic motivation is also facilitated on tasks that are comparable to real-world situations and meet needs for choice and control. Educators can encourage and support learners' natural curiosity and motivation to learn by attending to individual differences in learners' perceptions of optimal novelty and difficulty, relevance, and personal choice and control.[7]

This is a more cautious statement than their an draft that proclaimed that "individuals are naturally curious and enjoy learning in the absence of intense negative cognitions and emotions."[8] Still, constructivists assume that there is a mysterious intrinsic drive that makes human beings thirsty for knowledge. This is a reiteration of the Progressive hope to make all learning interesting, and, as I have shown in Part I, a utopian hope at best. Despite close attention to cooperative learning and impact of group dynamics on learning, constructivists largely remain unaware of the relational determination of learning. They have trouble overcoming the internal/external dichotomy. While acknowledging the importance of the "context" of learning,[9] constructivists place driving forces of learning securely within the individual student. Their sophistication in understanding human relations is represented by generalities like "Learning does not occur in a vacuum." The constructivist concept of learning is almost totally neutral to the type of institution where such learning might occur. One can conceivably practice constructivist teaching in an elite private school and in a poor rural school, in compulsory and in voluntary school, 300 years ago, and 300 years in the future. The constructivists are not really interested in how schooling shapes learning.

The weakness of educational theory has been demonstrated once again in the arena of educational reform. If something could be learned from the epic tale of educational reforming of the twentieth century, it is that educational systems cannot be improved by promoting any specific teaching or administrative model. Successful teacher behaviors do not transfer from one setting to another. The issue of replicability of educational research has never been adequately resolved. In short, attempts to replicate successful practices of a certain school or a certain teacher in other schools fail more often than not. This phenomenon is common to all social sciences but appears most vividly in education. Simply put, good teaching and administrative practices work well in some locations and do not work at all in others. In educational reforming, especially the kind associated with school improvement, context is destiny. Yet a meaningful description of such contexts has proven to be very difficult. Even when a researcher describes good schools with inclusion of the relational contexts,[10] it is very unclear what is generalizable about such a description. In other words, we do not quite understand how such descriptions can be useful for other educational practitioners.

The story of educational reforming took an interesting twist in the last decade of the twentieth century, when the idea of school-based reforming gained strength with the help of such theorists as Theodor Sizer and John Goodlad. Their proposals acknowledge the non-transferability of behaviors but do not really articulate the concern for relations. Instead, they suggest that if teachers in each particular school develop their own plan of actions, this will take care of the menace of non-replicability. An interesting idea, it assumes that thinking about a specific plan of action within a specific situation is better than thinking about acting in an abstract, general school. This is possibly true but misses the deeper paradigm crisis of educational theory. Teachers and administrators are asked to develop their own miniature educational theories that would take into account the specific relational context of their school. In a way, this is an acknowledgment that educational theory is quite useless. The model schools and their small-scale theories are no better than the old sort of theory—both are impossible to replicate because such theories prescribe what to do. As a result, some great schools produced very poor theories. Such a theory works as long as it is applied in the same context where it was created but not if transplanted elsewhere.

Educational theory experiences certain paradigm crisis—we, the theorists, are no longer able to give educational practitioners good advice. To be comprehensible, we simplify. Our simplifications often leave out much of the context, but in our field, context is everything. When we leave the context in, our writings become idiosyncratic. My intentions do not include providing some sort of proof of the theoretical crisis in educational theory. Anyone who has recently read educational policy documents or listened to school staff meetings can testify to how small a presence educational theory has in educational practice. Not many people in the field need convincing; how little we matter is a persistent theme of an educational conferences talk.

I happen to believe that lack of impact has nothing to do with policy making routine, with the language we are using, or with the ignorance of educators. Nor is there some exceptional talent drought among the educational theorists of the second half of twentieth century. For a long time, we simply did not have ideas that could capture imagination of educators and the public. We have lost the ability to give good advice. What is happening is something similar to what Thomas Kuhn describes as paradigm crisis.[11] It is a theoretical dead end rather than anything else, and we have just begun to see some ways out.

The old paradigm of educational theory frames educational processes in terms of doing. Teaching as well as learning is considered to be doing something. Human relations are obviously very important for any student of education, and yet relations have always served as a background, as a context of the theoretical picture of education. Consider the visual perception demonstration from your Psych 101 class, where one cup suddenly turns into two human faces, and the old woman suddenly becomes a young woman. No matter how much you stare into the background of a cup, it remains just that, the background. It is not really a matter of ignoring or not paying attention to the background. Only after some time, something clicks in your brain, and you realize that the background is the picture, and the picture is the background. Something like this is happening to educational theory. Once we can perceive relations as a text and actions as a context, we can see a very different picture of education. What we do with students is not that important; what sort of relations we build with and among them becomes very important.

The extensive Claremont study defined the main issues affecting American public education as seen from inside the classroom—by students, teachers, parents, and administrators. This allowed the authors to get away from the dominating rhetoric of school reform. The number one issue turned out to be that of relationships. "Participants feel the crisis inside schools is directly linked to human relationships.... This theme was prominently stated by participants and so deeply connected to all other themes in the data that it is believed this may be one of the two most central issues in solving the crisis inside schools."[12] There is a very practical need for educational theory centered on the notion of relation.

It is clear that the pedagogy of relation has a solid prehistory. One of the main intellectual trends in American educational philosophy may as well be described as a shift from the pedagogy of behavior to the pedagogy of relation. I am certainly not trying to create this shift; my aim is simply to point it out. Not a widely used term, pedagogy of relation nevertheless captures the shared intent of an otherwise widely diverse group of writers. It is mainly, but not exclusively, associated with feminist thinkers like Nel Noddings, Jane R. Martin, and Carol Gilligan. The feminist theory offers a remarkable attempt to place relations at the center of analysis.[13] Critical theory in its own way examines the relations among students and teachers, if only overemphasizing the social relations over what Martin Buber calls the interhuman relations.[14] Among non-feminists, one can mention a group of philosophers who support one or another form of proceduralism (often inspired by Jurgen Habermas),[15] Gert Biesta's communicative pedagogy,[16] and Frank Margonis and his relational ontology. A common thread of this broad trend is an assumption that education is a function of specific human relations and not a function of certain behaviors.

The feminist scholars responded specifically to neither the particular failure of the educational reforming nor the paradigm difficulties of educational theory. Rather, they sought to address the gender biases of educational theory and practices and in social life in general. However, in the process they have created an important tradition of concentrating on relationships. Noddings's examination of care, Martin's idea of the Schoolhome and its three C's of care, concern, and connection, and Carol Gilligan's ethics of care are examples of theoretical constructs that take human relationships to be the primary building blocks of reality. The observable human behaviors as well as cognitive schemata are to be interpreted against the more primary facts of human relations.

Nel Noddings writes about "taking relation as ontologically basic,"[17] although she chooses to develop the theory of a specific type of relation (care) rather than address more general implications of relational ontology. Frank Margonis makes an explicit link between the ontology and the pedagogy in his paper "The Demise of Authenticity." He calls for "adopting an ontological attitude towards educational relationships."[18] Margonis argues that teachers need to realize that the concern for primacy of relationships in education comes from the realization that relationships have the primacy of being. This link is important because it changes the most fundamental assumptions not just about education but also about our thinking about education.

In his critique of child-centered education, Margonis proposes what amounts to a relationship-centered pedagogy.[19] He critically examines the child-centered tradition of Rousseau and Dewey but also attempts to salvage what is salvageable there. The child's interest, he says, is a suspect orientation for pedagogy, because it assumes the universal child and her innate goodness and individualism. While Dewey to some degree overcomes Rousseau's individualism, he still believes in a "direction built into children's characters—the tendency to think scientifically."[20] Margonis uses a quote from Mike Rose that I would like to borrow as well:

> Teaching, I was coming to understand, was a kind of romance. You didn't just work with words or a chronicle of dates or facts about the suspension of protein in milk. You wooed kids with these things, invited a relationship of sorts, the terms of connection being the narrative, the historical event, the balance of

casein and water. Maybe nothing was 'intrinsically interesting.' Knowledge gained its meaning, at least initially, through a touch on the shoulder, through a conversation.[21]

Margonis suggests that relationships ontologically precede the intrinsic motivation for learning and should therefore be placed at the center of educational theory. I can only add that from the point of view of institutional analysis of schooling, the crisis of authority cannot be resolved by child-centered pedagogies. Rose's claim that nothing is intrinsically interesting can be supported not only theoretically but also by the troubled history of Progressive educational reforms. In her book *Left Back,* Diane Ravitch comes up with suggestions that, from my point of view, are very questionable, but her criticism merits close attention.[22] In other words, I see Margonis's call for a relational pedagogy as the only way out of the authority crisis in schools and the crisis in educational theory. We either learn how to make relationships work in schools, or schools will disintegrate.

Not all learning can be fun, and the older the students are, the more this is true. The search for intrinsically motivating learning activities is a worthy one and should continue; we just need to be clear that it has very definite limits. Extrinsic motivation associated with school authority is also largely gone. But this is not really a big theoretical problem, because human beings have always done boring and unpleasant things without threats of physical violence or expulsion. Why does my son take out the garbage when I ask him (well, ultimately)? Because he does not want me to get upset with him. Now, why doesn't he want me to get upset? Because he values our relationship and does not want to ruin it because of the stupid garbage. Another example: why do I look at my wife's art books and talk about art to her? Because the arts are part of her and therefore a part of our relationship. As long as I value this relationship, I will be interested in the arts. These two examples describe well what is happening in the best of schools. Students cherish relationships with their teachers and with each other and either become excited about what their teachers are excited about or (as in the example of the garbage) just do the work so the teacher does not get upset. More likely, it is a combination of the two or some other mechanism where relationships are at the center.

The pedagogy of relation begins with a postulate that learning motivation is mainly a function of relations in the sense Mike Rose demonstrated in his book. It is not, however, another theory of learning motivation. One cannot simply consider relations as yet another means of motivation. A purely instrumental interpretation of relations will defeat the purpose of the theory. We have to reconsider questions traditionally asked by educational theories. I am not asking, "what sort of relations shall we develop with and among students, so they can master curriculum better?" Rather, I would like to consider relations the aim of education.

Let us try to turn our thinking upside down, just for a moment. What if we suppose that education is a process of building relations? We need schools so that each new generation can work its way into the web of social and personal relations that constitute human society. Students learn to relate to each other, to their significant adults (parents and teachers), and to the rest of the world. Relations are semi-permanent structures of our world; individual human beings come and go. Life is slowly changing but is essentially the same play, only actors change. Education is a rehearsal. Of course, each new individual and each new generation change the web of relations. In the next chapter, I will further explore what it exactly means to follow Noddings's suggestion of "taking relation as ontologically basic." Yet, for now let us try to imagine that all curriculum, all knowledge and skills that students acquire have no independent worth or meaning. All of these are simply means of entering the world wide web of relations; these are simply tools, tokens, or signs that allow students to enter the relational fabric of human existence. It is hard for a Western mind to see itself as a temporary part of some larger whole. It is hard for anyone to admit that something so intangible, so ephemeral as one's relationships with one's parents, children, co-workers, the state, culture, or the world—that these relationships are not simply part of oneself but rather that one's self is an impermanent part of them.

If we can assume all this, pedagogy of relation may be more than simply building a good relation with and among kids so they can learn more arithmetic. Perhaps we can reverse the means and ends here and view arithmetic in the context of building relations.

Like many theorists, I fell in love with my subject. It is not enough for me now to show how relations can be used to motivate children to learn. No, I want to take the argument one step further, so that relations are even more important than learning itself. How can one resist the temptation to create a whole new worldview when trying to address a specific issue? The next chapter is an indulgence in such a project. Relation is not only the savior of education, it is also the building block of the universe.

NOTES

[1] Anthony Giddens, *The Transformation of Intimacy* (Stanford, CA: Stanford University Press, 1992).

[2] Giddens, *The Transformation of Intimacy*, 58.

[3] Giddens, *The Transformation of Intimacy*, 28.

[4] A good example of such literature is George Gazda, et al., *Human Relations Development: A Manual for Educators*, Sixth Edition (Boston: Allyn and Bacon, 1999, 1973).

[5] Robert E. Slavin, *Educational Psychology*, Fifth Edition (Boston: Allyn and Bacon, 1997), 162.

[6] Slavin, *Educational Psychology*, 391

[7] American Psychological Association. *Learner-Centered Psychological Principles*, 1997 (http://www.apa.org/ed/lcp2/lcp14.html).

[8] Slavin, *Educational Psychology*, 278.

[9] APA's Principle 6 is this: "Learning does not occur in a vacuum. Teachers play a major interactive role with both the learner and the learning environment. Cultural or group influences on students can impact many educationally relevant variables, such as motivation, orientation toward learning, and ways of thinking. Technologies and instructional practices must be appropriate for learners' level of prior knowledge, cognitive abilities, and their learning and thinking strategies. The classroom environment, particularly the degree to which it is nurturing or not, can also have significant impacts on student learning." American Psychological Association. *Learner-Centered Psychological Principles*, 1997 (http://www.apa.org/ed/lcp2/lcp14.html).

[10] A recent example of such a description is Shelby A. Wolf, Hilda Borki, Rebekah L. Elliott, and Monette C. McIver, "'That Dog Won't Hunt!': Exemplary School Change Efforts Within the Kentucky Reform," in *American Educational Research Journal*. Summer 2000, 37, 2, 349-393. A less recent but excellent example is Sara L. Lightfoot, *The Good High School: Portraits of Character and Culture* (New York: Basic Books, 1983).

[11] Thomas Kuhn, *The Structure of Scientific Revolutions,* Third Edition (Chicago: University of Chicago Press, 1996).

[12] Mary Poplin and Joseph Weeres, eds., *Voices from the Inside: A Report on Schooling Inside the Classroom. Part One: Naming the Problem* (Claremont, CA: The Institute for Education in Transformation at the Claremont Graduate School, 1992).

[13] See, for instance, Ann Diller, "Pluralisms for Education: An Ethics of Care Perspective," *Philosophy of Education 1992* (http://www.ed.uiuc.edu/eps/pes-yearbook/92_docs/Diller.HTM).

14. Martin Buber, *The Knowledge of Man* (Atlantic Highlands, NJ: Humanities Press International, 1988).

15. For a good summary of the proceduralist argument, see Clive Beck, "Difference, Authority and the Teacher-Student Relationship," *Philosophy of Education 1994* (http://www.ed.uiuc.edu/eps/pes-yearbook/94_docs/beck.htm).

16. Gert Biesta, "Education/Communication: The Two Faces of Communicative Pedagogy," *Philosophy of Education 1995* (http://www.ed.uiuc.edu/eps/pes-yearbook/95_docs/biesta.html).

17. Nel Noddings, *Caring: A Feminine Approach to Ethics and Moral Education* (Berkeley, CA: University of California Press, 1984), 4.

18. Frank Margonis, "The Demise of Authenticity," *Philosophy of Education 1998* (http://www.ed.uiuc.edu/eps/pes-yearbook/1998/margonis_2.html).

19. Frank Margonis, "New Problems in Child-Centered Pedagogy," *Philosophy of Education 1992* (http://www.ed.uiuc.edu/eps/pes-yearbook/92_docs/margonis.htm).

20. Margonis, "New Problems."

21. Mike Rose, *Lives on the Boundary* (London: Penguin, 1989), 102.

22. Diane Ravitch, *Left Back: A Century of Failed School Reforms* (New York: Simon & Schuster, 2000).

CHAPTER 7.
ONTOLOGY, ANTHROPOLOGY, AND EPISTEMOLOGY OF RELATION

Relational ontology assumes that what primarily exists is relation, not entities like things and individual human beings. The entities neither can know nor can be known; they neither can be changed nor can they change something outside of the relation. The elemental reality of this world is relation, although we cannot directly see or experience relation. Relational ontology is, fundamentally, an acknowledgment that an observer cannot take herself out of the picture. It is giving up on Cartesian "I think" and "I am," not to mention the "therefore." It is also abandoning the project of monological identity formation and of the authentic self. This chapter sets out to offer a brief list of the ontological, epistemological, and anthropological issues that arise if one places the notion of relation at the center of one's philosophy.

Harold Oliver in his *A Relational Metaphysics* contrasts object-subject and relational paradigms through both physics and philosophy. He starts his investigation with a Newton-Leibniz debate and follows both paradigms to quantum mechanics and systems philosophy.[1] He shows that philosophy and much of science are still dominated by Newtonian subject-object scheme, while twentieth-century physics has set the stage for a relational paradigm. I invite everyone who is interested in the history of relational paradigm to read Oliver's book. This book, however, is on educational theory, and my intentions do not include a comprehensive treatment of these issues. Subsequently, I leave out large chunks of pertinent literature, including writings of Heidegger and Levinas, and touch only superficially on Buber and Bakhtin.

In the twentieth century, the roots of relational ontology can be traced to Martin Buber: "In the beginning is relation."[2] Buber's main claim is: "To man the world is twofold."[3] *I-Thou* and *I-It* are two pairs of primary words that separate two very different modes of existence. Hence, *I-Thou* or just *Thou* refer to the realm of the dialogical relation, while *I-It* or *It* refer to the realm of subject-object experiences. Buber's approach was to concentrate on two types of relations (*I-Thou* and *I-It*) to show how human existence depends on which relation is in place. He majestically succeeded in establishing the primacy of relation. However, he had to rely on sharp opposition of the two types of relation to make the point that relations truly matter. Buber described an almost magical transformation that occurs when people shift from the world of regular *I-It* relations into the higher world of *I-Thou*, as if an invisible and ineffable switch flipped. As a result, his theory of relations lacks nuance. It is either *I-Thou* or *I-It*, all or nothing. There is nothing else and nothing in between. In his later work, Buber tried to enrich this binary model by introducing the notion of the *Zwischenmenschliche*, or the interhuman. The interhuman consists of elements of every-day life that may lead to a genuine dialogue or, as Buber describes it, *I-Thou* relation. But the interhuman is not an *I- Thou* yet; it just opens up some possibilities of moving toward *I-Thou*. Buber then distinguished again two essentially different areas or dimensions of human life, the social and the interhuman. In other words, Buber tried to overcome the extreme duality of his relational taxonomy, although he replaced it with yet another, if less extreme, binary opposition.

Buber's bipolar logic resulted in his deep pessimism about achievability of dialogue (genuine *I-Thou* relations) in the situation of educational encounter. Essentially, he claims that full mutuality is impossible between a student and a teacher (as between a therapist and patient—anywhere certain power asymmetry exists). This is where Buber's version of relational ontology ceases to be helpful for educational theory. He may be right in his pessimism, and I will examine the problem of power imbalance separately. However, it becomes clear that pedagogy of relation cannot be based on the typology of relations offered by Buber. We will need a more nuanced taxonomy of relations. The dialogical relations Buber examined in contrast to monological or instrumental relations are only a particular case of relational worldview. From my point of view, Buber's idea of the primacy of relations over things (and individuals) is a much more promising foundation of educational theory than his theory of dialogue itself.

I will treat the notion of dialogue as a specific case of relations. Buber and Bakhtin, the authors of two most fundamental concepts of dialogue, are ambivalent about their respective interpretations of dialogue. Both independently of each other claim that dialogue is both a universal feature of human life and a rare occasion, a highest point in human life. Bakhtin writes that every meaning is co-authored; every word uttered by an individual belongs in part to somebody else. "[The dialogical relation]—is almost a universal phenomenon, penetrating all of human speech and all the relationships and manifestations of human life; generally, everything that has sense and meaning."[4] Similarly, Buber argues that I-Thou is a natural way of life, represented both in the history of primitive men, and in the individual history of a child.[5] "There are not two kinds of man, but two poles of humanity. Every man lives in the twofold I."[6] "All men have somewhere been aware of the Thou."[7] Without delving into detailed analysis of their respective theories,[8] I will simply assume that when they talk about dialogue in the broader, universal sense, they discuss relationality. The narrow sense of the word describes the dialogue proper, a specific kind of relation, characterized by mutuality and opposite of instrumental *I-It* type. I will return to Buber in the Part III, but first, what is a relation ?

In *Categories,* Aristotle undertook first serious analysis of the relation, which in turn, produced an interesting discussion among medieval philosophers on the nature and status of relations. The discussion unfolded mainly along the realist–anti-realist divide. Jeffrey Brower describes a shift away from Aristotelian understanding of relation that occurred in the fourteenth century: "...instead of thinking of relations as the items responsible for relating two or more substances, they now begin to think of them as items existing only in the mind—that is, as mere beings of reason or concepts."[9] The relational ontology of Buber, on which I rely, is an example of a radically realist argument, which not only acknowledges the reality of relations, but also considers relations primary to substances.

According to V.I. Chernov the category of relation belongs to "the simplest and most general abstractions in the world," which are difficult to define but are so clear that they can be used to define other philosophical terms.[10] Yakov Kolominskii adds that perhaps the intuitive clarity is exactly what makes a category difficult to define.[11] This makes sense: with such categories as relation, the philosophical ladder, so to speak, ends, there is nothing more fundamental on which one could base a proper definition.

According to Avenir Uemov,[12] our world consists of things, qualities, and relations. All three could be described through each other. A thing could be presented as a sum of qualities; a quality is an aspect of a thing, and a relation is a quality of a system of things. From the logical point of view, there is no clean definition of relation, because it can only be defined through things or qualities, which, in turn, can be defined through each other and relations. Generally, relation is understood as a meaningful connection or association between two or more things.[13] My working definition is this: relation is the aspect of reality brought about by plurality. Admittedly, a certain reality comes from unity and sameness of being. However, another and, in my view, more important aspect of reality is determined by the differentiation of being, by otherness of being. This second aspect of reality can be described as relation.

Relations cannot belong to one thing; they are the joint property of at least two things. Relations are located, so to speak, in between things and are located in neither of the things joint into a relation. Any relation is an object of joint custody. More precisely, relations are not located at all; they have existence without location. For humans, existence is closely related to location—we know that something exists if we can place it somewhere. However, this is only a consequence of a geographic bias of a species developed in a relatively stable system of co-ordinates. Our sense of reality tends to ignore the relational aspects of material things' existence. For instance, when one says, "The goat is there," this phrase really expresses certain perceived spatial relation between the goat and the surface of the Earth. What really exists is a specific relation between the goat, the Earth, and the observer. The relation is not located, but it definitely exists.

Existence itself is a relation, too. "To be" is a form of relation, not a quality of a solitary thing. A thing that does not enter into any relations with the rest of the universe does not exist at all. The thing-in-itself is an interesting concept, but it is clearly beyond being. Any existence can only be conceived as "existence-among," as co-being. The line between existence and non-existence can be cleanly drawn with the help of relations. The only way to exist in this world is through others. The quality of existence does not belong to the thing that exists—this sounds paradoxical only at first. Existence is an honor, bestowed by others; it is impossible to achieve on your own.

Ours is a relational universe that relinquishes absolutes and yet demands a new sense of reality. We have made the crucial step from the stable universe of things and found ourselves in an unstable relativist universe, where everything is found to be relative. The next small step is from the relativistic to a relational view of the universe. It was quite easy to realize that the goat may or may not be there, depending on one's point of view. Much harder is to understand that "the goat is there" is not about the goat, and not about the observer, and not even about the Earth. It is a statement describing a real relation, if not real things.

By describing something as "relative," we implicitly doubt its reality. To say, "Well, it is relative" is to question how real that thing is. However, when corporeal certainty escapes us, we often fail to see the glimpse of a newfound relational certainty. A realization of uncertainty is nothing but finding another certainty; one cannot be without the other. Einstein postulated that there is no absolute rest in the universe, that there is no single thing in relation to which objects can be said to move or to rest. Thus the relations among things took the place of the absolute co-ordinates. Indeed, it is impossible to say whether the train moves and the station rests or the train rests and the station moves. But the train and the station certainly move away from each other.

In the new universe, relations are primary and things are secondary. To exist is to relate; nothing can exist outside relations. Relations truly exist; things only co-exist, or exist partially. Relations constitute the underlying fabric of the world, while things are but knots of relationality. Should you untangle each knot, you will find only a multitude of intertwined relations. Things are relative, but relations are absolute—absolute in a sense that they are complete, while things are always part of some relation. A thing is a part of many relations, but each thing cannot be whole. Non-relational existence is unthinkable, for thinking is a product of relation.

When I see a goat and think, "the goat is there," who is doing the thinking? The temptation is always to attribute thinking to myself. Yet, in the relational universe, it is the *relation* of the goat, the Earth, and I that does the thinking. The relation thinks, and I am only one part of the relation that happens to have a better brain. This may seem like a strange argument, but consider the following: One can consider my brain or its front lobes to be the agent of thinking; one can also locate thinking in the whole of my body. The choice of location of the thinking agent is quite arbitrary. Going deep inside my body will not produce an exact location of thinking. The assignment of thinking to a human being is also arbitrary; it is defined by the boundaries of my skin. Why not go outside of my body as well? Why do I draw the line at my skin or at my skull? Wouldn't it be much more reasonable to believe that the whole system of things that constitute a relation thinks? Just like my brain is an organ of thinking, the whole of me is an organ by which the world thinks. I am no more real than the I-and-the-goat system, or, rather, my existence is no more factual than the existence of the larger system.

Chuang Tzu had his famous dream in which he was a butterfly, and woke up with a question: "Was I before a man who dreamt about being a butterfly, or am I now a butterfly who dreams about being a man?"[14] The point of the story, as I read it, is not to say that there is no difference between dreams and reality; it is that the reality of the man and butterfly does not reside in the man alone. In the relational universe, things do not have solitary existence; therefore I do not ever exist independently of all objects and of other people. Taking this reasoning one step further, one may argue that things as we are used to seeing them, do not constitute reality, but relations among and between things do.

Because of certain accidents of our physicality, our species has developed a special blind spot where it comes to relationality. Our eyes look outside, and we do not see ourselves in most of our interactions with the world. In most practical matters, this blind spot does not matter and can even be beneficial. In our everyday life, it is usually clear what is moving and what is resting. We tend to fold a description of a relation into a description of a thing. However, when we enter the world of social relations beyond traditional homogeneous society, the sense of non-relational reality often fails us. One has to learn now to recognize, where one is speaking from in each particular situation, with each particular partner. The drive for such a sensibility to relations is one of the most remarkable social phenomena of contemporary America. Its beginnings are humble and necessarily simplistic: how does a man speak to a woman, a white person to a person of color, etc. With all the simplifications and inevitable flaws of such thinking, it establishes an important practice of paying attention to relationality of social life. Such a practice questions the concept of the authentic self and invites us to think about the possibilities of a relational self.

A relation between two people could be described as a puppeteer who directs two puppets simultaneously. He is invisible and disembodied; he can only hear through his puppets' ears, and see through their eyes. He has no voice of his own but can only speak with the voices of his puppets. He lives through the puppets, but he is a real being. He breathes life into the puppets, creates their characters, determines their actions, and gives them dreams. When he is tired and does not want to play anymore, they go limp and lifeless. The puppeteer also has a personality; he can change, grow, get sick, or die. He has his moods, his skills, his handicaps, successes, and failures. The puppeteer creates the rules of his game.

The relational concept of the self I am trying to advance presents the self in a way that disallows its independent existence. The self is an abstraction like "weight" or "color." We know that there is no "blue" as such; there are only things that are blue. The same is true about the self. The self is a quality that relations have. It is a very special quality but a quality nevertheless. The self is the point of intersection of a multitude of relations. It has constancy and coherence to the extent that multiple relations have points of connection and intersection. The self is a means of connection among relations. In a certain sense, the self can be understood as a relation among multiple human relations. It is a meeting point, a place of interaction of various relations. It serves as an anchor in the boundless sea of human relationality. The self is psychophysical embodiment of relations among relations.

The self cannot be understood as a separate entity; studying an isolated self is like studying "blueness." Only analysis of specific relations in their interaction can provide a glimpse of the meaning of the self. Education cannot be successful if it uses the model of stand-alone self. The aim of education is not to shape the self but to shape a certain bundle of relations that include the self. I believe it is time to abandon the Enlightenment infatuation with the self and the closely related infatuation with education. A human being is not a measure of all things; a human relation is. Relational ontology is counterintuitive for teachers, because we will have to cease to think of individual students as depositories of the final product of teaching. Instead, we will have to learn to create certain relationships, certain human communities here and now, and be content with them as true aims of education.

The ontological peculiarity of relations creates certain epistemological difficulties. Margonis identifies one epistemological problem with relations—our knowledge of relationship always remains partial and limited.[15] I can only add that any sort of knowledge is also partial and limited, but Margonis is right in pointing out that we have no available apparatus to assess validity of knowledge about relations. The efforts of Barbara Thayer-Bacon can at least partially address this problem. She is developing the relational epistemology, which "is motivated by the desire to expand what epistemology means to include the qualities of knowing that have historically been viewed as detrimental or distracting to the obtaining of knowledge—qualities such as feelings, emotions, and intuitions which are usually linked to women rather than men."[16] Thayer-Bacon infuses knowing with relationality, which may help us better understand relations. However, correcting the process of knowing with inclusion of relationality does not necessarily solve the problem when relations are the objects of knowing. In other words, following Thayer-Bacon, we can know better all classes of objects, but her approach does not give us any special tools in understanding relations. Relational understanding is not the same thing as understanding relations.

How do I know if my classroom relationships are those of trust, respect, or care? The difficulty here is that I cannot know it alone. The language of subject-object epistemology simply does not apply here. The knowledge about relations can only exist as collective knowledge, as a multitude of voices engaged in a complex multivoiced dialogue. Certain knowledge cannot be held or comprehended by one person. I want to appeal once to Bakhtin's theory of polyphony and polyphonic truth that is born "in the point of touching of different consciousnesses."[17] His argument is that the multitude of individual consciousnesses has some epistemological meaning. What could be known by the means of dialogue cannot be known by any other means. This may or may not be true about all kinds of knowledge, but it would be very reasonable to suggest that at least with respect to relations, polyphonic truth is a much more workable concept than any other form of knowledge.

Relations thus are not describable by one person. Relation in general is possible only in the presence of difference. Totally identical entities cannot relate to each other. Relations result from plurality, from some tension born of difference. Therefore any relation between or among human individuals will include certain non-coincidence of their reflections of the relation. None of the individuals involved in a relation possesses the truth about this relation, but all of them together do. This is not a matter of averaging or finding the truth somewhere "in between." According to Bakhtin, truth is not a result of a dialogue, truth *is* dialogue. If I hear two people discuss their relationship, I can grasp some truth about their relationship, although this truth is not to be summarized into a monological description.

Participants of a relation can describe it in dialogue, but then one person can describe their description. It is important to understand that one can translate the polyphonic truth into a form comprehensible by one individual. After all, Dostoevsky, who served as a model to Bakhtin, was a single author of his polyphonic novels. In other words, an epistemology of relation does not totally preclude individual knowledge of relations; it simply requires the special form of knowledge organization. The knowledge of relation is an internalized dialogue about the relation. Thus, the truth about relations is not a sum of internally consistent statements; rather, it is a set of mutually engaged but contradictory statements. To know something about relations is to be able to reconstruct many possible dialogues about this relation that include all participants. For example, a teacher cannot know or describe her relation with students using her consistent monological voice; there can be no truth in such knowledge. However, the teacher can present a dialogue between the students and herself, which presents different but engaged and dynamic opinions about the relation. The polyphonic knowledge is one where the other is made present.

If we are to give advice to teachers about classroom relations, this is all but impossible without including students in some dialogue about relations. Whatever knowledge of relations theorists will be able to generate is not easily transferable to improve classroom relations, at least not through teachers alone. Generally, we write our books and papers for teachers; educational theory never fancied to have students as its audience. I am not quite sure why this is so. No marriage therapist will work on family relations with just one family member. However, we are trying to improve education while speaking to a tiny majority of people involved. Teachers and administrators make no more than 5 percent of the total population of schools. No matter how important their role is, we cannot assume that they represent the remaining 95 percent of the equation. One can imagine a book intended for an audience of teachers and students and meant to be read by a whole classroom.

But what about theory of educational relations intended for adults only? How does relational epistemology play out here? How can the multivoiced description translate into prescriptive knowledge? How do we tell anyone about better relations and ways of achieving them? It is relatively easy to know what we should not tell to teachers. As I have stated earlier, we cannot tell them what to do. No action could be prescribed as good or bad in itself. Nothing that a teacher does or does not do has meaning outside of the relationship. Instead, we can offer advice on how to relate to students: how to like them and how to be liked, how to trust and how to be trusted, how to include and how to be included.

A particular relation can be described and therefore known. Moreover, the history of such a relation can also be described and known. In other words, one can determine what specific consequence of action led to this specific relation. Yet this knowledge is not generalizable. One can never assume that the same set of actions will lead to a similar relation for other people. However, the knowledge of relation can be generalized to a skill. The old but vague analogy between teaching and art can be given more serious thought. A future artist will benefit from watching a master working. How exactly will she benefit? She will not simply repeat the master's actions, but she will acquire a skill. She will not necessarily understand how a good picture is made. Her knowledge of a particular process will translate into a skill. In a certain sense the knowledge of the particular can be generalized to a skill.

There are many examples of such knowledge-to-skill generalizations. Reading many legal arguments will help a lawyer to learn how to build an argument without a set algorithm or general knowledge. A psychiatrist will learn some theory, of course, but also observe many therapy sessions to develop the needed skill. To think of it, skills *are* a form of knowledge. Moreover, some skills are a form of *generalized* knowledge. Good artisans, good salespersons, good teachers, and good doctors know something *generic* about achieving good results in unique, one-at-a-time circumstances. The evidence of such general knowledge is manifest in the results of their work. They know something because they can do it. Such knowledge cannot be expressed through a text though. A skillful artisan cannot tell us exactly how he does what he does. Polanyi[18] brought attention to this type of knowledge and called it tacit knowledge. However, it is different not because it is implicit. The skill can be just as apparent and as visible as a theory. The difference is in how this knowledge can be expressed and verified.

The knowledge of educational relations is unlikely to turn into a highly formalized theory with principles, laws, taxonomies, and algorithms. It could develop into a highly sophisticated field of teacher training. Future teachers will observe and read about hundreds of cases of human relationships in schools. They will learn to "read" relationships, to reflect on these cases, to talk and write about relationships. The key skill here is the ability to reconstruct the other voice. A teacher must develop this ability to hear what has not been said, to formulate what his students are not able to articulate, to engage in a dialogue when the other party may not be willing or ready to engage. The ability to understand human relations relies heavily on the heightened ability to hear and respond without preconceived notions of truth.

This model of teacher training will stay away from using random "situations" that crowd pages of today's educational textbooks. The situations are problematic because they are highly decontextualized, often artificial, and just plain weak. Future teachers will train their imagination and sense of reality. They will have a general idea what will or will not work in different circumstances. However, they will also learn that each relationship requires special attention and creative thinking. They will learn to develop plans of actions to improve specific relational contexts. The student teachers will be judged by how well they could get along with kids and how this good relationship was beneficial to the kids. Epistemology of relation borders praxeology, which does not preclude one from knowing and understanding relations.

As a teacher, I should be concerned primarily about the quality of relations that exists between myself and my students, as well as the quality of relations among my students, and those relations my students have with the outside world. Of course, such an interpretation of education implies different qualities, different levels of relations. The critique of authenticity and recognition I offer also implicitly uses some notion of better and worse relations. It will be among my tasks to establish the taxonomy and the hierarchy of relations.

NOTES

[1] Harold H. Oliver, *A Relational Metaphysics* (The Hague: Martinus Nijhoff Publishers, 1981).
[2] Martin Buber, *I and Thou* (New York: Collier Books, 1987), 69.
[3] Buber, *I and Thou*, 3.
[4] Mikhail Bakhtin, *Problemy poetiki Dostoevskogo* (Moscow: Sovetskii Pisatel', 1963), 56.
[5] Buber, *I and Thou*, 22–28.
[6] Buber, *I and Thou*, 65.
[7] Buber, *I and Thou*, 53.
[8] I have done my share of Buber and Bakhtin scholarship in Alexander Sidorkin, *Beyond Discourse: Education, the Self, and Dialogue* (Albany, N.Y.: SUNY Press, 1999).
[9] Jeffrey E. Brower, "Medieval Theories of Relations," *Stanford Encyclopedia of Philosophy* (http://plato.stanford.edu/entries/relations-medieval/), 2000.
[10] Vladimir I. Chernov, *Analiz filosofskikh ponatii [Analysis of Philosophical categories]* (Moscow: Nauka, 1966), 44.
[11] Y.L.Kolominskii, *Psikhologiia vzaimootnoshenii v malykh gruppakh. [Psychology of Mutual Relations in Small Groups]* (Minsk: TetraSystems, 2000), 28.
[12] Avenir Uemov, *Veshchi, svoistva i otnosheniia [Things, Qualities, and Relations]* (Moscow: Izdatelstvo Akademii Nauk SSSR, 1963).
[13] Microsoft *Encarta Dictionary* (http://dictionary.msn.com).
[14] Jay Deuel, *Tai Chi Page* (http://www.utah.edu/stc/tai-chi/stories.html), 1997.
[15] Frank Margonis, "The Demise of Authenticity," *Philosophy of Education 1998* (http://www.ed.uiuc.edu/eps/pes-yearbook/1998/margonis_2.html).
[16] Barbara J. Thayer-Bacon, "Navigating Epistemological Territories," *Philosophy of Education 1995* (http://www.ed.uiuc.edu/eps/pes-yearbook/95_docs/thayerbacon.html).
[17] Mikhail Bakhtin, *Problemy poetiki Dostoevskogo*, 107.
[18] Michael Polanyi, *The Tacit Dimension* (Gloucester, MA: Peter Smith, 1983).

CHAPTER 8.
BETWEEN EROS AND ATHENA:
THE ECONOMY OF RELATIONS

So far, this book has concentrated on the importance of relations and relationality for education, especially for schools. If my work will simply help educational theorists and practitioners to pay more attention to the relational side of education, I will consider it a success. However, a substantive discussion of the educational relations is needed to understand how relational pedagogy may work.

I will use the metaphor of economy to emphasize certain characteristics of relations: they are not subjective and unpredictable; they work according to some hidden mechanisms that could be discovered and used for the purpose of education. Another motive I have for using this metaphor is to remove the connotation of sentimentality and pop psychology from the notion of relations. The relational network of a school is a complex mechanism to be studied and transformed, but it is neither mysterious nor ineffable. People attribute certain problems to relationships in a sense that this is something not fully understandable, requiring the intuition of a genius. The word "relationship" is used with an air of complexity in the negative sense as something beyond our understanding and control. Sure, relations are very complex; they consist of myriads of small and big events, conversations, looks, and gestures, just as the economy consists of billions of big and small individual transactions. However, there are certain rules that govern the complexity of the marketplace. Each individual actor tends to follow a real or perceived concept of rationality. Similarly, there must be some rules that govern the development of relationships.

There exists a complicated economy of school relations, the intricacies of which are yet to be understood. Students like some teachers and dislike others, cooperate with some, and rebel against others. Some kids are popular and some not; friendships are forged and dissolved; alliances formed, the intrigue brews—much without proper educational analysis and planned intervention. All I am prepared to do at this point is to give the sketchiest outline of this economy. My hope is, of course, that someone will be interested in pursuing field studies of such economies. However, it is much more important that practicing teachers realize that the matter of teacher's gossip about the human relations in schools are not just on the periphery of education but perhaps the most important thing to talk about at staff meetings.

My general suggestion is that teachers should at least be as cunning and knowledgeable about relationship matters as the most sophisticated child sociologists. They should know who is popular and why, how the popularity is achieved, what it takes to get into the popular crowd. They should also know who the outsiders are and why they are outsiders, whether they form alternative centers of influence, is there a rivalry between two or more groups, etc. Every teacher should have an idea about what his or her relations are with individual students and with whole groups of kids and where those relations ought to be going. Teachers must have a reasonable strategy of linking all the groups and forces of students into some sort of school community. Most significantly, the teachers should figure out how the process of creation of such a community can be made to serve educational purposes. In other words, what we need is love, of course, but more importantly, some sophisticated analysis and well-planned strategies of relational pedagogies.

What we commonly call the market is possible only as long as there is some differentiation among the commodities. If every producer manufactured the same thing, no exchange would be possible. Similarly (but not identically) the richness of relational life depends on the variety of relations that exist and the easiness with which they convert into one another. I assume this to be the basic principle of the economy of relation: a social organization such as school must contain a typological multitude of relations; these relations must be mutually convertible.

At the foundation of the economy of relation lies an assumption that a certain driving force compels individuals to take part in relations in schools. The metaphor of "economy" only makes sense when one assumes that individuals have certain interests they pursue in relations with each other. Recall the description of bullying in Chapter 5. Although basic aggressive desires definitely play a role, I suggest that the incidents of bullying are instances of rational violence. The bullies simply pursue their own interest of power maintenance, and the practice of bullying itself is no more than a means to achieve certain goals. In a sense, this is also true about relations we would call positive. Of course, we all possess the gift for altruistic sympathy and human solidarity. Students and teachers do like (and dislike) each other without any reason and do establish unmediated relational bonds. However, one must not ignore the strong rational underlining of many human relations. An example may be helpful here.

A physics teacher who is also a basketball coach rarely has disciplinary problems in his class. Here is how he could describe this: "They need something from me—to be able to play the sport they love. But I also need something from them, which is to show me respect in the classroom and to do their schoolwork. The eternal 'you scratch my back, I'll scratch yours' type of relationship explains why coaches often have better relations with kids and make better teachers." This is an example of the economy of mutual interest that does not require massive coercion but is also free of utopian assumptions about self-motivated learning. Some believe that all children would be eager to learn about poetry, logarithms, and enzymes if correct teaching methods are applied, or if proper demands are made. Let such people believe what they want, but the cynical basketball coach seems to be so much closer to reality than those curriculum theorists.

Coaches do not hold a monopoly on motivational power (and not all coaches can play this game sensibly). In fact, all good teachers *give* something to kids in return for sometimes-boring schoolwork. Some do it through other extracurricular activities; some simply find a way to give the students the respect, recognition, and companionship they need. This is an economic mechanism oiled by interpersonal relation but powered by mutual interest.

Coaches tend to believe that this works because of their great teaching and disciplinary skills and their charismatic personalities. However, the reality is very simple—the coach has something students want, and they have something he wants. It has little to do with how likeable the person is, or, rather, his likeability will only have an effect within a certain relational situation. Now, a non-athletic student will likely respect the coach as well because, of her relations with the athletes (more on this in the next chapter). One cannot offend friends of one's friend, so the relational bonds tend to extend well beyond immediately interested parties. Let us assume that, no matter how skeptical this may sound, people tend to like each other more if their relations are mutually beneficial.

Here is where my thinking about human relations deviates from that of Buber. For Buber, dialogue is a relation that is characterized by mutuality, directness, presentness, intensity, and ineffability.[1] Yet mutuality implies exchange and thus contradicts directness. Human beings do not enter relationships because they are disinterested. One cannot ignore the place desire plays in human relationships. Individuals seek pleasure in conversation, help, alleviation of suffering, sexual pleasure, and intimacy. Buber's descriptions of dialogical encounters radiate with sheer ecstasy of being; he speaks the language of Eros. He denies that people engage in the dialogical relation with a specific goal in mind; however, his version of dialogue is clearly sensual. Desire fuels the economy of relations.

Every time a teacher asks a student to sit down and be quiet, she expends a certain amount of relational currency. Every time the same student receives something he wants from her, he spends some currency. These mechanisms of exchange are often confusing and sometimes totally invisible for the participants as well as for the observers. On several occasions, my wife and I have been able to get something from our teenage kids just by reminding them of the mechanism of exchange. For instance, our son refused to go to a theater performance with us, because he suspected it was going to be boring, and he would rather hang out with his friends. "Okay," we said, "fine, you can stay home, but next time you need to go to a party we are not driving you." This was a very appealing argument, because our son realized that his parents have something he needs beyond basic obligations of parenthood.[2] This goes beyond simplistic questions of who has the power and authority and how much. I would argue that successful teachers engage in transactions of this sort every day, and I see nothing morally wrong with such an arrangement. Most of these transactions are unspoken and indirect. After all, my wife and I simply tried to demonstrate a principle and not complete a specific exchange of one theater show attendance for one trip to a party. The economy of relations does not resemble barter; rather, it operates through complex symbolical interchanges that signify mutual indebtedness and obligations.

If anything, the economy of relations resembles precapitalist economies, where traditional obligations do not allow for exactly measured and impersonal exchanges of goods but where a whole community is tightly bound together with a mixture of expectations, personal likes and dislikes, rivalries, micropolitics, and blood ties. Such economies are still based on mutual interest, not on direct violence of an outside authority. The precapitalist economies are based on the threat of exclusion, which implies that being included has some tangible benefits.

The bottom line of the economy of relation is that teachers need to have something to offer to the students. The fundamental flaw of contemporary schooling is the strange situation when adults have very little of what students really want. I will address later the institutional changes that could remedy the situation. However, on the level of everyday teaching practices, any teacher will benefit from a balance sheet of sorts. She needs to know what she has that students want. These are her assets that can be used in exchange for something she wants from her students. Russian teachers' slang used to have an expression that literally translates as "to buy the student." When teachers trade stories of some difficult kids in a classroom that had been converted from foes into friends, this act of conversion would be described as "This is how I bought him," meaning, this is how I won over the student's respect and cooperation. One only needs to figure out what we have that kids want.

Sometimes they just want our personal attention, sometimes some tokens of respect and affection. Little kids want hugs, older kids need a sympathetic ear; almost everyone needs attention. They might be interested in what we know and what we can do. We can lend them our influence, our connections, our advice, or opinion. We can give them candy and stickers. We can teach them how to play a new game or tell them something new about their athlete hero. We can talk to their girlfriends and evaluate their boyfriends. We may have information they need, or we can keep secrets they entrust to us. In short, there are a million small and big things a kid may want from an adult. The trick is not so much to figure out what they want and what we have, but to jumpstart the exchange. In other words, having the merchandise does not automatically guarantee a deal. Not unlike real economies, the economy of school relation will work only when it is well oiled with personal relationships.

In this chapter, I focus on the elemental cell of the economy of relations, the individual student-teacher relationships. It is, of course, an abstraction, for the economy requires a multitude of players who enter into complicated multilateral relations. To set the stage for this task, I will start with the discussion between Chris Higgins and Kal Alston at the Philosophy of Education Society meeting in 1998. Higgins asks a question, "What types of love are educative?" He then uses Freud's paper "Observations on Transference Love" to answer the question. In short, Higgins agrees with Freud that the professional considerations prevent teachers (like therapists) from entering into romantic relations with students. However, Freud stated that a therapist cannot simply reject his patient's advances either. Higgins concludes the paper with the following summary:

> As teachers, we are fundamentally transitional objects, we may love and be loved, but these loves arise in the service of attaching a student's love to what is good in a wider world than that of the classroom or the teacher-student relationship. As teachers, we are at most a station along the track, or perhaps with a few students a kind of switching point, but when we begin to think of ourselves as a destination, we have lost sight of something central to the practice of teaching. As teachers, our love for our students as learners, as fellow searchers on a quest to understand themselves and their world, as human beings in the process of widening their experience and deepening their capacity to think and feel, is our best reason not to let this love be replaced by another.[3]

Higgins's thinking about Eros in a student-teacher relationship is constructed in terms of limits, while Freud thought about it in terms of acceptable use. Higgins asks us not to forget the transitionary nature of education, with which I am in full agreement. Yet, in the end, he advises teachers, so to speak, not to go there or to go somewhere else instead. Freud's idea of transference has another dimension. He sees love as something necessary and valuable to be transformed and used for therapy.

Kal Alston, in her response to Higgins,[4] points out that teachers are not therapists; the latter do not disclose their true personality, while the former must do it in order to be good teachers. I am not sure if an effective therapy can happen without the therapist disclosing her true self; however, she is right about teaching. Alston's own recommendations are these: "the teacher must help the student to understand the value of the educational relationship, as well as the distortions and distractions that are possible when combined with romance." Teacher-student relationship is more contextual, she says, and the teacher cannot simply tell her student that his feelings are not really directed to her as Freud might suggest. In the end, however, it is not clear what Alston wants a teacher to do in this situation.

I will take several points from this discussion. A teacher-student relationship is both personal and teleological. By personal, I mean not only that the teacher must disclose her true personality to students but also that this relationship is necessarily imbued with Eros—not necessarily with romantic love but with Eros in the larger sense of the word as used by Freud and Marcuse, not in the narrow sense closely linked to sexuality. The student-teacher relationship is also teleological, which means that it serves some purpose; it is not a relationship for the sake of relationship, not the "pure relationship" in the sense defined by Giddens.[5] This relation is temporally and spatially limited; it has a beginning and an end, a direction, and a purpose. This is the central tension of the student-teacher relationship—the tension between mutuality and instrumentality, between dialogue and authority, between Eros and Athena.

I will roughly cut all school relations into two groups—erotic and athenaic. Eros is the god of love, and Athena is the goddess of arts, crafts, war, and wisdom—her dexterity nicely matching the range of activities that make up an education institution. These two layers of relationships mix easily and, as I will argue later, necessarily. Moreover, no relation could be purely erotic or purely athenaic. However, I will ask the reader to accept that people can be drawn together in two different ways. One is out of affection ranging from sexual love to amity. These relations are motivated by the immediate pleasure humans draw from being with each other, from enjoying each other's bodies, souls, minds, and company. *Immediate* is a key word here, for Eros does not need a reason, for he operates out of deep-seated instincts of intermingled sexual desire and sociality.

Athena, however, appeals to humans because of their proclivity to making and knowing things. She is, in a sense, a goddess of vocation. Athenaic desire is love for arts and crafts; it is evident in pure pursuit of knowledge, sports, and other pleasures not directly embodied in another human being. Eros lets us enjoy other people; Athena lets us enjoy other things. In athenaic relations, individuals are bound together because they need one another for something else. One needs a partner to play chess or soccer or music, to exchange magic cards or to play videogames, to learn something from, or to have an audience. Again, in real-life human relations, these two reasons for connection tend to mingle, complement each other, and transform into one anther. What starts as help with homework can become romantic love, then perhaps a marriage; an athenaic relationship becomes an erotic one and then a hybrid one. Both relations can range from exploitative to mutual; both can be extremely oppressive and manipulative, as both can be rewarding and help human lives flourish. The distinction between erotic and athenaic relations is not along ethical lines. The success of relational pedagogy depends on how well the economy of relations can work, which, in turn, depends on how well the two types of relations can enter this economy.

Any human relation is always bipolar; it is always imbued with tension. Parties of a relation, by definition, can never be identical to each other; therefore they will never totally agree on what their relation is, what it means, and what it should be. All relations are contentious and ambivalent. Relations are interpretive fields that draw on history of personal and group interactions. Relation is a special form of history recording used to interpret the present and to construct the future. Of course, relation is a reflection of a constructed history, a history of which people made some sense. Nevertheless, the existence of a relation depends on a certain flow of events, on change. Relations make sense in the context of time; they are functions of time and change. A static relation is an oxymoron. If a relation between you and me today is the same as it was yesterday, this means that nothing happened between us yesterday, which, in turn, means that we had no relation. Relation is engagement; engagement implies events; events bring change. Therefore, relational dynamics is not something extrinsic to the nature of relations, they change not because "everything changes," but the change is constitutive of relations.

Like any other relation, the educational relation (and, specifically, the student-teacher one) cannot be understood and described in terms of what it ought to be. We cannot assume that a particular type of relation is always desirable. Instead, a theory of educational relation must describe a process of changing relation—where it begins, how it should change, and where it is going. The educational relation ought to be different at different points of the educational journey. What is good and appropriate at one point could be wrong and inappropriate at another. Both Higgins and Alston make the same mistake of treating the dynamics of educational relations as something spontaneous, to which a teacher must react. An ability to react is important, but it is more important to understand the laws that direct the intrinsic dynamics of educational relations. Each type of human relation has its vector; in order to understand the educational relation, we must define its vector.

Relational teaching and learning can be described as transformation of erotic relations into athenaic ones. A student-teacher relationship develops along the line that separates and connects Eros and Athena. Genetically, athenaic relations derive from erotic ones. The love of doing or knowing is a projection of human love onto non-human objects. In this sense, all love is social. Athenaic drive can be properly called the secondary eroticism. When one loves gardening, for instance, it really comes from loving the idea of a person who loves gardening. Perhaps the Freudian idea of sublimation has merit, and the restraint of civilization somehow transforms our erotic desire into creative impulses. However, I am looking here not at inexplicable bursts of creativity but rather at much more mundane facts of pleasure that people derive from doing something with non-human objects. This sort of love does not come from repressed libido; it comes from Eros spilling over onto the non-human world. This is how we learn to enjoy reading, writing, making violins, driving racecars, and taking care of the infirm; this is how we learn to love beauty, truth, and justice. Teaching has to include the education of desire; it has to be an introduction to a more varied and sophisticated desire. Good teaching is panerotic.

One cardinal flow of contemporary organized education is that schools rely heavily on athenaic relations and are trying hard to be utterly unerotic. As I am trying to argue throughout this book, academic learning makes a very weak foundation for athenaic relations because it is poorly motivated. Yet even if schools boasted a great variety of intrinsically motivating activities, they would not create a sustainable relational ecosystem without erotic relationships. The neglect of Eros is a serious flaw of educational theory and practice, although it is also an easily understandable cultural phenomenon.

The struggle against exploitative forms of sexuality has had some unintended consequences. An example of such a consequence is an overdeveloped taboo of erotic relationships in schools. Yet not all that is erotic is sexual; moreover, not all that is sexual is exploitative. It is one thing to forbid full-blown sexual relationships between teachers and students; it is quite another matter to pretend that no sexual desire could exist. I refer to the discussion between Higgins and Alston cited previously for various reasons why romantic love is not a good idea in a student-teacher relationship. My intention is simply to point out that there is something awfully repressive in reducing the riches of Eros to the excesses of Dionysus. If love in schools was a road, it would be as foolish for a teacher to go all the way as not to go at all.

Let me return to the interplay of erotic and athenaic relationships. Theoretically, there are two models of relational transformation, (1) erotic to athenaic (E-A) and (2) athenaic to erotic and then to a new athenaic (A_1-E-A_2). The first one describes a case of an attractive, sociable, and enthusiastic teacher whose love of knowledge seems to be contagious. Such a person can jumpstart the educational process using her personal appeal. Indeed, a few exceptional teachers can hold enormous influence over their students just by sheer force of their personality. It always amazes me how blind these successful teachers are to the secret of their own success. Many of them truly believe that it is their methods, techniques, and knowledge that create success, whereas in reality it is the individuals' attractive personalities that often do the trick. Students can only learn to love something from someone they love.

One would be irrational to count on such teachers to make a difference in schools. There is something sinister in all schemas that count on extraordinary personality, enthusiasm, and sacrifice. Even if teachers' salaries are raised significantly (which is very doubtful), one simply cannot count on recruitment of millions of extraordinary talented people to become classroom teachers. The schools should be able to make the economy of relations work in such a way that an average teacher can enjoy respect from students, feel good about herself, and be an effective instructor. Teachers should be able to succeed just as an average professional can be reasonably successful working for a corporation, a government agency, or managing a small business. Although the E-A model is real and can be effective, I doubt that it could work for most teachers. The fact that some teachers can pull it off does not mean that everyone can. A teacher must have too much erotic capital in the first place. This type of relational economy will not work because it is resource-poor.

Only few teachers possess sufficient erotic capital to sustain relational economy of teaching. Such teachers constitute an important exception that only reaffirms the rule. Most teachers cannot count on their charisma and personal appeal to provide reliable motivation for learning. This is true not only because the number of star teachers is limited. The position of a favorite teacher is a social role ascribed by students. No school could tolerate an all-star faculty; this is not how relational matrices work. In every school, there have to be a few favorites, a few teachers that no one likes, and some in the middle. Nevertheless, much of the teacher training is constructed around observing and replicating the best teaching practices. The assumption I find erroneous is that all can do what the best can. I will not deny that straight transformation of erotic relation into athenaic one is possible, but I will deny that such a transformation could be seriously counted on.

A much better model on which I am preparing to place my bet is the second one, where teachers build athenaic relation based on preexisting interest of students, then transforming that relation into the erotic one, and finally transforming it back into an athenaic relation but based on a new interest. Let me return to the example of the coach who is also a physics teacher. His relations with kids around the sport begin as athenaic—they would like to play sports, not necessarily to hang out with the teacher. However, a successful coach will also gain some erotic capital through the common experiences of the team. He will make sure to use athenaic relations for building a much more personal and less instrumental connection. And only after that will he carefully construct athenaic relations around physics lessons. I know this may not sound too realistic; after all, how many football players fall in love with physics. I was only trying to demonstrate a mechanism. If it does not work all the time, it is only because teachers lose sight of all the elements of the transformation.

One quote may help to explain the economy of a good school. A student from school number 825 in Moscow, where I conducted a few interviews several years ago, was asked: "What subjects do you dislike?"

"Chemistry," she answered rather quickly. "But you still do your chemistry homework, don't you? Why?" "Well, you see my chemistry teacher is such a great person; if I don't do my homework, she gets upset."[6] This demonstrates the economy of relations that exists in a good school. Parts of learning are inevitably boring; they are nothing like personal liberation, or search for knowledge for the sake of knowledge. However, the girl I spoke with exchanged her labor of learning for some other very tangible benefits that she received from school. She gets paid for her learning by the quality of relations she enjoys at school. We do the unpleasant things for our family and our friends without the expectation of a monetary repayment. We do it because we believe that this is the price we must pay for the continuation of our relations. This is precisely what happens in a good school. Students do boring, unpleasant, and as I have argued, not so useful things, because they like their teachers, each other, and their school. Teachers need to do the very best to be liked instead of repeating the empty incantations of "higher expectations."

The background of this particular school could explain the situation. Vladimir Karakovskii, the principal, has created a system where teachers and students have multiple opportunities for developing close personal relations with each other in the context of shared activities. Most upper class students, for instance, have a very intensive spring retreat with teachers. The school does not make a distinction between curricular and extracurricular activities; all are considered to be equally important. The chemistry teacher has acquired some erotic capital she did not naturally possess. She appears to be nice to the girl not only because of the sheer force of her charisma, but mainly because the girl had an ample opportunity to be with the teacher. They have a set of common memories and an emotional bond they both value. The relational equilibrium between the two is such that upsetting the teacher seems undesirable. The boring chemistry homework figures neatly into the equation as a small price for maintaining a great relationship.

The elemental cell of the relational economy is the mutual transformation of erotic and athenaic values. Unfortunately, just by looking at behavior alone one has no way of telling which transformation occurs. Let us consider a simple observable fact: a history teacher asks her student to open a book and read a paragraph, and he complies. We do not know what is going on at the relational level. This may be a remnant of official authority, which, as I have argued, is dying but is very far from being dead. This may be an instance when the teacher cashes in the personal erotic capital she has with the student, and he does it just out of respect and affection. Or, the student may already be thrilled with history, with this specific book, and it is the teacher who is doing him a favor within the athenaic relations. Most likely, we witness some complex combination of the above scenarios, and it may very well be the case that the student and the teacher interpret the exchange in diametrically opposing ways. Yet behind every little transaction, one can see the silent figures of Eros and Athena quietly exchanging the invisible goods of human relations.

Pure Eros is both unethical and ineffective as Higgins demonstrated. Pure Athena is unachievable as I have tried to show. A static mix of the two is too simplistic, because it does not explain the dynamics involved in educational relations. What we need instead is a creative transformation of one into another. Educational relations are metamorphic; they need to change as students grow with them.

NOTES

[1] Maurice S. Friedman. *Martin Buber: The Life of Dialogue* (Chicago and London: The University of Chicago Press, 1976), 57.

[2] One has to appreciate the fact that in dealing with their children, middle-class parents have many more bargaining chips than parents of poverty. Of course, if the human side of relations is destroyed, bribery does not work. However, bribery does help under many circumstances.

[3] Chris Higgins, "Transference Love from the Couch to the Classroom: A Psychoanalytic Perspective on the Ethics of Teacher-Student Romance, " *Philosophy of Education 1998* (http://w3.ed.uiuc.edu/EPS/PES-Yearbook/1998/higgins.html).

[4] Kal Alston, "So Give Me Love, Love, Love, Love, Crazy Love: Teachers, Sex, and Transference?," *Philosophy of Education 1998* (http://w3.ed.uiuc.edu/EPS/PES-Yearbook/1998/alston.html).

[5] Anthony Giddens, *The Transformation of Intimacy* (Stanford: Stanford University Press, 1992).

[6] Alexander Sidorkin, Razvitie *vospitatel'noi sistemy shkoly kak zakonomernyi protses. [Development of a School as a System: Driving Forces and Contradictions].* Candidate of Educational Sciences Dissertation (Moscow: Research Institute for Theory and History of Education, 1990).

CHAPTER 9.
RELATIONAL FIELDS

This chapter will take one step away from the abstract treatment of educational relations as those existing between two individuals. Relations are never isolated from other relations; there is always a relational continuum in which human beings live. In the end, every relation is a function of all other relations. I will try now to offer an analysis of the communal properties of relation. Relations connect individual people, but they also connect with other relations. Of course, no description is possible without simplification. For the purposes of this chapter, I will simplify the communal aspect of relationality so that the physical boundaries of a school will serve to limit the scope of my analysis. In reality, of course, the continuity of human relations does not stop at school walls.

Most teachers recognize the value of establishing personal relationships with students. Invariably, though, they bring up a question of how difficult it is to cultivate any sort of relationship with every student. This is a very serious question that has little to do with how effectively a teacher's work is organized. An answer would require something more than simply advising teachers to make an extra effort. The fundamental fact of schooling is that one adult teaches and supervises many students. The early school was nothing but a form of division of labor: while most adults worked, some were charged with minding the children and teaching them some skills. This essential configuration precedes humanity and is very common among social animals. This fundamental fact changed very little throughout human history. Teaching still involves facing a multitude of children, thus creating the problem of dividing one teacher's attention among many students.

I will draw here on a specific tradition of Russian educational theory, the theory of the collective. The notion of the collective has acquired somewhat derogatory meaning in the West, mainly because of its association with totalitarian Soviet Communism. The Cold War sealed the negative connotation of the word, and *Star Trek,* the movie, with its semirobotic faceless members of the Collective finished the job. However, the Russian theory and practice of the collective draws its roots clearly from American and European Progressivism and social psychology of the early twentieth century. This is not a good place to tell the full story of the educational collective. I only would like to point out that its basic theoretical premise made a lot of sense.

Early Soviet practitioners of collective education correctly reasoned that meaningful education requires personal relationships, but it is difficult for one teacher to influence many children at once. It is difficult not only because of the difference in numbers, but also because children, and especially adolescents tend to resist adult influences. However, children and adolescents are very likely to be influenced by peers. Therefore, educators must try to create a modified peer group called the collective. This peer group will generally support the educationally desirable influences and limit negative ones. In other words, the collective education is simply a way to use peer-group relations for educational purposes.

This line of reasoning is not entirely unknown in the West. Some recent examples could include various peer mediation and peer counseling programs, the Just Communities experiments by L. Kohlberg and his associates,[1] and the experiences of many volunteer youth organizations (see, for instance, McLaughlin et al., *Urban Sanctuaries*[2]). However, Western equivalents of collective education have never entered the mainstream educational practices with the exception of rudimentary student governments. Consequently, Western, especially English-speaking educational theorists never realized what kind of potential lies in the peer groups modified for educational purposes.

The Russian collective education from the very beginning had two schools of thought, one authoritarian and one democratic. Anton Makarenko, one of the founders of collective theory and practice, believed that collective development goes through two stages. During the first stage, creation of the collective itself is the aim of teachers' efforts. The second stage turns the collective into a tool for educational purposes oriented toward an individual student. The authoritarian school of thought emphasized the first stage and viewed the collective as an excellent instrument of behavioral control. Practical results of this theory were quite unsuccessful; to control students, Soviet schools always relied on formal adult authority rather than on the peer group. The democratic wing of the theory was looking for the forms of communal life that would facilitate individual development. The democratic collective theory also had only limited influence on the mass schooling (mostly because of ideological concerns of the authorities), but it produced a number of spectacularly successful examples of working democratic collectives. Sometimes no more than difference in emphasis, sometimes a bitter political issue, this basic division between two theories of the collective survived to this day in Russia.

The heyday of the collective education is associated with the so-called Communard movement, which I had an opportunity to describe in some detail elsewhere.[3] In my opinion, the story of the Communard movement is one of the most fascinating episodes in educational history of the twentieth century. Despite large numbers of publications in Russian, it still awaits its proper historical investigation in Russia; it is almost totally unknown in the West.

The movement's humble beginning coincided with the period of the political "Thaw" of the late 50s. By the end of the 80s it had influenced hundreds of thousands of children. A culturally idiosyncratic educational method, it cannot be directly replicated in any other country. However, it did show that the aims of collective education are indeed achievable on a large scale. Teachers can significantly modify peer groups so that the peer relationships are included in the sphere of education. In other words, to the question of how does a teacher create personal relationships with every student, the Russians had an answer—not the only answer, I hope, but an answer nevertheless. You do not have to have a close personal relationship with every student. Instead, together with the kids, create a specific type of community where an educationally appropriate style of relationship will automatically be recreated without your personal involvement in every little detail. In other words, you can teach kids to take care of each other so that the educational goals will also be served.

The educational collective is a human machine that reproduces educational relations. To some extent, it blurs the distinctions between teachers and students; some students begin to act as teachers toward other students, but teachers have to share some of their authority with students. The Communard educators found that the right relations are created from other relations. The raw material that goes into the new relation is other, previously existing relations. This makes sense: people know how to make friends and fall in love because they have observed other people make friends or fall in love. Now, kids who have never in their lives seen or experienced a democratic educational community, have never *known* how to have friendly relationships with adults, could never be able to create such bonds. They simply had no models.

The same was true for adults as well; the Communard type of relationship was impossible to explain. The Communards realized that the type of relationships they thought educationally valuable have to be demonstrated rather than explained or described. The Communard way had never become a program to be distributed through books or seminars. Ironically, it was a constant suspicion of disloyalty on the part of the Communist Party that prevented the movement from becoming yet another program. The lack of official recognition and support prompted the Communard educators to develop another way of dissemination. Instead of printing brochures, and developing guidelines, they would usually send whole teams of kids and teachers to a new place, where such a team lived out a certain type of relationship while trying to recruit other adults and students. The Communard spirit proved to be like a living organism that could reproduce relatively easily but is impossible to recreate artificially. Virtually every known Communard group needed "yeast" (a small group of experienced Communards) to rise. The only serious limitation of the Communard model was that it was difficult to implement within a regular school. Most (but not all) groups existed in the world of after-school youth centers and organizations. Democratic practices and creative spirit of the Communards clearly contradicted authoritarian and traditional Soviet schools. This problem also indicated that the theory of collective education is not sufficient to make a difference in mass schools.

Yet the collective education also produced many excellent democratic schools. Although only a few were designed along the Communard lines, their experiences revealed the same basic features of educational collectives. For example, each good school would have adult leaders who paid intense attention to relationships with students. Each good school featured one or the other form of altered peer culture. All schools have good teachers, but good schools have no bad teachers, mainly because teachers act as a group rather than individually.

Liudmila Novikova, who in the 70s became an unofficial dean of the democratic wing of the collective theory, by the mid-80s realized that the language of the traditional educational theory was no longer adequate to describe the new realities of Russian education. I do not think she ever stated explicitly her reasoning, but here is my interpretation based on many conversations with her. Novikova always made it a point to keep very close ties with several excellent schools throughout Russia, both to conduct research and to try out her ideas in schools. At some point, she and people around her realized that good schools had become too different from one another. As educational experiments diversified, it became more and more difficult to say that certain things work in all schools.[4] The traditional language of the collective education was very sophisticated and well suited to analyze peer relations and student-teacher relational dynamics.[5] However, it was structured so that a theorist could recommend specific behavioral strategies for teachers (which is how North American educational theory is unfortunately structured, too). As the real-life educational collectives were becoming more and more diverse, the theory of the collective ran into some problems. Frustrated by the lack of observable commonalities among the best schools and the difficulties the Communards faced while trying to work in schools, Novikova started to use the systems approach in an attempt to understand deeper structures of schools as social organisms. For that purpose, she created a special laboratory of the educational systems in the mid-80s within the Russian Educational Academy, where I had a chance to get the Russian part of my graduate training.

Novikova's group took schools to be holistic social systems, where all components are interrelated and equally important for education—formal curriculum and informal peer interaction, school walls and inside jokes, assemblies and rumors, little habits and serious traditions. They saw the school as something like a living organism, with its own culture and ecology, its own natural cycles of activity, its line of development from birth to death. Education was thought to be a function of the entire system, not only of conscious and organized efforts of teachers and administration. They realized that a school is not fully controllable, at least not with the means of direct management. The good schools did not become such strictly by design; there was always an element of the unexpected. The mechanisms of self-control and self-regulation were found to be much more effective than tools of administrative control.

Novikova's group quickly realized that emphasis on complexity (non-determinism) of school systems and interdependency of all components presents a specific theoretical problem. Any sort of description implies separation of important from unimportant, of figure from the background, of key features from secondary features. Yet the assumption of the system theory was the interdependency of all components, small and big. But how does one describe such a system, let alone give recommendations on how to create or improve one? It is one thing to give examples of seemingly unimportant details of school life that turn out to be educationally significant; it is very different to give a more or less comprehensive description of a school. With so many elements to consider, school systems could become indescribable, and therefore untheorizable. This theoretical problem is similar to one the Western educational theory is experiencing now—acknowledgment of contextuality of education made it very difficult to produce any prescriptive statements.

To address the problem, one could use the methods of qualitative research, and Novikova encouraged her doctoral students to use those extensively: "I don't really believe in numbers," she would often say, "you better be able to describe what's going on in that school." Yet even an ethnographic study would have to come up with some theoretical framework that could explain the system as a whole. And this is something very difficult to do, because the holistic assumptions also imply some sort of ineffability of the examined object. The systems approach forbids reducing the whole system to the sum of its components. However, no description is possible without breaking down the whole into some sort of components. Novikova's group set out to search for new units of analysis and for methodology that would avoid traditional analytical breakdown of the whole into parts. The search is still going on with various degrees of success.[6] What follows is not so much a rendition of Novikova's group findings as an examination of some possible implications of the group's research.

One fundamental implication of Novikova's work was finding that good schools have to maintain certain levels of complexity. The good schools cannot be monolithic and homogeneous. Rather, they are conglomerates of heterogeneous groups, including peer groups, teacher friendships, clubs, sport teams, etc. Significantly, all these groups have overlapping memberships and means of communication with each other. Karakovskii, Novikova, and Selivanova describe this as a "web of memberships and relations enveloping a student."[7] The multiplicity of school activities seems to ensure that no rigid hierarchies of successful versus unsuccessful groups will emerge. In Russia, it was always assumed that schools cannot and should not limit themselves to strictly academic learning. Novikova's associates found empirical evidence suggesting that, outside of the selective elitist schools, only schools with a sufficient variety of activities can be successful both socially and academically.

Another implication is that school as a system cannot be meaningfully presented in one coherent description; instead, it should be presented at least as two different, complementary descriptions (school as an organization and school as a community). This distinction is similar to the German notions of *Gesellschaft* and *Gemeinschaft*.[8] The important point here is epistemological—a system as a whole cannot be adequately described only once. Three-dimensional computer imaging could serve as an imperfect analogy. In order to get a 3-D image, one needs to take numerous 2-D pictures of an object. Just one very good image, even an X-ray does not create the sense of reality of the 3-D object. With complex social systems, the same principle applies. One description of the system, no matter how detailed or how sophisticated, does not do justice to the complexity. Two or more different descriptions, however, can do just that.

Any school can be described as having "core activity" and "relationships." The notion of core activity (*Vedushchaia, kliuchevaia* or *sistemoobrazuiushchaia deiatelnost*) has a long history in the Russian theory of the educational collective. The core activity makes creation of the school community possible, because in some way it requires collaboration, differentiation of roles, and motivation. Here is how Alexander Pashkov explains the role of core activity in education: "Cultivating humanity in various kinds of activity helps the transition from objective, super-personal knowledge to subjective, personalized, phenomenological knowledge of experience. This involves understanding activity as a special mechanism that transforms outside influences into internal developmental changes."[9] One can clearly see the connection to the Vygotsky and Leontiev traditions of Russian psychological theory of activity. Learning is understood as a function of social activity and not as just any kind of cognition. Simplifying to the limit, this is the position "learning is doing," where "doing" is understood as a collective action.

Novikova's group took the activity theory beyond the problematic of learning into the theory of educational systems, which could be viewed as applying Vygotsky's idea of the zone of proximal development to large social systems. They consider the core activity the main systemic factor.[10] This simply means that a school must be held together by some sort of shared activity. A good school, in their view, has both a variety of activities and one common core activity.

Now, the other side of the school system is usually described in Russian as simply "relations" (*otnosheniya*). To distinguish this from the individual relations considered in the previous chapter, I will introduce a notion of a *relational field*. Let me return to the claim at the beginning of this chapter that each relation is a function of other relations. A newlywed friend told me once: "When you marry a divorced man, you also marry his ex-wife." This is a rather dramatic description of a universal phenomenon of intersecting relations. Every person who enters a relation brings along all other relations, past and present. In Chapter 7, I advanced the understanding of the self as a congelation of human relations. The self is a point where multiple relations intersect and influence each other. The self in this sense is a relation among other relations; the self is a meta-relation. Therefore, human relations do not exist as isolated phenomena. Rather, one can think about the existence of the *philosphere*,[11] a global network of human relations. Ultimately, everyone is connected to everyone else. However, one would succumb to mysticism to take such a universal connection too seriously. The philosphere varies a great deal in intensity of relations. Even in the age of the global mass media, the closer interpersonal relations remain much more connected to each other than distant ones. Each individual community, family, each circle of friends, neighborhood, or a workplace produces its own distinctive relational field, a sphere of influence that greatly affects all individual relations formed within such a field.

Organization theory, social psychology, sociology, and cultural anthropology each in their own way addressed this phenomenon under different names. The notion of culture is most commonly used to describe behavior patterns, practices, beliefs, institutions, etc. Like any overused words, "culture" could mean almost anything. All that characterizes human societies can be included in the concept of culture. My focus is much narrower; I want to capture the prevalent patterns of relations within a certain group of people. This is where the metaphor of the field is helpful. In physics, a field is an area that exerts a certain force on objects that enter it. Without unduly stretching the metaphor, let us accept that social groups can produce more or less strong relational fields that color all individual relations that are formed by the members of such groups with each other. From the educational point of view, such fields can also be positively or negatively charged; that is, the fields can be beneficial or detrimental to human flourishing. Ms. Smith's classroom, Mr. John's gym, and Parkview Elementary can generate more or less potent relational fields that put all individual relations in a certain order. Similarly, a magnetic field lines up metal particles in a certain pattern. Each relational field consists of smaller relations between individuals, yet their totality is greater than the sum. When relations form patterns, aided by organizational structures, cultural influences, and the procession of events, they merge into organized fields.

The way relational fields operate does not necessarily bring harmony or tolerance. In Chapter 5, I demonstrated how an unfortunate relational field could create bullies and victims. Similar mechanisms work for teachers, too. For example, every school has a popular teacher, a hated teacher, and a teacher of whom students will take advantage. Who ends up in which position does not depend exclusively on the personalities of the teachers but also on which roles are available. In general, if A likes B, it is only because there is a C that A does not like. Human attachments are products of choice and of giving preference to someone over the other. Relations cannot be totally homogeneous, and every social group will produce a certain range of available relations. The relational fields can be understood as a matrix that determines all available repertoires of relations allowable in a given group. Of course, the intrigue and drama of social life begin where people attempt to change the matrices, but one would be well advised to realize that such a matrix exists before attempting to change it.

I will now return to my earlier claim that the relational field directly depends on the type of the core activity. In other words, a volunteer fire department and a criminal gang will produce two different types of relationship not only because they are populated by different people but because the nature of common activity implies different relationship. Schools differ not because they implement dissimilar policies or have dissimilar social makeup; they differ because they have dissimilar core activities *and/or* dissimilar relationships.

In my earlier research, I hypothesized that schools are self-regulating systems; the type of relational field will generally follow the type of core activity. This does not mean though that there is an automatic link between the two. A school succeeds as an educational community if it has an important common project (the core activity) but also if it is able to realize an adequate form of relational field. Any misbalance between the two will create tension and conflict. The internal driving force of the school histories is the tension between the core activity and the relational field. The latter tends to mutate much more rapidly than the former, and school's communal mentality outgrows the activity-based foundation of the community.

Now, this or any other description of relational fields and their intricate connections with the core activity has nothing specifically educational in it. In fact, this is an example of the general sociological theorizing that is often applied to educational institutions without considering their specificity. What are the specifics of the educational relation when such relation is considered in its communal aspect (as a relational field)? In other words, how can the pedagogy of relation be realized *in schools*? Now I believe that unlike any other organization, schools have it backwards: their relations should come first and the activity second. In the next chapter, I will explain the logic of such reversal.

As I was trying to show in Part I of this book, certain doom hangs over the whole project of education, especially that organized into schooling. If you accept my argument, schools are theaters of absurd, where children and adults are thrown together against their will, without a reason for being together, compelled to engage in an activity that lacks purpose and motivation. Even worse, this activity makes a very poor social glue, because it does not invite collaboration. Worse yet, schools are quickly losing the means of traditional control (based on exclusion and violence) they had in the past. After saying all this, I invite my readers to believe that schools will be saved by pedagogy of relations, a mechanism of transforming the erotic relations into athenaic ones. The schools have to learn how to establish effective and humane fields of relations that will provide for the education of all children. For a measure of credibility, I will have to show how one can turn absurdity into Eros.

Relational fields of schools must solve the essential problem of education—how to establish relations around the non-relational. Schools are communities that do not matter to the outside world, and yet they have to live as if they do. Schools are places where kids are stored so they don't break anything, and no matter how well adults hide this fact, it cannot be hidden. Consequently, good schooling is manufacturing of relevancy. The schools are communities that should live and thrive despite their *raison d'être*. An existentialist will object by saying that *all* human relations are about confronting the absurdness of existence and about creating some meaning out of the meaningless. This is true, and I do not want to overemphasize the uniqueness of the educational world in comparison to the rest of society. However, every type of social group faces this general task in its own special way.

A good school's relational field is created by a cathartic revelation of absurdity. A good school is a community of laughter and defiance, one that does not take itself and the whole project of schooling too seriously. It is a group of people that simply uses education as a pretext to get together like a company of friends going fishing or playing cards. They play the game of schooling while fully realizing that this is only a game. Such communities move the essential absurdity of learning outside of parenthesis by calling it what it is. A good school is always a victory of collective human spirit over dehumanizing conditions imposed by organized education. The relational field of a good school lays out the grid of relations so that most important ones have little to do with learning, teaching, and official authority. One's position in a good school usually has little to do with one's academic achievement, one's instructional aptitude, muscle power, or outside connections. A good school is not a community of learners; rather, it is a group of people who, despite being called a "school," made a decision to develop their own sense of identity and invent a purpose for being together.

NOTES

[1] Clark Power, Ann Higgins, and Lawrence Kohlberg, *Lawrence Kohlberg's Approach to Moral Education* (New York: Columbia University Press, 1989).

[2] Milbrey McLaughlin, Merita Irby, and Juliet Langman. *Urban Sanctuaries: Neighborhood Organizations in the Lives and Futures of Inner-City Youth* (San Francisco: Jossey-Bass, 1994).

[3] Alexander Sidorkin, "The Communard Movement in Russia," *East-West Education* 16, Fall 1995, Number 2: 148–59.

[4] Interestingly, a similar discovery was made in the United States about the same time, which resulted in the movement of school-based educational reform and, perhaps, the site-based management models.

[5] Liudmila Novikova, Pedagogika Detskogo Kollektiva. Voprosy Teorii. [The Pedagogy of the Children's Collective: Theoretical Issues] (Moscow: Znanie 1978).

[6] See, for instance, Vladimir Karakovskii, Liudmila Novikova, and Natalia Selivanova, *Vospitanie? Vospitanie... Vospitanie! Teoriia i praktika vospitatel'nykh sistem. [Character Education: Theory and Practice of Educational Systems]* (Moscow: Novaia Shkola, 1996).

[7] Karakovskii, Novikova, and Selivanova. *Vospitanie?*

[8] Sidorkin, *Razvitie vospitatel'noi sistemy shkoly.*

[9] Karakovskii, Novikova, and Selivanova. *Vospitanie?*, 115.

[10] Karakovskii, Novikova, and Selivanova. *Vospitanie?*, 25.

[11] I borrow the word from the *Philosphere Publishers*, www.philosphere.com, although my use of it much more prosaic: "philos" simply means love and affection.

CHAPTER 10.
DESCHOOLING SCHOOLS

In most of the other social institutions, people are brought together by common interests such as economical, political, cultural, or combination thereof. Their relations are built a on more or less tangible foundation of what they do together. The normal logic of human connection is this—shared activity, then personal relations. In schools, this logic is reversed: relations come first, then the common activity. Only a very limited range of social phenomena is based on pure human relations, not mediated by material interest—friendship is one example, love the other. Yet notice that no one ever attempts to create large social entities the size of army regiments based on friendship or love. Well, schools are such impossible utopian enterprises. Hundreds of people are brought together without any common interest or an identifiable project and are expected to maintain social harmony and peace. Sometimes the utopia works; in many cases it works in a limited way, within a single classroom. In most of the cases it does not, because it cannot. We all will be better off understanding the intrinsic limitations of the great utopian project called "school."

Utopias are fragile because they lack a solid mundane foundation of material interest. For this reason, they tend to shift either toward cruelty or toward great human communities. There are not that many schools in between. Even perfectly dull and uneventful suburban schools at close scrutiny harbor one or another form of concealed cruelty, but they can also present an unassuming beauty of a truly caring community. The cruelty sometimes erupts into awful acts of school violence. The great but not flashy schools rarely draw any attention. One problem is that it is hard to discern a difference between the two. In any school, students lack (and will always lack) intrinsic motivation for learning. This is the basic condition of schooling. There are only two ways for teachers and school administration to get over that obstacle. The first way is to force students to learn, using a host of direct and indirect forms of violence educators invented over the centuries. The second way is to build a community where kids will love their teachers, and then these kids will agree to do the school stuff, too.

My worry is that contemporary educational policies nudge schools toward the first way. This may be driven by the needs of maintaining the nation's economic and technical capabilities. My concern is that in pursuit of keeping a competitive edge, too many schools will become factories of cruelty. I am not sure at all if this may weaken the American democracy or economy; it may very well be the case that education does not affect democracy or the economy at all. Yet this country should learn to look at its schools as not only means of social and economic progress but as places where millions of its citizens spend much of their lives. Education is mainly an issue of students' quality of life.

The American practical mind does wonders for the economy and a comparatively decent job in solving many social problems. However, it has demonstrated very little creativity solving educational problems. The no-nonsense educational policies aimed at testing, basic skills, more hours, fewer students per class, etc., may bring unexpected results. The educational policies I am talking about are based on the assumption that there is nothing unusual about schools. Approaches that worked in economy, in welfare reform, in environmental and health regulations should work in education a common assumption holds. This assumption is wrong. School is a very different animal altogether.

For the economy of relations to work, specific changes must be made to school organization. One common assumption that I want to question is that the learning has to be at the center of an institution like school. The division of labor in the instance of education has gone too far. Schools have become institutions too specialized to remain viable. Schools are for learning—what could be more obvious? However, this may not be such a self-evident truth. We need to stop thinking of schools as exclusively educational institutions and instead make them centered on a much more complex idea of a good life. The capitalist economy is not the whole social life; learning activity is not the whole of the school life.

In order to outline the reform implications of the pedagogy of relation, I will briefly discuss the types of educational reform. There are two main concepts of school reforming: policy driven and movement driven. The former implies that certain policies will produce certain effects. If a policy had a certain effect in one instance, it will produce a similar effect in all other instances. Reforms fail either because of the faulty policy or faulty implementation; the individual differences among schools are "noise." The movement-driven concept of reforming has similar assumptions: schools are simple, deterministic, and homogeneous systems. One school's success could be translated into few key components, which then could be transplanted into another school. The only difference between the two concepts is that the movement-driven one believes that individual schools select for themselves which model to assume and whose success to follow.

I would argue that it does not matter whether schools are given an exact directive from above or teachers truly believe they can emulate someone else's success. For most reformers, most of the deep relational structure of a school remains invisible. For example, schools can be on different periods of their development and have different core activities and relational fields. To understand a school, one needs to attend to its relational field, which is unique for each school.

The matter is complicated by the fact that many successful educators often do not realize the reason for their own success. Some of the great school principals, who were able to create wonderful, vibrant school communities, sometimes have extremely eccentric ideas about why they were able to succeed. As successful principals, they enjoy tremendous respect and acquire followers. Unfortunately, great principals are not necessarily good theoreticians (and vice versa, of course). In fact, it is very difficult to be enmeshed into complexities of everyday reality of one school's life and be able to produce meaningful generalizations. We all tend to pay much attention to what we do and very little or none to in what sort of relational context we do those things.

In short, the trouble with educational reforming is not with where the models come from, it is with how those models are produced. The movement-driven reform (or a school-based reform) is just as unlikely to bring satisfactory results as the top-down reforms. Both types of reform make mechanistic assumptions about schools. Educational reform, from my point of view, should be based on assumptions of the systems approach: every school is a complex non-deterministic system, the key dimensions of which are the core activity and relational field. To change a school means to change its core activity and relational field. One cannot arbitrarily change the relational field without changing the core activity. However, introduction of a new activity does not necessarily bring about a change in relational field. One cannot count on changing the relational field (and therefore the culture) of a school if the foundation of an activity is missing or does not fit. At the same time, just changing the core activity is not sufficient; the new and adequate relational field is also needed.

The appearance of schools and the routines of school life give an observer an inaccurate impression that all schools are the same. Indeed, in many ways schools all resemble each other. Despite all the differences in size, socioeconomic and racial composition, location, etc., schools are remarkably similar. The system approach I advocate here is not so much about emphasizing the uniqueness of each individual school. Rather, I want to concentrate on the fact that schools, like other organizations, have deeper structures that cannot be arbitrarily changed. Most importantly, the line that separates a great school from a bad one does not lie in what the two respective schools (or their teachers) *do*. The educational reform has been sidetracked by paying excessive attention to what successful teachers and schools exactly *do* rather than what sort of relations they construct.

Of course, the systems approach brings its own set of problems. For the sake of the argument, I will accept a common assumption that a school is a system where education is the central organizing process. This means simply that what we call a "school" is a certain group of people, buildings, and other things when they are brought together for the purposes of educating students. Of course, they enter into a number of other relationships that have nothing or little to do with education, but educational relations proper take precedence over all others. In other words, teaching and learning normally take a privileged position in schools.

This initial assumption does seem self-evident and circularly defined. Yet the next logical step that directly follows this assumption is something I find troubling and am willing to dispute: The more organized the school is as an educational system, the more educationally effective it is. Why I dispute this will become apparent later, but for now I need to state another assumption. Following the critical theorists whose argument stems from the Marxist analytical tradition, education may not be understood as limited to transmission of value-neutral knowledge and skills to students. There is no value-neutral knowledge; therefore education will inevitably involve the core of human personality—the beliefs, agency, and the ability to choose. If one was to understand education as simply training, my argument will make very little sense.

The language of efficiency, effective schools, and effective education is the foundation of many current trends in educational policy making. As John Goodlad comments: "Much of so-called effective schools movement that grew out of some solid research on factors characteristic of good schools foundered on efforts to reduce complexity to a few simple concepts."[1] A school that wants to get recognition is pressured to come up with a simple explanation of its success. Yet most successful schools are very complex and not fully explicable.

The notion of school accountability, a rhetorical pet of the 2000 presidential campaign, is based on some idea of effective schooling. To hold schools accountable, one must not only believe that schools control the outcomes of education but also that effective schools are good for student's education. Let us imagine that schooling would have been found to be a necessary but also dangerous and unreliable technology, say, like nuclear power plants. In such a case politicians would not be able to speak only about efficiency but also about containing the negative aspects of the technology such as waste disposal and risk of accidents. Nothing like this shows up on the radar of educational politics; the speeches about education improvement are strikingly uncontroversial. I never, for instance, heard any politician mention the educational risks of standardized testing (some mention the monetary cost). Schools are simply assumed to be unequivocally good, free of side effects, fully controllable, and therefore the public is free to pursue the goal of effective schools without limitations. But what is an effective school? Can there be different interpretations of effectiveness? And, most importantly, are there limits of school effectiveness?

If we understand schools as social systems clearly organized around their educational purposes, then their unchecked effectiveness is detrimental both to democracy and to personal development. On one hand, extraordinary successful schools will inevitably reduce pluralism by imposing a particular set of values on all students. On the other hand, effective school education will limit the freedom of choice. Paradoxically, schools cannot be organized as purely educational institutions. Consistently effective education cannot be the main principle of school organization. To the contrary, schools must be systems that prevent education from being overly successful.

Paradoxically, good schools cannot be very effective. Education itself is a paradoxical process as I have shown previously. Its purposes are contradictory. Education must normalize, make everyone somewhat the same, and provide the same knowledge and train the same skills. The idea of public education is in many ways a reflection of this normalizing side of education. At the same time, education has a differentiating side. It has to make everyone different, free, and able to make independent choices. When such a contradictory process as education is used as a cornerstone for building a social system such as school, one discovers quickly that it is not easy to do. How do you "align" a system in relation to a contradictory set of goals? Most often schools simply ignore the second set of goals and pretend that education is all about normalizing. This happens not because educators do not value individual free agency, but because they are faced with a much more immediate task of building an organization called "school." And the organization must be coordinated, run smoothly, have a clear set of priorities, be controllable, and effective.

Luckily, schools comprise a multitude of conflicting interests of teachers, administrators, different groups of students, parents, political and ideological parties, etc. Not many schools are very effective organizations, but such "imperfection" exists entirely by accident and for the wrong reasons. No one *consciously* tries to prevent schools from becoming effective. Moreover, I worry about a relatively recent school-reforming trend that is called different names in different states and has no clear identity beyond being clearly influenced by business quality management techniques. Sometimes this trend is openly aligned with the Total Quality management movement; sometimes it is called something else like continuous improvement planning. Its essence is to let schools and school districts develop their own ideas and procedures of self-reforming under strictly defined guidelines. This is not a classical top-down reform but a reform developed at the local level. Here is the catch: the *process* of developing every school's ideas is strictly prescribed and monitored. This reforming trend should be properly analyzed in another work. I only want to suggest that it may prove to be effective, at last, and thus very dangerous. The industrialized nations have grown so used to very ineffective attempts of educational reforming that they may miss a moment when one particular reform will be successful and will wipe out any complexity from schools.

My critique of pure education in Part I shows that learning and teaching do not make a strong organizational foundation for schooling. Adults find it is perfectly acceptable to go to highly specialized economic institutions in the morning and then enjoy their civic and personal lives later in the day. For kids, who are not paid for their work, such separation is utterly unfeasible. The labor of conveyer-belt assembly is an example of how dehumanizing the division of labor can be. Schooling is another example of this phenomenon of alienated labor although the cause of alienation is different. I admit that the logic of social development demands massive segregation of unskilled workers who are charged with the task of producing mountains of useless things. What I have a hard time understanding is that such factories of the absurd will disallow any other activities that could make the sentence more bearable and sensible. School reforming around efficiency and accountability is the capitalist efficiency going berserk. Schools' strong orientation to learning has to be diluted by a multitude of other things to do and by relations outside of learning.

From the point of view of school as an organization, learning is impossible to sustain as an all-encompassing activity around which everything is centered. Yet what I find the most worrisome is the steady decline of extracurricular activities and other "peripherals" of school life like rituals and celebrations, the extermination of places and periods of times. Most kids get up in the morning and go to school so they can be around their friends and a few good adults. The community and fellowship are by far the strongest attractor and the hardest currency schools can offer in exchange for their incessant demands. Yet schools become obsessed with increasing "on-task" time and getting rid of everything non-educational. Even after school programs, such as those created by the massive federal Learning Centers Initiative, are tied to boosting kids' academic achievement.

Interestingly, among the large number of best Russian schools studied by Novokiva's group, only very few had learning at the center of their communal life.[2] Now, all the schools had excellent academic achievement levels, sometimes despite unfavorable socioeconomic odds. However, the overwhelming majority of good schools did not place academic learning into the center of their lives. This can be explained by the specifics of academic learning as an activity that does not invite much cooperation, especially on the scale of the whole school. My own research suggests that good schools as social systems are not really aligned around the educational purposes as educational rhetoric often suggests.[3] Moreover, my intuition tells me that the worst of schools are rigidly geared up toward educational goals, while the best of schools keep many other things in mind. For a great school, the education of students comes as almost a by-product of some other interesting and engaging activity. I argue for less education in schools.

One can question the assumption that schools and other educational institutions should exist exclusively for pursuing educational goals. Life in schools may or may not be wholly oriented toward education of children. I suggest that viewing schools only as educational institutions is very limiting and dangerous, because such a view allows for inherent flaws of educational relations that take central place in school life. In reality, every organization serves a multitude of purposes. For instance, every corporate office is also a social club, an educational enterprise, and an entertainment establishment. We understand, however, that the central function of the office clearly dominates all the others. People come there to work, before everything else. Of course, schools are also such multipurpose places. The difference is that a corporation can afford to allow its productive side to dominate all other sides; schools cannot. Any school functions as a school, with its policies, schedules, rules, and roles. At the same time, a subtle network of interpersonal relations flourishes, constituting very elusive but real phenomena.

The educational function of school does not have to be the central one. Moreover, in light of certain inherent limitations of education that I outlined above, this purpose cannot serve the function of a "social glue" that is capable of holding a school together. Why not think of schools as places that are aligned toward the ideal of a good life rather than the educational ideal? I want to take Goodlad's metaphor of a village further than he would perhaps have liked to take it: as a village, a school is centered around the goals of common well-being and not around any specific goals like education.

One thing I believe should happen is a slow emergence of a hybrid social institution, something between a regular school and a voluntary youth association based on shared interests of its members, commitment, and voluntary acceptance of authority. The youth and adult voluntary associations have been in existence for a very long time and comprise the loose network that makes the civic society function.[4] *Urban Sanctuaries* by McLaughlin, Irby, and Langman[5] gives an excellent description of voluntary associations for inner-city youth that work. The trick is to invent a hybrid institution that could be both a voluntary, interest-based organization, and a school that teaches in the traditional sense of this word. Overly simplified, the school and the "boys and girls" club should become one organization run by the same people and sharing the same relational field. This will solve the crisis of authority, because no adult leader of a volunteer youth organization has any trouble exercising his or her authority. Kids want to be there and therefore agree to follow rules. Importantly, the kids want to be there not because they like every activity or every rule. They often want to belong to a community and/or enjoy whatever the main activity of such a community happens to be.

Such a hybrid school provides a multitude of benefits for young people—a place to hang out, to make friends, to create and to think but also, among other things, a place to learn. Learning is something one has to do to be able to attend—it is work, a form of compensation students have to provide to the organization. Yet both adults and young leaders of such a school realize that they need some other powerful reasons for students to be there. Such a school will be less educational in the sense I outlined previously but a good place to be. Of course, some things need to be changed to create such schools. The schools need to be small, personal, allow for student choice and teachers' experimenting with a multitude of non-educational activities. These may very well be more expensive schools, but the corporate world that benefits the most must pay at least something.

An interesting implication of the relational pedagogy is that one cannot simply create effective educational relations out of thin air. The direct interpersonal relations are just too unpredictable and accidental to serve as a foundation for the relational schools. The hybrid schools must create a variety of situations where relations could be formed and developed. For example, one can imagine much longer lunch breaks and recesses with built-in opportunities for teachers and students to interact informally. Teachers need to think of a wide variety of opportunities that students want in addition (not instead of, like Progressives thought) to traditional academic subjects. The schools must become less specialized in regard to teaching and more concerned about the quality of their communal life.

NOTES

[1] John Goodlad, *Educational Renewal: Better Teachers, Better Schools* (San Francisco: Jossey-Bass, 1994), 204.

[2] See, for example, Liudmila Baliasnaya, Editor, *Vospitatel'nye sistemy sovremennoy shkoly: Opyt, poiski, perspektivy [Educational Systems in Contemporary Schooling: Experiences, Explorations, Perspectives]* (Moscow: Russian Educational Academy, Institute for Educational Theory and Pedagogy, 1995).

[3] Alexander Sidorkin, Razvitie *vospitatel'noi sistemy shkoly kak zakonomernyi protses. [Development of a School as a System: Driving Forces and Contradictions].* Candidate of Educational Sciences Dissertation (Moscow: Research Institute for Theory and History of Education, 1990).

[4] For a detailed analysis of connection between voluntary associations and democracy, see Robert D. Putnam, *Making Democracy Work* (Princeton, NJ: Princeton University Press, 1993).

[5] W. McLaughlin, M.A. Irby, J. Langman, *Urban Sanctuaries: Neighborhood Organizations in the Lives and Futures of Inner-City Youth* (San Francisco: Jossey-Bass, 1994).

Part III. Polyphony

CHAPTER 11.
THE PROBLEM OF EDUCATIONAL AUTHORITY

In this part of the book, I will attend to a number of difficulties the pedagogy of relation faces. This exercise will allow a closer analysis of relations in education. My basic claim is that the type of relation most beneficial in educational encounters is dialogue. The first problem is how to reconcile dialogical relation with power asymmetry.

In educational theory, the problem of relation has been confusingly entwined with the problem of power. Educational relation is fundamentally different from a number of other social relations where power imbalance is concerned. Emancipatory movements of the twentieth century demanded more equality in the distribution of power among classes, races, genders, and sexual orientation groups. Certainly justified in the larger social contexts, the equality of power distribution simply does not apply to education. Teaching and learning directly imply certain power asymmetry, so empowerment of students is an appealing but not sustainable ideal.

Elizabeth Ellsworth's influential paper may serve as a demonstration of this point.[1] Even "emancipatory" authority is still imbued with power asymmetry, but how does one remain a teacher without some sort of authority? Burbules and Rice[2], then Clive Beck,[3] then Clifton Tanabe,[4] and a number of others tried to reconcile the power imbalance with educational relation. Indeed, the contradiction between power and relation is essential for understanding education, and I find the debate very interesting. However, I am afraid it will not be very productive because we do not have an adequate apparatus for describing relations in education.

By concentrating on power relations, we make a theoretical leap and oversimplify the picture. One simply cannot assume certain generic social relations among people and analyze the role of power in them. Educational relation needs to be understood in its specificity. This book is an attempt to do so, but clearly, more work needs to be done to address educational relation.

Margonis realized that the problem of power imbalance in educational relation is hardly solvable without first examining the concept of relation. His call for a relational ontology assumes that power is an aspect of human relation and, as such, cannot be understood without assigning a privileged ontological status to relations.[5] In other words, he is saying that we do not know much about relations and do not take them seriously enough.

The debate on compatibility of teaching with power is not a surprise though. Theory develops in somewhat parallel ways with educational practice. The continuous debate about the imbalanced power relations indicates the anxiety of American educators about the loss of control over students. Sensitive teachers who cannot get their students to be quiet project their own sense of powerlessness onto students. The real-life relational vacuum promotes the issue of power on top of the theoretical agenda. The main problem of student-teacher relationships is not so much that they are tainted by power imbalance; the problem is that such a relationship often does not exist.

However, the problem of power asymmetry does exist. Buber identified the central problem the ontology of relation poses for education, which I will call the paradox of an imbalanced relation. Buber indicated that mutuality is necessary for educational relation. However, he also argued that true dialogue is impossible between a student and a teacher or between a patient and a therapist, because of the imbalance of authority in the situation of their encounter. To set a stage for the discussion I use the transcript of the 1957 dialogue between Carl Rogers and Martin Buber.[6] Rogers suggests that therapist-patient relations can be an *I-Thou* relation as described by Buber. Throughout their exchange, Rogers insists that a patient-therapist relation may become truly equal and that not only the patient but also the therapist can become open to profound personal change.

> ...it seems to me that when another person is really expressing himself and his experience and so on, I don't feel, in the way that you described, different from him. That is—I don't know quite how to put this—but I feel as though in that moment his way of looking at his experience, distorted though it may be, is something I can look upon as having equal authority, equal validity with the way I see life and experience. It seems to me that reality is the basis of helping, in a sense.... And I do feel there's a real sense of equality between us.[7]

Buber considers this impossible because the very objective situation of a helper and one being helped excludes the possibility of genuine *I-Thou* relations. He states his case rather forcefully:

> You have necessarily another attitude to the situation than he has. You are able to do something he is not able. You are not equals and cannot be. You have the great task, self-imposed—a great self-imposed task to supplement this need of his and to do rather more than in the normal situation. But, of course, there are limits, [...] the limits to simple humanity. To simple humanity meaning being I and my partner, so to speak *alike* to one another, on the same plane. I see you *mean* being on the same plane, but you cannot. There is not only you, your mode of thinking, your mode of doing, there is also a certain situation—we are so and so—which may sometimes be tragic [...]. You *cannot* change this.[8]

Buber had a keen sense of reality. However, this sense has little to do with positivistic interpretations of reality. Rather, he saw the context of human relations as ontologically fundamental. Thus, his talk about the *situation* is yet another reference to the underlying relational reality. Relations are not endlessly pliable and have a certain objective structure. They are neither objective, nor are they of the world of subjectivity.

All that Buber says about the therapeutic situation applies to the situation of educational encounter. The tragic side of such a situation is that, regardless of teachers' intentions, the relationship cannot become equal and truly dialogical. I believe we do injustice to the concept of education when we do not appreciate its tragic overtones. The inequality is built into the educational situation. Of course every teacher can develop a fully dialogical relationship with a student but only at a price of ceasing to be a teacher.

For Buber spontaneity is an important characteristic of dialogue: "...for what I call dialogue, there is essentially necessary the moment of surprise."[9] One cannot have a plan of dialogue; neither can one set a purpose for dialogue. In contrast to this, teaching by any definition remains a purposeful and planned activity. As teachers, we *must* keep in mind the educational implications of one or another activity, of any relationship we have with students. Of course, teaching may be full of surprises and improvisations, but it does not cease to be a purposeful activity. Teachers always have a hidden agenda, a second-plane educational thought, while in contact with students. This is another side of the same limitation of teaching. As teachers, we cannot enter a true dialogical relation with students and remain teachers.

Buber was not a philosopher who valued literal consistency among all his writings. In his conversation with Rogers, he says: "You see, I am not a quoted man who thinks so and so and so."[10] His position on a possibility of dialogue in education may have been complex and changing, depending on the context of a conversation. On another occasion, he proclaims "The relation in education is one of pure dialogue."[11] In other words, he does not think that asymmetrical situations preclude mutuality. Teachers and students can relate to each other in a direct and mutual way. Yet mutuality does not overcome the asymmetry of relation; it does not solve the power imbalance problem.

I have to clarify the notions of authority and power that I use in two distinctly different contexts and with different meanings although they are synonymous in the general use. In Chapter 4, I argued that teachers lack authority in schools, which necessitates developing the pedagogy of relation. Now my claim is that there is always an imbalance of power in student-teacher relations, which means that teachers have more power. By "authority" I mean the ability to control student behavior, while the word "power" is reserved to express a more general ability to exercise influence over another person. Yet despite this terminological trickery, there is a real contradiction here. Teachers have very little power over the students *until* they create a strong personal bond with the latter. Once in the relationship, teachers tend to face the opposite problem of too much power. I suspect that everyone who has been a successful teacher at one point or another realizes with horror that students begin to believe what she or he says. Being in a position of authority of knowledge and moral authority is both coveted by teachers and makes them uncomfortable once achieved.

The postmodern philosophers made the challenge of imbalanced relation one of the central themes in philosophy. Outside education, many more if not all forms of human relation were found to be imbued with authority imbalances, even those considered to be egalitarian and based on neutral assumptions. Foucault is, of course, a prime example of this line of reasoning, but so are Lyotard and Derrida. Buber's dream of dialogue suddenly appeared to become less and less realistic. The postmodernists discovered so many contaminants in human relations that the pure *I-Thou* relation took on the air of utopia.

The realm of education has its own distinctive form of the universal problem of power vs. dialogue. To a degree to which teaching can be understood as shaping another person's agency, it is laden with a paradox. Human agency is by definition something not shapeable by others, because it implies exercise of the free will. This chapter is intended to show that such a paradox is not merely an exercise in formal logic but may have important implications for the theoretical understanding of education. The paradox itself is a mere reflection of the contradictory nature of education.

Of course, one may understand teaching differently, as having nothing to do with shaping the other person's agency. One can conceive of teaching in a number of ways, including those ways that totally avoid discussion of whether a student exercises free will in the process of education and whether teaching implies any sort of limitations to that free will. Yet many would agree that at least some parts of education as it is commonly understood involve deep changes in the student's self, changes that are influenced by a teacher. I tend to believe such experiences to be the core of the educational project. For those who consider these experiences to be a peripheral or unnecessary part of education, my argument will have a sphere of application as limited as the place they assign for such experiences of personal change.

Despite Buber's caution about the impossibility of a true dialogical relation with students, teachers must enter such a relation. Paradoxically, dialogical relation is necessary if we hope to access the moral core of a student's self. In those instances where an act of education makes an impact on the student's agency, it must at least *look* like a genuine dialogical relation to the student. None of us likes to be formed, shaped, or educated if we know one of these is occurring. One tends to accept influences in the context of genuine dialogical relation, where one's partner is truly open to the possibility of changing, too.

The self possesses certain protective mechanisms that prevent it from changing by simply conforming to others' demands. The notion of agency at least partially signifies the ability to resist the influences of others and to stand on one's own feet. Of course, these mechanisms are not perfect, thus allowing for crude propaganda to be effective sometimes. Nevertheless, such mechanisms do exist, which, among other things, makes teaching a challenging occupation. The self jealously guards its inner space from attempts at direct control.

At the same time, the self contains the mechanisms of change. The self is a relational phenomenon. The meaningful change comes only from relationships with others. The self is deeply ambivalent toward the outside influences—it limits and yet welcomes them. To facilitate such an ambivalent act, the self employs specific devices to filter the influences. Our instinct for mutuality, for dialogical relation—arising from something Buber called "simple humanity"—this instinct makes sure that our partner in conversation is not armed with hidden agendas, plans, and preconceived notions of what the conversation should produce. Therefore, we open up only to those who are reciprocally open. Only when we experience a true dialogue do we let our guard down.

Of course, one can learn a technical skill from someone and be perfectly aware of the educational, and therefore unequal, nature of the interaction. However, where it comes to deeper situated layers of our selves, we all generally loathe to be influenced. Acting on free will means acting without someone else's gentle push. A teacher can say, "I will teach you to read," but rarely will she or he say, "I will teach you to want to read." One cannot really teach to want something—not explicitly anyway. The same applies to any sort of moral or value judgment. As soon as students realize this is not simply a talk but the teacher attempting to drive home a lesson, the effective teaching is over, because the filters of students' selves will not allow the desired influence. Teachers are in the position "You're damned if you don't and you're damned if you do." We cannot establish true dialogue with students, and yet we have to.

Of course, I want to teach a kid to want to read, but I never say so and never show so. I want to affect student's morals and values, but the student must not suspect anything. The better the teacher is, the more sophisticated is her or his exhibition of the dialogical relation, the deeper her or his educational agenda is hidden. Some of the best teachers are not even aware of the specific position of "helper" they occupy. Carl Rogers, for instance, managed to do just that—he is not a helper even in his own eyes, and yet, in reality he remains a therapist with the therapist's agenda.

Using the Buberian language, teaching is *I-It* packaged as *I-Thou*. It is a dialogue with a predictable outcome, which is an oxymoron. At the crucial points in educational relations, teachers act as if they are genuinely excited, truly upset, or honestly puzzled. On the level visible to students, teachers pretend to be partners in dialogue; on the deeper level, teachers have definite plans how this relation should affect students. Education is profoundly ambivalent; at its core, educational relation is a manipulative one, albeit with best of intentions.

Let me reiterate that teachers frequently do experience genuine feelings. They do get upset, excited, and puzzled. Just like Rogers, many teachers indeed experience the education relation as one of mutuality and true dialogue. "No doubt of it," Buber replied to a similar charge, "but I am not speaking now about feeling but about a real situation."[12] Such a reply implies the existence of certain reality of a situation independent of what people involved in it feel. Such a way of thinking gives dialogue a certain objective status, which is counterintuitive. How can it be a non-dialogue and yet feel like a dialogue?

This argument goes back to Buber's ontological understanding of dialogue as a mode of being and not merely a form of communication. This is his assumption that does not have to be shared by everyone.

However, I want to point out that Buber's insistence on the existence of certain "real situations" has nothing to do with the objectivist notion of reality. For Buber, the only reality is the reality of relations, not the reality of things. He does not allow for a disengaged subject to have a view from nowhere. Likewise, he does not allow for existence of things out of context of relations with each other and with people. Being for him is relating.

And for being to make any sense, it must be differentiated. Therefore, Buber must insist that different modes of being (relating) fundamentally differ from each other. Thus *I-It* and *I-Thou* are two parallel realities, so to speak, and one is not free to pop in and out of these realities at will. From my point of view, one's ontological assumptions require making a choice: either the things are fixed and relations fluid, or things are relative but types of relations are stable. This is a choice that many "particularists," especially postmodernists, neglect or refuse to make at the expense of losing the grasp on *being* itself.

Following Buber's sense of reality, I will accept that teaching cannot *really* be based on a dialogical relation. It is a manipulative *I-It* relation, but because the "It" part is another human being (a student), and because what the teacher wants from it has to do with voluntary change, to the student this relation has to *look* like a genuine dialogue. When I presented similar thoughts to a senior colleague several years ago, he was appalled by my cynicism. "Do you mean to say that we can educate children effectively as long as we lie to them?" This is indeed my conclusion.

I will attempt to salvage the primacy of relation in the face of the postmodernist critique of power imbalance using Bakhtin's idea of polyphony. Bakhtin's account of author-hero relations in the *Problems of Dostoevsky's Poetics* can be used to outline a solution for the paradox of imbalanced relation. My theory is that in presenting the author-hero relation in the polyphonic novel Bakhtin describes the general way of mutuality in an imbalanced relation. Essentially, Bakhtin disassociates dialogue from equality. The problem of imbalanced relation is not to be countered with power sharing based on considerations of equality; it needs to be addressed with polyphony, the principle of engaged co-existence of multiple yet unmerged voices. Polyphony is a fascinating fusion of ethical and esthetical considerations applied to human relations.

Bakhtin's principle of polyphony offers a new way of reconciling power imbalance with mutuality of relation. According to Bakhtin, an author of the polyphonic novel creates heroes who are fully independent of their creator. The problem of authority imbalance may be misstated; it is the specific kind of monological authority that eliminates mutuality, not authority itself. The polyphonic authority *creates* mutuality, and only this kind of authority should be used in education.

In *The Boy Who Would Be a Helicopter,* Vivian Paley gives an example of her best teaching moment, a story of Jason and the mother pig.

> The pig is in a story of Katie's, and Jason is the boy who tells us every day that his helicopter is broken. "Come listen to Katie's story," I call to Jason. "This mother pig does something that reminds me of you." He approaches the story table blowing on his blades, one of the many ways to repair a broken helicopter, and I read what Katie has just dictated to me.
>
> There is the three pigs. And the mother pig is there. Then the wolf huffs down the brick house. And the mother puts it back together.
>
> "That makes me think of the way you fix your helicopter," I say. Jason and Katie smile at each other, and I am a step closer to my vision of connecting everything that happens in this nursery school classroom. My habit of drawing invisible lines between the children's images is, I think, the best thing I do as a teacher.[13]

Paley, the teacher is also a novelist. She has a roomful of characters, each capable of creating his or her own worldviews. What she does is not only encourage them to tell their stories but provide a way of connecting them together. She clearly exercises a great amount of power (influence) over her students. She is, after all, a strong and creative teacher, which, by definition, means a person with power. But her power concentrates on encouraging students to write their own stories, which means giving them the tools of interpretation and, therefore, the power to redefine classroom relations.

Paley does two things: she encourages kids to write their stories and provides an opportunity for these stories to meet each other. Thus she shifts the center of gravity from the student-teacher relationship to the student-student relationship. She relinquishes her monological authorial voice in favor of the polyphonic multiple voices of the novel. Paley thinks of her classroom as a novel, not an epic, not a drama, not a short story. Her novel is populated with a number of fully independent characters, each with his or her own story to tell, his or her own version of the common events. There are many distinctive yet intersecting storylines. Paley's classroom is an epitome of polyphony. The essence of her teaching is making dialogue possible.

Her authority is based on her usefulness to children—she is the only one who can write, and she can give their story-telling some time and space. "Drawing invisible lines" between students' stories seems to be where her authority is mostly applied. Her relations with children are not easily described in this framework of power imbalance. Rather, they all seek to combine their strengths against the common enemy of isolation, muteness, and incomprehension. Their relationships make more sense if described as division of labor. Someone can tell a good story; others can act it out; some can write while others will dictate. It is within this division of labor that the teacher gets to set some rules, to allocate time and resources. She does what others cannot do, but they do what she cannot do. In Paley's classroom, people seek to add their powers, not measure them against each other. The teacher's authority makes sense as a function of that joint power. To get to that point, they need to write a novel.

What we see here is a transformation of the athenaic relations into erotic ones. The very logic of the athenaic relation *allows* certain power imbalances, because the common goal supercedes the considerations of power for the sake of power. Paley does not seek the authority; she is asked by students to assume it.

The tricky part of the educational novel is that the teacher cannot be simply an author but is also one of the main characters. As such, she will have to produce some statements that could be described as authoritative. To illustrate my understanding of relational authority, I will draw on Bakhtin's analysis of authoritative statements in *Problems of Dostoevsky's Poetics*. He uses the *Demons* and *The Brothers Karamazov* to illustrate his points.

> We shall direct our attention to the following point. At first Smerdyakov perceived Ivan's voice as an integral monological voice. He hearkened to his preachments on the permissibility of all things as to the word of a called and self-confident teacher. He did not at first understand that Ivan's voice was divaricated and that his convincing and confident tone was intended to convince himself, and not at all as the completely convinced transmission of his view to another.
>
> Analogous is the relationship of Shatov, Kirillov and Petr Verkhovensky to Stavrogin. Each of them follows Stavrogin as a teacher, accepting his voice as integral and confident. They all think that he spoke with them as a mentor speaks to his pupils; in fact he made them participants in his endless interior dialog, in which he was trying to convince himself, not them. Now Stavrogin hears his own words from each of them, but with a firm, monologized accent. He himself can now repeat these words only with accent of mockery, not conviction. He was unable to convince himself of anything, and it was painful for him to listen to people who have been convinced by him.[14]

This describes the tragedy of a teacher, which many try to avoid. Teachers know only too well how words can be taken too literally, how students can sometimes only hear a part of what one says and ignore other voices in the teacher's internal dialogue. And yet I state again, that the problem lies not with the authoritative statements themselves but with the way the internal dialogicality of such statements is misunderstood or misrepresented. What is missing is the right relational context. It is a teacher's responsibility to make sure that authoritative statements are presented as cues of larger dialogue—forceful and passionate but never finalized and unanswered. Authoritative statements without dialogue are indeed very dangerous. A teacher should sound like a hero from Dostoevsky's novel:

> Accents of profound conviction in the speeches of Dostoevsky's heroes are in a huge majority of instances merely the result of the fact that the words are a part of an interior dialogue and are intended to convince the speaker himself. The intensification of the convincing tone is evidence of the internal opposition of the hero's other voice. A word completely independent of these internal struggles is almost never found in Dostoevsky.[15]

There is a need and a place for authority in the world irreversibly immersed in plurality. The need is there, because the plurality is not a plurality of independent parallel worlds. We as individuals and as groups need each other for our very existence. And if so, we need each other fully, with all the mistakes and biases. The place is there, because authoritative statements, if presented and understood correctly, are only parts of a big dialogue. It is neither Smerdyakov's fault nor Ivan Karamazov's if things with authoritative statements regularly go wrong. Their relations lacked the polyphonic dimension that Paley was able to establish. In Bakhtin's view, authority does not preclude dialogue; only certain kinds of authority do. This agrees with Buber's general position that mutuality does not imply symmetry.

The dialogical authority of a teacher should be directed not at a student but at student-teacher relations. Dostoevsky's plan is to write a polyphonic novel, to investigate certain questions about the human soul. He has no idea how the events will develop. He gives his invented heroes as much agency as he possesses himself. His authority is consciously self-limiting. It imposes the genre but does not dictate action or belief. Dostoevsky passes no judgment that would be more authoritative than those of the heroes. Similarly, Paley does not have a specific plan for each child. Her authority is just as self-limiting as that of Dostoevsky. Paley imposes the genre of relationship, hoping that the genre will be good for students' growth. In a certain sense, teachers' authority imposes freedom. She has the authority over the relationship but not over the student.

Are these not the same thing? How is the authority over relations different from the authority over people? Even if we can impose mutuality and dialogue on our students, should we do it? Who is to say that engagement is better than separation? Who has the right to force the other to speak when she prefers silence? I will address similar questions in Chapter 13. Let me just note that these are all questions thinkable in the relativist universe but not in the relational one. In the relational universe, the absolute duty of each human being is to relate to others. All language games, all cultures, all opinions possess equal rights to exist. None has the right to exist in isolation. Thus, the ethical justification for the dialogical authority is the axiomatic acceptance of the value of relation. This cannot be proved, and I won't try.

NOTES

1. Elizabeth Ellsworth, "Why Doesn't This Feel Empowering?" *Harvard Educational Review* 59 (1989): 297-324.
2. Nicholas Burbules and Suzanne Rice, "Dialogue Across Differences: Continuing the Conversation," *Harvard Educational Review* 61, no. 4 (1991): 401-2.
3. Clive Beck, "Difference, Authority and the Teacher-Student Relationship." *Philosophy of Education 1994* (http://www.ed.uiuc.edu/eps/pes-yearbook/94_docs/beck.htm).
4. Clifton Tanabe, "Social Power and Education," *Philosophy of Education 1998* (http://www.ed.uiuc.edu/eps/pes-yearbook/1998/tanabe.html).
5. Frank Margonis, "The Demise of Authenticity", *Philosophy of Education 1998* (http://www.ed.uiuc.edu/eps/pes-yearbook/1998/margonis_2.html).
6. Buber, *The Knowledge of Man*, 156-175.
7. Buber, *The Knowledge of Man*, 162.
8. Buber, *The Knowledge of Man*, 162.
9. Buber, *The Knowledge of Man*, 168.
10. Buber, *The Knowledge of Man*, 163.
11. Martin Buber, *Between Man and Man* (London: Kegan Paul, 1947), 98.
12. Buber, *The Knowledge of Man*, 163.
13. Vivan Paley, *The Boy Who Would Be a Helicopter* (Cambridge, MA: Harvard University Press, 1991).
14. Bakhtin, *Problems of Dostoevsky's Poetics* (Ann Arbor, MI: Ardis, 1973), 220-221.
15. I cannot help making a comment here. Perhaps postmodern critics of grand narratives ignore this inner split, the inner dialogue in the great modernists' writings? Perhaps Kant, Hegel, Freud, Marx, and others have some other voices within their writings that we do not read very well?

CHAPTER 12.
ON THE VALUE OF DOUBLE MESSAGES

The second problem of relational pedagogies is reconciling polyphony with teacher authority; it is principally a question of integrity. Will polyphony of relations fragment the student's self in a harmful way? In other words, if teacher refuses the monological authority, won't the student's life be shattered from confusion?

Here is what happens to a teenage boy. He discovers the internal universe of the self, which turns out to be complex and rather confusing. Everyone around the kid, including parents, teachers, counselors, and peers insist that he must define his true, whole self. Most people find the idea a sensible one, and this is how the teenager gets thoroughly confused. The whole world keeps asking, who are you? What kind of a person are you? Where do you belong? The adolescent looks inside and finds...not much there. We learn about ourselves from experience, and this is something sorely lacking in adolescents by definition. Am I a dreamer or a practical person? Am I a coward or a courageous person? Do I like arts or sciences? As all these questions arise, parents and teachers more often than not urge kids to answer them. In this American culture, knowing who one is is highly valued.

One should keep in mind that knowledge of our selves has clear limits, just like any other kind of knowledge. We do not know how we would react to a grizzly bear turning into our hiking path until we actually run into the bear. Most ordinary folks go through life without the slightest knowledge of the bear-response part of their identity. Only in our imagination can we try to find out more about our selves than the horizon of our everyday experience allows.

Further, even if you had the grizzly experience once (and made it out alive), there is no guarantee, not even a reasonable certainty that you will react the same way next time another grizzly decides to check you out. The unpredictability of human behavior is one fact that does not raise any controversy among scholars and any number of knowledgeable people. This looks like a basic fact of human nature. When someone claims to be an honest person, this simply means, that in a limited number of similar situations, the person is more likely to act honestly. A statement like "I am an honest person" is a gross overgeneralization, not unlike saying "all Englishmen are fat" after meeting a couple of overweight Englishmen.

A teenage girl looks inside and finds totally contradicting opinions inside her head, most of which sound suspiciously like someone else's. She finds different things convincing at different times. Today's beliefs become ridiculous tomorrow. The adults tell her this is associated with the adolescent search for the self. So to grow up you have to grow out of it, become a unified, consistent, stable self, right?

The truth is, most adults do not know what they are talking about when it comes to the self. They know how to build a ship and how to clone a sheep. But when we enter the murky waters of psychology and philosophy of the self, we encounter a completely different sort of knowledge, where there are no hard facts. I would put a big warning on every psychology/education/self-help book: "The contents of this book may turn out to be completely untrue and may cause injury and death." There are just not many established facts about the human self. The need for a unified true self is just one of these facts that are opinions rather than facts.

Another truth is that most of the adults, including those well-adjusted and successful individuals, are themselves deeply confused about their own integrity. Fact one: adults' beliefs about what they are do not coincide with their own behavior. Most decent folks occasionally lie and cheat. Most terrible people have done something noble. Fact two: adults' behavior is inconsistent; they may do one thing today and something totally opposite tomorrow. Every time they would find justifications for both actions. Fact three: adults say different things to different people. If they don't, they are probably stubborn idiots. All these three observations are especially apparent when applied to the ways the teenager's own parents treat her. Most of the parents have no consistent rules for their children. Some have rules but no consistent enforcement. Most of them feel guilty about it but for some reason do not want to change the situation.

Perhaps there is a powerful need to be inconsistent, of which they are not even aware? Those who, despite great struggle, do adopt and enforce consistent rules for their children are the worst kind of parents, nervous wrecks and control freaks. Most healthy adults never solve the problem of an authentic self, which they claim to be an issue specific for adolescence.

In addition, my third big argument against integrity is that today's teenagers live in a different world that demands and will demand even more in the future a new type of personality structure. What only few philosophers knew only 30 years ago is now obvious to any smart teenager. The human world is based on irreducible, fundamental multiplicity. There is no unity in the world. If you are in one of the large urban school districts, just look around you in the school halls. You see kids of all races and combinations thereof, of many different religions, languages, political and cultural persuasions, etc. Some people still believe that it is worthwhile to find the underlying unity for all these people, something in common among all of them. But as a practical matter, we all know, there is nothing you can do to make all of them agree on any one thing. This planet was always incredibly diverse, but it is only recently that we were hit square between our eyes with this diversity. Many violent conflicts of the past grew out of an idealistic dream of bringing all the nations together under the auspices of some universal idea or a universal truth. It never worked out. Philosophers call this newly discovered feature "the postmodern condition."

The postmodern world demands the postmodern self, whose integrity is a rather secondary concern. The postmodern self needs to navigate in the world of irreducible differences, and the only way to do it is to match external diversity with internal complexity of the self. Yet, what educators try hard to do is to avoid double messages. The notion of "double message" is commonly perceived as a negative one in the educational context. Of course, double message is something one has to accept if my theory of the dialogical authority is true. Many believe that an educational institution and, even better, a whole community, must convey a consistent moral message to the youth. This chapter aims to show that the consistency of a message is not always good and that a truly educational moral message is always a double message, an ambivalent and self-contradicting one. To preserve the polyphony of a moral message, I argue, is more important than to observe the cohesion of such a message.

Greater Expectations by William Damon[1] presents a strong argument in favor of moral consistency. Damon advocates for a "youth chapter," that is, a unified consensus on core values conveyed to youth by the society.

> Children everywhere seek a coherent framework of guidance. Without a strong community, there can be no such coherence. A parent may offer a sterling example for the child, a teacher may provide a moving insight or admonition, but in the long run the child will experience confusion unless the child finds synchronous notes elsewhere in the community. This confusion sows the seeds of demoralization. In turn, demoralization inevitably will lead to either apathy or rebellion, depending upon the child's inclination and circumstances.[2]

Damon acknowledges that contemporary society is by nature pluralistic. Yet this pluralism for him does not exclude the possibility of reaching a consensus about the basic messages communities convey to their youth. The expressions of a community's moral voice, for which he advocates, should adhere to three principles: (1) The expressions must come from a variety of sources. The variety will ensure the "cumulative influence," enhance each other's credibility, and help the youngster "to understand the various ways that moral aims may be pursued in different relationships and circumstances." (2) These expressions must be consistent with one another, which means that "parents, teachers, peers and others should advocate roughly the same goals and expectations for young people." Damon has "core" goals and expectations on his mind here, as opposed to cultural and political matters "about which civilized adults differ." (3) A community must express its moral voice in a manner understandable and compelling to youth.[3]

As Ralph Waldo Emerson once noted, "A foolish consistency is the hobgoblin of little minds, adored by little statesman and philosophers and divines. With consistency a great soul has simply nothing to do."[4] I would like to argue several related points in connection with Damon's claim that the inconsistency of moral message leads to confusion and demoralization: (1) a consistent a moral message may also lead to confusion and demoralization, (2) an inconsistent moral message (a double message) does not necessarily lead to confusion and demoralization, and (3) any truly educational moral message is intrinsically inconsistent and ambivalent, although not all inconsistent moral messages are truly educational.

Damon offers some examples of the consistent moral voice of a community. He approvingly quotes Frank Furstenberg's description of a working-class community in Philadelphia, one of the many that "have fought hard to preserve their safety and their solidarity in the face of deteriorating societal circumstances."[5] This is a community where people watch out for other people's children. "On matter of core standards, the community speaks to the young with one voice."[6] And yet this particular community manifests "fierce racism" that helps contain discord among neighborhood residents. Damon does not see a connection between the two facts. For him, the consistency of the community's moral voice is one (good) thing, and the racism is another (unfortunate) thing. From my point of view, these two are intrinsically linked. This example raises the red flag about the price of the consistent morality of tightly knit neighborhoods. This example also makes one wonder about the golden age of America's fifties, to which Damon constantly refers. Did that paradise consist of communities like the one from Philadelphia? Being kind and attentive to your neighbor's kids while being cruel and unjust to the kids from another neighborhood, whose skin happened to be of another color—is it not the kind of society to which Damon wants us to go back?

The consistency of a moral message for the young people was just the other side of the exclusion of whole groups of people. How else could you achieve the consistency of moral values that are to be conveyed to youth? Consensus is agreeing on one position, one point of view. Even if one assumes such an agreement is possible to achieve voluntarily (which I doubt very much), still the question remains, what would happen to all those *voluntarily* withdrawn dissenting voices? Even a voluntary self-exclusion from the conversation is still a form of exclusion. Consensus and general harmony sound wonderful, truly utopian. And any utopia leads to cruelty, which our century's turbulent history proves only too well. I will not go into generic postmodern criticism of "grand narratives," confining myself to yet another specifically educational example.

I grew up in a society that promoted the same consistent moral messages methodically, consistently, and repeatedly. In the Soviet Union, the moral voice of community was about as coherent as it is practically possible to achieve. As a child I was never confused about moral principles, they were explicitly stated and promoted by mass media, school, and other institutions. And yet the Soviet Union of the 70s and 80s was a very cynical society. The coherent message of moral authority was completely irrelevant to the complex lives we all lived.

One may object by saying that the reality of Communist domination itself conveyed a message in contradiction to that of Soviet educators. However, there will always be a gap between a moral message we convey to our youth and the realities of the adult world, regardless of political and economical arrangements. After all, Damon does not propose to reform the society so it reveals itself to the youth in a better light. He persuades us to *tell* something different to the youth, not to *become* different. Thus if we treat the notion of a message in its precise sense, as something being intentionally communicated to the youth, the Soviets achieved remarkable consistency in their educational message.

This line of argument does not imply in any way that everything Communists did was wrong simply because it was done by the Communists. On the contrary, historical experiments of autocratic societies such as that of the Soviet Union may offer valuable illustrations to some "what if" questions. Reasons similar to those offered by Damon motivated the Soviet educational policy makers. There is no reason to believe that American attempts to do the same thing would have a much different effect.

Soviet scholars had developed an elaborated educational theory about "the uniformity of educational expectations," which was promoted in the sphere of moral education.[7] It was very much a part of educational rhetoric and practices at the time when I was a student in the 70s and when I began my own teaching career in the mid-80s. It was also the least successful of all Soviet educational policies. Soviet educators did not fail to get their message across because it was a morally deficient one. Quite to the contrary, it boils down very much to what Damon calls "core values"—work, honesty, integrity, respect for elders, personal responsibility, altruism, social activism, etc. The hope was that if only the same message is repeated over and over again, from different sources, so that youngsters would have nowhere else to go, then such a message would be accepted. This hope has never been realized.

It is the wholeness and internal consistency of the message and not its content that makes it implausible. A fully consistent message simply does not capture the complexity of moral life. Consistency cannot always be considered an advantage, and moreover, as I am trying to show, there are a few deep problems with the very idea of consistency of a moral message intended for youth. Consistency was grossly oversold as an educational value. One of the main reasons for such overvaluing of consistency is a simplistic understanding of the plurality of moral voices in the community. One insists on consistency because one considers plurality to be superfluous and accidental.

Damon accepts plurality but certainly does not view it as something intrinsic to a moral voice of community, perhaps only as something inevitable. For him, it is not plurality of moral voices but rather plurality of sources from which the same moral message is reiterated. Bakhtin offered a very different way of viewing plurality. I will rely here on Bakhtin's notions of dialogue and polyphony, developed in his *Problems of Dostoevsky's Poetics*. Bakhtin suggested that one single voice is not capable of telling the truth. Only a multitude of simultaneous voices together may constitute truth. In other words, no message alone can be truthful. The capacity to produce truth is directly linked to the multiplicity of voices that deliver the message or, rather, a number of messages. This suggestion contradicts the very definition of truth fostered by European thought for centuries. Truth was always supposed to be singular in contrast to plurality of errors. However, Bakhtin thought that truth is a number of simultaneous and inconsistent messages rather than one unified message. Bakhtin elevates pluralism to the status of necessary prerequisite of a truth rather than simply a condition of truth, external to the content of the truth. Now, for Bakhtin, truth is an ethical category when it reflects a human being and not merely an inanimate object. Ethics and epistemology resist separation when we deal with people rather than with things.

Bakhtin's theory warrants a revision of our understanding of the moral self. An individual should internalize the multiplicity of voices to sustain his or her capacity for moral judgment. One might argue that moral consciousness consists of several interacting but mutually contradicting voices. A moral person is one who can bring up an internal dialogue among these voices every time the situation of moral choice arises. The outcome of such debate is unpredictable by definition. One or the other internal voice may win this particular round of debate, which does not guarantee its right to win in all future debates. For instance, one may keep both pro-choice and pro-life arguments active in one's mind; that is not as simply a number of abstract arguments but as an ongoing dialogue between the two. Moral mind functions not unlike a democratic government, where separation of powers makes sure none of the major voices gets too powerful. None of the three branches alone is democratic, only the combination thereof makes democracy possible (although does not guarantee it). Similarly, the very multiplicity of internal voices makes moral consciousness possible. No single voice is moral; neither the masculine voice of rational reasoning nor the feminine voice of love and mercy; neither principles nor attention to particulars. None of these voices is moral *by itself.* Only simultaneous representation of many, preferably *all,* relevant voices can constitute a moral self.

Now I must go back to the issue of moral message for youth. Even with such a revised notion of the moral self I cannot simply sing praise to all double messages. In this regard, Damon is right; the abundance of double messages *as such* does not do anything good for our children. Double messages are a necessary, but not sufficient condition of moral education. I need to find criteria that separate the "good" plurality from the "bad" plurality, a "good" double message from a "bad" double message. There must be an underlying principle of organization of multiple voices other than consistency. Such a principle should work both for the internal polyphony of a moral mind and for a community that tries to organize its polyphony of voices in an educationally sound moral message for youth. In search of such a principle I will turn to Margret Buchman and Robert Floden's article, which explores the notion of coherence in opposition to the notion of consistency in the context of developing teacher education programs. Consistency, from their point of view, implies logical relations and the absence of contradiction, while coherence allows for many kinds of connectedness.

> Educational coherence is found where students can discover *and* establish relations among various areas of sensibility, knowledge and skill, yet where loose ends remain, inviting a reweaving of beliefs and ties to the unknown.[8]

I find it a useful distinction. However, Buchman and Floden settle for the notion of coherence that looks like a compromise, a not-quite-consistency, rather than a qualitatively different kind of connectedness. They view coherence as an overlapping number of metaphors or messages, which are not logically consistent and yet partially agree with each other or show common themes and patterns. Bakhtin had something else in mind when he wrote on the notion of polyphony. Here is how Bakhtin describes Dostoevsky's ability to see the polyphonic truth:

> Where others saw a single thought, he was able to find and feel out two thoughts, a bifurcation; where others saw a single quality, he discovered in it the presence of a second and contradictory quality. Everything that seemed simple became, in his world, complex and multi-structured. In every voice he could hear two contending voices, in every expression a crack, and the readiness to go over immediately to another contradictory expression; in every gesture he detected confidence and lack of confidence simultaneously; he perceived the profound ambiguity, even multiple ambiguity of every phenomenon. But none of these contradictions and bifurcations ever became dialectical, they were never set in motion along a temporal path or in an evolving sequence: they were, rather, spread out in one plane, as standing alongside or opposite one another, as consonant but not merging or as hopelessly contradictory, as an eternal harmony of unmerged voices or as their unceasing and irreconcilable quarrel. Dostoevsky's visualizing power was locked in place at the moment diversity revealed itself—and remained there, organizing and shaping this diversity in the cross-section of a given moment.[9]

Bakhtin's polyphony is not a multitude of overlapping metaphors. He thought of a multitude of different disagreeing voices, each existing through and with another voice. The very notion of difference he perceived as another form of connectedness. For him, being different was not a reason for an independent and isolated existence. Rather, one can only live out one's difference through others. In other words, just like sameness and similarity can serve as both grounds for connection or as grounds for separation; similarly, the difference may be both an excuse to part ways and a reason for relations. The relational understanding of difference is the foundation for Bakhtin's notion of polyphony.

I will now attempt to characterize this principle of organizing the multitude of voices without consistency. I will call it the non-teleological dialogicality principle, which provides three things.

1. *Perpetuity.* Dialogue in its polyphonic, Bakhtinian sense should have no end. The voices in it never merge, never achieve a formal consensus, and if such a consensus arises, it is a by-product not an aim of dialogue. Dialogue has no purpose but continuation of dialogue; it is not a means toward some other aim but an aim in itself. Although it may serve a useful purpose, dialogue may not be treated as a means toward some other end. One should place higher value on dialogue compared to all practical aims achieved with its help.

2. *Mutual addressivity.* Voices of dialogue do not simply present themselves to each other as finalized principled opinions. They define themselves with and in relation toward each other. One should never have an opinion about anything unless one knows the audience, who listens, and what is another opinion on the matters discussed. Voices should explicitly or implicitly address each other.

3. *Inclusion.* Truth in the dialogical sense is approachable when most or all of those who have something to say on the subject are included. For instance, when a conversation turns to gay rights, and none of the participants is gay, one can feel a void, a missing voice, without which truth is unachievable. That is why one could feel compelled to recreate the absent voice, to speak from a gay person's position as well as one could. This may not be a best solution, and yet such "modeling" of a live voice is much better than simply representation of an abstract argument of gay activist group or ignoring gay voices completely.

The non-teleological dialogicality is not an absence of any connection. It is a principle that allows for inconsistent messages to be organized in a non-hierarchical and inclusionary manner; it is a way of staying engaged and talking while not leading toward more or less violent or more or less exclusionary consensus. A community must present its complex and contradictory moral voice as a multitude of mutually addressed voices, not as a unified and consistent whole. Instead of avoiding giving youth double messages, we must pay attention to how we construct our double messages.

One can imagine a society that is not concerned with how to overcome differences but, rather, with how to sustain its polyphony without losing any of the voices. Such a society will have only one shared moral belief, namely, that all its groups, movements, political parties, etc., must abandon their claims for universal truths in any form except for the sake of an argument. This postmodern pluralism will imply that there will never be an agreement among its members on most fundamental values. However, the postmodern pluralism forbids both exclusion and withdrawal from a conversation. In fact, one's beliefs and values will only then come alive, when one constantly brings them into contact and interaction with values and beliefs of other groups and individuals. People will generally loosen up their attachment to principles, valuing change and challenge over consistency and stability. Adults will not even consider trying to relate a single unified moral message to the youth; they will make sure the variety of beliefs and opinions will be properly conveyed to the young generation, with all the connections, past discussions, and contradictions among them.

This postmodern pluralist society will still have to enact laws and make other collective decisions. Yet it will generally consider dialogue that might have preceded such a decision to be more important than the decision itself. Making a collective decision will be perceived as a sad if inevitable fact, as a necessary closure of possibilities, always imperfect and always open for further revisions. The postmodern democracy will discuss and change the rules of discourse as often as it changes other laws and policies. The definition of good life for all will include the value of never-ending dialogue.

NOTES

[1] William Damon, *Greater Expectations: Overcoming the Culture of Indulgence in America's Homes and Schools* (New York: Free Press, 1995).

[2] Damon, *Greater Expectations*, 227.

[3] Damon, *Greater Expectations*, 239.

[4] Jone Johnson Lewis, *Transcendentalists web site*, 1995-2001 (ttp://www.transcendentalists.com/emerson_quotes.htm).

[5] Damon, *Greater Expectations*, 232.

[6] Damon, *Greater Expectations*, 233.

[7] See Viktor M. Korotov, *Pedagogicheskoe trebovanie [The Educational Expectation]* (Moscow: Prosveshchenie, 1966).

[8] M. Buchman and R. Floden "Coherence, the Rebel Angel" *Educational Researcher* 21 (1992), 8.

[9] Mikhail Bakhtin, *Problems of Dostoevsky's Poetics* (Minneapolis: University of Minnesota Press, 1984), 30.

CHAPTER 13.
LYOTARD VS. BAKHTIN

Another challenge to the pedagogy of relations comes from the relatively new appreciation for diversity associated with postmodern thought. Many thinkers seriously doubt the possibility of human relations across differences. The dissolution of the absolute makes it difficult to conceive of the need and the justification for human relations. In the recent past, assumptions about a universal human nature also allowed for relations across and despite the differences. Now the very plurality of human worlds seems to threaten the possibility of a certain relation that Buber calls the interhuman. This chapter is an attempt to show that the diversity does not prevent relation.

Postmodernity for me is not as much a concept as a vivid image. It is a memory of a particular high school recess through which I was walking a few years ago. It was a warm spring afternoon, students standing at their lockers, a tall student languidly dribbling his ball, some voices angry, some joyful, a kid dancing, and a kid doing martial arts moves. The commotion was both pleasantly exciting and somewhat threatening. Mine were the eyes of a sub—strange enough to notice the familiar and familiar enough to remain unnoticed. Nothing really happened, just a walk through rather narrow and crowded school halls, yet I can still hear the sounds and feel the commotion. Many other school experiences blended together into that one walk when one simple realization came to me. The spectacular and unabashed multitude of languages, accents, styles, dresses, shades of skin color, racial features cumulatively made a powerful statement one would have to be blind and deaf to miss: "we are here to stay."

Diversity itself is not new in urban America as it is almost anywhere in the world. However, only recently has diversity firmly announced that it will not go away or diminish. I looked at the students and realized that they will grow up as different as they are now, and there is nothing in the school's power to become the melting pot once again.

Diversity has been perceived as temporary and superficial. It appeared temporary, because in a historical perspective, the differences would all but disappear in favor of American or mankind's unity. It appeared superficial, because deep down inside we all were supposed to be the same; universal human nature, if only properly understood, would make our differences only skin deep. This is just one way to invalidate difference. Another way of doing it is to proclaim diversity significant but only as a problem in connection with the great difficulty teachers must face to overcome this diversity. "We have a very diverse student population," a school principal says, meaning, "what can you expect of *these* kids?"

Many still perceive diversity as a curious anomaly. For instance, consider a political speechwriter's cliché: "Diversity is our strength." At least two assumptions can be recovered from this cliché. First, diversity is reduced to a means toward some other goal. Without a useful function, diversity would have no reason to exist. Second, diversity is *our* strength, that is, some other nations do not possess it and, therefore, are somewhat lesser nations. The idea of diversity can then serve as a basis for exclusion. This brief example shows that there are many ways to overlook and dismiss diversity, including the ways of glorifying or utilizing it. Yet when I walk in the hallways of a school, the plurality of human worlds presents itself as an inescapable reality regardless of whether one perceives it as strength or as a threat. It simply demands respect, which, in turn, demands making sense of diversity.

Making sense of diversity brings a nagging feeling of worry. What is education if not normalizing? How is education at all possible in the postmodern world? This chapter attempts to bring together the views of Lyotard and Bakhtin in order to develop a notion of engaged diversity as a foundation for postmodern education.

Postmodern philosophy has made a very effective effort to pay due respect to diversity. Lyotard's now-famous definition states: "Simplifying to the extreme, I define *postmodern* as incredulity toward meta-narratives."[1] This is a negative statement, and negative statements never make good definitions. Such formulaic negativity brought about a good deal of criticism against postmodernism, much of it deserving. However, one should bear in mind that this same statement springs from a perfectly positive assumption, namely, that difference, diversity, pluralism, etc., truly matter. "I wonder, if the failing of modernity," writes Lyotard, "could be connected to a resistance on the part of what I shall call the multiplicity of worlds of names, the insurmountable diversity of cultures."[2] For the purpose of this chapter, I will define postmodernism as the concern for the significance of difference and diversity.

In order to show that human diversity is neither accidental nor superficial, postmodernists emphasize the depths of difference. Lyotard, for instance, makes a point that various language games are incommensurable. Then he develops the notion of *differend*, that is, essentially, an impossibility of true understanding across discourses. His logic seems to be the following: the difference is significant, because it runs so deep, to the point of incommensurability. This is a perfectly acceptable move, and it sits well with observable facts of our lives. Examples of incommensurability are easy to find and hard to deny.

In reviews of an earlier version of this chapter, it was pointed out to me that Lyotard could not support total heterogeneity of discourses, because this would make movement from one discourse to another all but impossible. This is true; nowhere did Lyotard attempt to exaggerate the incommensurability. However, Lyotard's defense of diversity comes from the fact that he perceives diversity to be an important fact of reality. Lyotard respected diversity because it is there. My aim is to suggest that Lyotard's way of showing the significance of diversity is not the only conceivable way. Something might be of great importance for reasons other than the scope of its existence. Mikhail Bakhtin presents an example of such an alternative logic. He respected diversity whether it is there or not there.

As far as I know, Bakhtin never commented on postmodern philosophy. He shared some of the basic assumptions of postmodern writers but also significantly differed from them. It is not among my goals to properly "classify" Bakhtin in relation to postmodernists, who are remarkably hard to classify in relation to each other. Very few people would be interested to find out whether Bakhtin was a modernist, a postmodernist, or something else. More important is that Bakhtin's writings possess a potential to contribute significantly to the debate on diversity in education, and this potential remains little noticed.

Bakhtin clearly understood the indefensibility of the modern concepts of universal truth. For instance, the following passage could be as easily found in Lyotard's texts as in Bakhtin's: "The consolidation of monologism and its permeation into all spheres of ideological life was promoted in modern times by European rationalism with its cult of unified and exclusive reason, and especially by the Enlightenment."[3] Bakhtin was obsessed with finding variety, difference, and polyphony everywhere he looked. As Caryl Emerson points out, "For Bakhtin, [...] what grace there is must be found in *drugost'* and *inakovost'* (otherness and 'otherwiseness'); an ideal coming together is always predicated on subsequent departure and vigorous differentiation."[4]

However, let us consider on what grounds Bakhtin critiques modernity. Arguing about the ways ideas are used in monological writing, Bakhtin states that, in idealist philosophy, which for him was the quintessential modernity, the unity of existence is replaced by the unity of consciousness.

> "From the point of view of "consciousness in general" this plurality of consciousness is accidental, and so to speak, superfluous. [...] In the ideal, a single consciousness and a single mouth are absolutely sufficient for maximally full cognition; there is no need for a multitude of consciousnesses and no basis for it."[5]

The general direction of Bakhtin's and Lyotard's thought is similar—there can be no universal truth as there is no "consciousness in general." Now, Lyotard rejects the universal truth because it does injustice to other, separate, and incommensurable truth claims. In other words, he rejects the overarching or universal truth because of other competing truths. He rejects the universal truth not because of its content but because of what is happening outside of it, namely, the existence of other truths. One can plausibly continue his thought by saying that if there would be no other discourses, no alternative truth claims, then the universal truth of modernity would be acceptable. Unlike Lyotard, Bakhtin rejects the absolute truth because of its internal structure, namely, that it speaks in a single voice. If the multiplicity of human cultures and discourses would vanish, if only one very homogeneous group of people would survive some global disaster, even then Bakhtin would reject the type of monological truth developed by modernity. In fact, Bakhtin's criticism is not limited to the case of modernity, which is just one, the most prominent, case of monologism.

There is a subtle but very important difference between Lyotardian and Bakhtinian concepts of truth. For Lyotard, there is a multitude of discourses, each of them capable of producing its own truth claims and criteria of validity. In effect, he allows each of the many truths to play a role not unlike one played by the old universal truths of modernity with one difference: the former do it within the circle of their language games or discourses, while the latter played such a role across the discourses. Lyotard demotes modernity one level down without changing its monological nature.

For example, in his critique of Habermas, Lyotard endorses local consensus:

> We must thus arrive at an idea and practice of justice that is not linked to that of consensus.
>
> A recognition of the heteromorphous nature of language games is a first step in that direction [...] The second step is the principle that any consensus on the rules defining a game and the "moves" playable within it *must* be local, in other words, agreed on by its present players and subject to eventual cancellation.[6]

I see several objections against the local consensus idea. First, let us look at the distinction that Lyotard makes between the universal truth and a local, or a particular one. Assume there are other forms of intelligence in the universe. Then, on the larger scale, the great narratives of Enlightenment are just local narratives of our small planet. From a great distance, the differences among cultures, political orientations, etc., may seem quite insignificant. Thus, the distinction between the universal and the local is a rather questionable one. Locality and universality signify quantitative, not qualitative difference.

Second, the local consensus never happens even in the smallest of the games. There is *always* a minority, a voice of dissent, unless someone takes measures to silence it. Finally, the voluntary nature of a local consensus is not in any way different from grand narratives of modernity, for the *voluntary* acceptance of the rationality through education is exactly what Enlightenment philosophers envisioned.

While Lyotard's critique remains very powerful, his own solutions are less than convincing. Moreover, the type of solution he proposes (local determinism, small temporary consensus instead of global determinism, universal consensus) shows that he views diversity as a multitude of discourses that are different from each other but each of them is homogeneous inside. In his afterword to Lyotard's *Just Gaming*, Sam Weber raises a similar criticism—"Otherness, then, is not to be sought *between* the games that are supposed to be essentially self-identical, but *within* the game as such. This amounts to saying that the game is necessarily *ambivalent* from the start."[7] Thus, diversity, according to Lyotard, presents itself as a multitude of totalities.

The language games are not only separate from each other, they also *should* be kept separate, says Lyotard:

> Here the Idea of justice will consist in preserving the purity of each game, that is, for example, in insuring that the discourse of truth be considered as a 'specific' language game, that narration be played by its 'specific' rules.[8]

This idea of justice, which is remarkably similar to that of Michael Walzer,[9] views plurality in the same general way the classical liberal theory views the separation of powers. Many language games should be put against each other, so none becomes dominant and domineering. This postmodern version of "checks-and-balances" concept calls for several objections.

I really fail to see how allowing for several parallel discourses without changing the nature of each discourse addresses the basic problem of difference. How is the domination *within* a particular language game better than domination *across* different language games? How a grand narrative, developed within a particular group, is better than the grand narrative intended for the whole humanity. The scale of monologism and domination does not matter that much. Some of my friends create elaborate metanarratives in their own families. Corporations, private associations, and schools do that all the time. And, finally, many individuals produce utterly dominating internal discourse, where one main idea of the self excludes any sort of plurality within the person's inner world.

Lyotard (and Walzer) may object to this by saying that the plurality of independent discourses allows a person to move from one discourse to another to avoid possible totality of either one. However, this very ability to shift from one discourse to another, from one language game to another, goes against the idea of separate "pure" discourses. What is the point of changing language games if you cannot take anything from one to another if you cannot mix them together and speak across several ones? I also doubt that small language games are easier to escape than the big ones. The mechanisms of "terror" can essentially be the same within each small language game and within the grand narratives of modernity.

Again, plurality cannot be limited to only one level. What Lyotard does not properly address is that the plurality of discourses should go all the way down. This comes from his emphasis on unpresentability and incommensurability. He makes an attempt to show that difference among language games is significant, but the type of significance is tied to the degree of difference. As a consequence, by blowing this particular level of difference out of proportion, he dismisses other forms and levels of difference. For when you speak of incommensurability of discourses, to what exactly do you contrast it? Apparently, the assumption is that there exists full commensurability of statements within each discourse or each language game. Such an assumption is at the very least dubious.

There are some unpresentable things, asserts Lyotard. According to Bakhtin, nothing is ever fully presentable, in a sense that a true and full understanding is impossible. Any understanding implies co-authorship. In the moment of understanding, one who understands co-creates meaning with one who is being understood. Which in turn means that what Lyotard calls the *differend* is not an exception but rather a universal practice: any understanding includes misunderstanding; any presentation includes misrepresentation. This "gap" in understanding is omnipresent and does not necessarily lead to exclusion. In fact, this gap is the only thing that makes a conversation possible. The *differend* is not an obstacle but a condition of true understanding, because, according to Bakhtin, to understand something means to embrace two or more incongruous views on the subject. Thus only presence of what Lyotard calls *differend* makes understanding at all possible.

Lyotard assumes multiple but whole truths, while Bakhtin says that truths are not only multiple, but every one of them consists of a number of statements. Let us turn to his concept of truth in more detail:

> It is quite possible to imagine and postulate a unified truth that requires a plurality of consciousnesses, one that cannot in principle be fitted into the bounds of a single consciousness, one that is, so to speak, by its very nature *full of event potential*, and is born at a point of contact among various consciousnesses.[10]

A couple of clarifications need to be made. First, "unified" is better translated here as simply "one." Second, what Caryl Emerson translates as *full of event potential*, is actually one Russian word of Bakhtin's own invention, *sobytijna*. This is an adjective deriving from *sobytie*, which generally means *event* but literally translates as *co-being*. Bakhtin is not simply saying that truth arises momentarily as something happens (with this much Lyotard would certainly agree). He implies that 1) the truth can never be expressed as one statement, but it can be expressed as a certain set of simultaneous and contradictory statements; and 2) the truth is not a set of disconnected statements but a set of statements that came to certain interaction via their carriers in a course of an event.

The concept of polyphonic truth does not in any way imply anything like "the truth is somewhere in the middle." Quite to the contrary, Bakhtin explicitly rejected Hegelian dialectics with its idea of eventual synthesis of the opposites. The individual voices that make up the polyphonic truth never merge. In this regard Bakhtin definitely sides with Lyotard in his debate with Habermas. There is never a consensus, and consensus is not at all what validates the polyphonic truth.

Despite some similarities, Bakhtin's concept of truth also disagrees with Lyotard's. No one individual language game or discourse is capable of producing truth on its own just because no single voice has enough capacity to generate the truth. I cannot explicate the concept of the polyphony here at its full extent and will refer to Bakhtin's own work. Let us just try to think of truth as a number of simultaneous statements about the same thing without trying to reconcile or "average" them.

At this point Lyotard, without a doubt, would have asked, "What is the source of legitimacy of such truth, polyphonic or not?" How is it being distinguished from a non-truth? Indeed, if the truth is multiple statements, how do we distinguish it from a simple cacophony? Apparently, by denying internal consistency to the truth-statement, Bakhtin implied some other form of internal organization or connection between heterogeneous parts of the polyphonic truth. Simple mechanical juxtaposition of different points of view is no better solution than a metanarrative. Some of the less successful multicultural textbooks on U.S. history can serve as illustrations to this. Thus Bakhtin must show Lyotard some other "rules of the game" and than show that these rules do not exercise terror to exclude those who do not play according to the rules. Obviously, any concept of truth implies both existence and exclusion of false statements.

Bakhtin allows for one absolute, which he calls dialogue. Dialogue in his view is not merely a form of communication but the most fundamental human relation. At the end of his book on Dostoevsky he states: "To be means to communicate dialogically. When dialogue ends, everything ends.... All else is the means; dialogue is the end. A single voice ends nothing and resolves nothing. Two voices is the minimum for life, the minimum for existence."[11] Let me rephrase his logic: On one hand, no statement can claim truth without interaction with other, contradictory statements. On the other hand, no existing statement is refused to enter the big dialogue or the polyphonic truth. Yet for a statement to exist, it must be addressed to someone else. Statements and voices that do not possess this dialogic potential simply do not exist or have no significance. Thus at least statements that claim to be the absolute truth and thereby deny the possibility of a dissent are excluded when dialogue (in Bakhtinian sense) is the name of the game. This much exclusion may be problematic in itself, but it is something Lyotard should accept. Lyotard, for instance, presents Habermas's claims as invalid, therefore excluding at least one language game, one of modern rationality.

Am I creating another grand narrative of dialogue and polyphony with Bakhtin's help? Perhaps, not, because Lyotard explicitly defines metanarrative as a project, a certain vision of the future, the Idea, which has legitimating value.[12] Dialogue has no end and no other purpose but perpetuation of dialogue. Dialogue is a strictly non-teleological good. Bakhtin, not unlike Lyotard, rejects the linear time of modernity, where history has an end. Rather, he accepts the present as privileged time, as time of fullest existence.

Let me restate the description of the polyphonic truth: a number of statements will be considered to constitute a polyphonic truth when they are engaged in a dialogue. This means that the inclusion of all statements that allow themselves to be included will constitute the criteria of truth. In other words, if one wants to know the truth about something, one should attempt to solicit everything everyone has to say about it, make all these voices talk to each other, and include one's own voice as one among equals. One should listen to this big dialogue, not to get the main idea but only to get all the voices to address each other. There is always an element of the "dialogue of the deaf," when parties do not really hear each other. The ability to hear the truth depends on minimizing this effect. Everyone can probably remember such a high-intensity conversation when all the opposing positions present themselves as distinct and yet really address each other. At a certain point, one notices that in order to really talk, the voices should implicitly include each other, echo each other, so that the difference "travels down into depths," ultimately splitting every individual voice. And just before it falls apart again, the truth emerges as in musical polyphony, where the multitude of voices forms a higher of harmony.

Let us assume for now that the inclusion has some value. How then do we understand inclusion? For Bakhtin, inclusion would mean *mutual inclusion*, mutual penetration of different perspectives or voices. Lyotard, who defends purity of discourses, would find himself in basic disagreement with Bakhtin on this issue. The very point of plurality for Bakhtin is constant touching, shifting, penetrating, mutual inclusion of voices. His idea that the multiple voices never merge, never come to a grand ending of a grand narrative, does not in any way mean that the voices do not change each other. Quite to the contrary, the interaction is the truest moment of their being. To be changed is the destiny of all meanings we produce. One should speak in order to generate a dialogue. We must abandon this absurd desire to be fully understood or to express the truth. No one speaks in order to express truth. One should speak in order to provoke a response, so truth could be heard together.

In the end, Lyotard and Bakhtin both elevate diversity to the new status, making it a fundamental fact of human existence rather than a superfluous and temporary feature of the world. Nevertheless, they introduce substantially distinct understandings of diversity. Lyotard proves value of diversity by emphasizing the depth of difference. His diversity is a multitude of independent and incommensurable discourses. This is essentially a vision of disjoined diversity. Bakhtin, to the contrary, values diversity for its epistemological and ethical power. Difference is important for him, not because it is large but because it is more capable of capturing the truth. He does not address the degree of differences among various human agents, because diversity for him is unthinkable without engagement, without constant interaction. For Bakhtin, diversity is just another name for connectedness. In other words, Bakhtin implies that difference, just like sameness, is a form of connection.

Lyotard's version of diversity may present a serious problem for education. What is the justification for teaching? Education involves changing someone else's view of the world, but how is it possible without imposing overarching totalizing truths? It is fairly obvious that any school houses a multitude of language games and discourses. Some of them, like adolescent slang, are designed specifically to keep adults out. Youngsters invest significant energy into inventing new code words and learning the words invented by peers in order to protect the independence of their linguistic territory. On top of this, more and more students maintain and support their ethnic and racial identities, making it clear that teachers' authority will not transgress the group boundaries. Lyotard suggests that we respect such boundaries and keep the language games separate. This contradicts the very idea of teaching, for teaching involves crossing the boundaries between language games—crossing not in a sense of a light passing between them but crossing for the purpose of changing. Teachers either invade their students' discourses or cease to be teachers.

Bakhtin's version of diversity portrays a difference that allows for active interaction. The new status of diversity does not mean we leave our students alone in fear of imposing another grand narrative upon them. As I tried to show, difference does not arise and does not exist without the other, who is the co-author and attends to this difference. When my student wants to assert difference of his or her way of life from mine, it is my duty to engage, challenge, "distort" (which really means "co-author") his or her vision of difference. One can either invade other discourses or keep away from them. But these are not all the choices. One can invade with a purpose of destroying or with a purpose of engaging in dialogue.

Diversity makes sense when it implies engagement. But more than that, any group *must* allow for internal diversity, otherwise we simply break the metanarratives of modernity into a number of baby modernities, each capable of a little Auschwitz. Teachers must not be in awe of difference; they must instead develop a respectful but inquisitive stance toward it. Teachers should not be afraid to misunderstand, misinterpret, or corrupt someone else's culture. Rather, education is only possible as intense dialogue, where different voices intensely interact, change, and never merge. A teacher, walking down the school hallways, should keep in mind that his or her task is neither to reduce diversity nor to stand still watching diversity grow. A teacher's role is to convert it from simple diversity into diversity of the connected.

NOTES

[1] J.-F. Lyotard, *The Postmodern Condition* (Minneapolis: University of Minnesota Press, 1988), xxiv.

[2] J.-F. Lyotard, *The Postmodern Explained* (Minneapolis: University of Minnesota Press, 1993), 30-31.

[3] Mikhail Bakhtin, *Problems of Dostoevsky's Poetics* (Minneapolis: University of Minnesota Press, 1984) 82.

[4] Caryl Emerson, *The First Hundred Years of Mikhail Bakhtin* (Princeton, NJ: Princeton University Press, 1997), 212.

[5] Bakhtin, *Problems of Dostoevsky's Poetics*, 81.

[6] Lyotard, *The Postmodern Condition*, 66.

[7] J.F. Lyotard, J.L. Thébaud, *Just Gaming* (Minneapolis: University of Minnesota Press, 1985), 106.

[8] Lyotard and Thébaud, *Just Gaming*, 96.

[9] Michael Walzer, *Spheres of Justice* (New York: Basic Books, 1983).

[10] Bakhtin, *Problems of Dostoevsky's Poetics*, 81.

[11] Bakhtin, *Problems of Dostoevsky's Poetics*, 252.

[12] Lyotard, *The Postmodern Explained*, 50.

Chapter 14.
Multiculturalism, Postmodernism, and Critical Theory

Multicultural education theory sits uneasily between two philosophical chairs, one of postmodernism and one of critical theory. This is not the most comfortable position to be in, which makes multiculturalism quite vulnerable to various criticisms. This chapter, first, shows that such a foundational gap does indeed exist. Next, I argue that this gap cannot be bridged unless both of the philosophical components are revised. And finally, I attempt to outline how these components can be reworked with the help of Bakhtin's concepts of dialogue and polyphony. In other words, I am not interested in shifting multicultural education onto one chair or the other; rather, I am looking for a way for it to sit comfortably on both chairs rather than between them.

Some may object right from the start that portraying postmodern philosophy and critical theory as two separate philosophical traditions may be unjustified. After all, theorists like Peter McLaren consider themselves to be critical postmodernists or postmodern critical theorists. Moreover, for the purposes of this chapter, I lump all the postmodernists together, which is an oversimplification. Nevertheless, from the point of view of multicultural theory, one can assume the existence of two distinctive theoretical trends or two general directions of thought that could be called "postmodernism" and "critical theory" for the sake of convenience. My focus is not on properly defined theoretical concepts but on what one may call philosophical traditions if this is applicable to fairly recent theoretical developments. If the words "postmodernism" and "critical theory" mean anything at all, this is a fair play.

The fact that multicultural education includes some heterogeneous elements of postmodernism and critical theory is not especially controversial. For instance, Sonia Nieto writes that multicultural education both affirms pluralism and promotes the democratic principles of social justice.[1] However, she does not perceive it as a problem. Numerous other examples might be given of the same attitude: pluralism and critique of the Western canon, on one hand, peacefully coexist with adherence to critical theory with its liberatory metanarratives and claims of universal justice on the other. I am not saying that coexistence, or sitting on two chairs at once is impossible, impractical, or somehow wrong. The only comment I want to make is that it cannot be viewed as unproblematic for the reasons that follow.

The evidence of the theoretical ambivalence of multicultural theory is easily obtainable from external critics. David Sacks and Peter Thiel presented their charge against multicultural education as it was and is carried out at Stanford in *The Diversity Myth*.[2] The book is not only a good example of conservative critique of multicultural education practice, but it also raises certain related foundational issues that are of interest to this chapter. It is not my intention to judge whether such a critique is valid or whether it is sufficiently informed about what is really going on in the field of multicultural education. One can easily see a definite political agenda looming behind this critique, which I neither share nor consider being reasonable. One useful feature of such a critique is that because it misses some important nuances of multicultural theory, it arrives at basic questions that are not adequately answered by multiculturalists.

One of the main charges against multiculturalism is an accusation of relativism. This is certainly a common theme in critical literature on multiculturalism. Sacks and Thiel ask three fundamental questions:

> First, which groups (or cultures) count in the multicultural world? If it is said that they all do, then it may be asked: what are relevant criteria for distinguishing groups? Are Americans of Irish or Italian backgrounds multicultural groups worthy of 'proportional representation?' [...] More abstractly, since there seems to be no limiting principle, why are chess players not a group? ...[3]

> Second, how are differences between groups to be resolved? [...What] does one do when the desires of these groups conflict? If two groups are acting in a manner consistent with each one's own standards, what set of external standards exists to arbitrate disputes? Even if multiculturalists concede that this might be a theoretical problem, but claim that it is one that can be worked out in practice through compromise, they still cannot explain what to do with groups that reject compromise altogether. Who is to say uncompromising groups are wrong?[4]

Third, how are differences within groups to be resolved? If Chicanos, for instance, have a special 'perspective' to share, and if indeed most Chicanos can be found to agree on a particular issue, [...] what does one do with dissenters in the group who hold contrary opinions? [...] Which individuals within groups count?[5]

Finally, unable to find answers to these and other questions, authors conclude that multiculturalism is not what it claims to be, but, rather, a disguised form of radical political ideology of the Left.

Curiously, this critique completely misses the inconsistency of multicultural theory and becomes inconsistent itself. These critics charge multiculturalism with two supposedly mutually exclusive sins. How can one be both a relativist and a radical political activist? However, the lack of consistency is not the point here. Rather, the conservatives' anxiety demonstrates that multiculturalism surely appears to be an ideology, a certain movement with more or less defined political agenda. At the same time, its theoretical arguments often come from criticism of the universals, of the Western canon, of classical liberal thought.

From the critics' point of view, no one provides reasonable criteria for distinguishing groups "in the multicultural world." I must notice that this last charge is not entirely without merit. Despite a large number of works on multiculturalism, there is no widely shared understanding of criteria for distinguishing groups in respect to multicultural agenda. These groups are rather empirically defined for each individual country, which could be a pragmatic thing to do but which makes it difficult to evaluate claims of new groups to be considered in multicultural education.

In general, multicultural theorists are understandably reluctant to engage in discussions about their definitions of justice, democracy, and good life. Rejection of Western European imposed "universals" makes it a very difficult task to arrive plausibly at some new positive universals. This difficulty reflects the same tension between the liberatory narratives of justice and postmodern avoidance of the universals. Let me restate the question, how is it possible to appeal to such notions as social progress and justice and at the same time doubt the possibility of universal criteria equally applied to different cultures?

Further evidence of the philosophical trouble comes from disagreements between different branches of multiculturalism. For instance, Peter McLaren writes about conservative, liberal, left-liberal, and critical multiculturalism while clearly advocating for the last one to the exclusion of others.[6] He solves the problem by decidedly shifting the gravity center to the critical theory chair at the expense of the postmodern argument. Frank Margonis offers a similar vision of a critical theory in the age of the postmodern theorizing,[7] although he does not specifically focus his argument on multicultural education. He would probably object my lumping together Marxists and critical theorists like McLaren. However, for the purposes of this chapter I will consider all those who appeal to universalistic metanarratives of liberation and social justice to be under one big umbrella of critical theory. Margonis accepts charges of universalism and explanatory reductivism of the Marxist tradition as inevitable features of any "language of conviction" capable of generating real social change. Further, he acknowledges the power of the postmodern argument, but thinks it went too far:

> The postmodern prohibition of metanarratives is simply neglectful of the conditions of existence.... We must act daily, and our acts will serve good or ill. Our understandings and action will inevitably rely, to some degree, on oversimple generalizations about experience, humans, and society. Poststructural and postmodern critiques of totalizing theory serve as powerful checks on the arrogance of general theory, but that does not mean we can do without oversimple claims.[8]

Here I must say that European postmodernists like Lyotard, Derrida, and Foucault draw their verdict against metanarratives not only from a purely theoretical consideration. Their home continent has abundantly demonstrated in the last century, and beyond that any "general theory" always, without exceptions, regardless of the degree of its initial arrogance, becomes dangerous to human existence. They believe that what leads to Auschwitz are not one or another interpretation of nationalism or Marxism but the very content of the interpreted theories.

My own Russian sensibility tells me to be especially attentive to such an argument. A suggestion that Russian, East European, Chinese, Cuban, and other Marxist experiments were simply historical aberrations or products of immature interpretations of Marxism is not made explicitly any more but continues to be expressed implicitly. In fact, Russia alone attempted several different models of socialist society, and all these years remained internally a very complex society, with multiple forms of socialism in operation. Lenin, Trotsky, Bukharin, Stalin, Tito, Mao Tsetung, Khrushchev, Gorbachev, and others have undertaken serious theoretical attempts to revise Marxism. These were sophisticated, attentive to the reality, and creative attempts to implement Marxist theory. They all lead to concentration camps of some sort regardless of the leadership's intentions. A significant body of historical analytical work in the post-Soviet Russia argues this very point.

Now, the recent history of the United States' can prove the same connection between the "language of conviction" and various repressive practices. The enthusiasm about freedom, progress, and the Westward expansion helped to exterminate most of the native inhabitants of the continent. This nation, convinced of its civilizing mission, placed remaining Native Americans in boarding schools and tried to remake them into whites. United around the idea of fighting for democracy in the war, American people sent its compatriots of Japanese descent to internment camps. Radicalized by Senator McCarthy's activism, Americans engaged into a trivial witch-hunt. What makes one think that Marxism in America is somehow immune or can be made immune to such side effects? Rephrasing Margonis' assertion, I would reply that Marxist unreserved endorsement of metanarratives is also neglectful of the conditions of existence. This, of course, applies not only to Marxism, neo-Marxism, but to all critical theories that allow for metanarratives by making universalistic and reductionist claims.

Having said all this, I am not suggesting that the multicultural theory shifts completely from its critical theory chair onto the postmodernist one. Although I had trouble finding such a suggestion explicitly defined in the literature, it is plausible to imagine a tendency to go completely postmodern at the expense of the critical component. Here, both Margonis and McLaren would easily pinpoint the postmodernists' Achilles heel. None of the postmodern writers gives us a reason to act. They just are not useful in our dealing with very real problems of injustice and human suffering. They do very little to address racial or gender discrimination or to redeem inherent economic injustices of capitalism. Margonis is right, only large-scale organizing, impossible without the "language of conviction," can bring about tangible progress toward justice.

Moral arguments against the postmodern position can amply complement the political ones. Most multiculturalists set certain limits to pluralism on moral grounds, excluding what they consider to be oppressive or reactionary points of view. All multiculturalists, especially those of critical orientation, make implicit or explicit truth claims, thus setting certain limits to cultural pluralism. For instance, Sonia Nieto writes:

> A multiplicity of perspectives approach can indeed be an important strategy to use in multicultural education but, when used uncritically, it can result in accepting all perspectives as equally valid, no matter how outrageous. People and events can, in the process, lose their moral center. For example, some might call for "equal time" for the Nazi point of view during World War II or for the plight of White segregationists during the civil rights movement, claiming that all viewpoints have equal validity, including contentions that Holocaust never happened or that the impact of slavery in U.S. history has been given too much play in newer curricula.[9]

What is the criterion that allows us to include a curriculum on the impact of slavery and exclude the white segregationist viewpoint? The appeal to the moral center is the same in the Right as it is in the Left, although neither can plausibly justify its preferences for what is moral. Yet, this does not diminish the validity of Nieto's question.

This, of course, is a part of a larger philosophical problem raised by the postmodern debate on how one can be both a liberal and an ironist, as Richard Rorty puts it.[10] How can contingency of language, of selfhood, and of community be comprehended along with the need for human solidarity? How can we both value diversity and have moral grounds to stand on? Rorty himself does not see a point in attempts to synthesize the two polarities. From his point of view, one should be a liberal in one's public life and an ironist in one's private life. His is an elegant compromise that does not do much for the burning issues of multicultural education. Education does not know a clear delineation between the private and the public. A teacher cannot be a liberal the first period and an ironist the second when she or he constantly moves between the private and the public. In the context of education, the contingencies of the postmodern demand that teachers take moral stands.

It is clear that both the critical and the postmodern chairs have much to offer. It may be less clear that both have serious faults of their own, which I had hoped to demonstrate. I see no way to bridge them in any meaningful way without first revising both of them. The two philosophical chairs that multicultural education sits on need to be fixed first, before they could carry the weight. Critical theory remains a grand narrative and does include certain claims of universal truth. Multiculturalism will remain a suspect as long as it shies away from becoming a political ideology, like postmodernism, and trying to bring about justice, like critical theory.

One way to think about such reworking is drawing on the ideas of Bakhtin, who was neither a postmodernist nor a modernist. Moreover, he used an entirely different set of references to talk about difference, culture, and justice. Bakhtin places his peculiar concept of dialogue in the center of his world and arranges everything along the monological-dialogical continuum. I have tried to imagine what Bakhtin would have to say to a postmodern philosopher and to a critical theorist, based mostly on *Problems of Dostoevsky's Poetics*. This is, of course, pure speculation, because Bakhtin has openly commented on neither postmodernism nor Marxism. He noted, however, in the second edition of his Dostoevsky book,

> We see no special need to point out that the polyphonic approach has nothing in common with relativism (or with dogmatism). But it should be noted that both

relativism and dogmatism equally exclude all argumentation, all authentic dialogue, by making it either unnecessary (relativism) or impossible (dogmatism). Polyphony as an *artistic* method lies in an entirely different plane.[11]

This brief remark contains the seeds of his criticism of postmodernism (or relativism) and the critical theory (dogmatism). The two variations of the same monological approach, despite their apparent dissimilarities, nevertheless share certain assumptions. Indeed, postmodernists are pessimistic about a possibility of a true dialogue because, from their point of view, true understanding is impossible across various discourses or across language games. In the context of multicultural education, this means that there cannot be a dialogue across various cultures, because each culture has its own set of values and meanings that are not communicated across cultural boundaries without violating their authenticity. Critical theorists, however, tend to argue from a position of absolute justice that either needs no dialogue or views dialogue only as a vehicle toward general consensus (Habermas). This last interpretation of dialogue is unacceptable for Bakhtin, who saw it as an end, never a means.

Bakhtin would agree with postmodernists, who are asserting the irreducible multiplicity of human worlds, cultures, word games, languages, and discourses. Difference demands respect, and does not allow reducing itself. Difference resists being brought to a unity, to a synthesis. Indeed, there exist certain incommensurability of discourses; the *differend* is a real and fundamental condition of human existence. More strongly, we cannot be human unless we differ. The postmodern suspicion towards the grand narratives of modernity is fully justified.

The postmodern theorists undertook a strong critique of modernity's universalistic failures. However, the postmodern vision of human diversity remains within the monological realm. For instance, postmodernists assert that defining truths across discourses is impossible. Such an assertion implies that finding the truth is possible, in principle, at least *within* one particular discourse. The postmodern writers substitute the impossibility of universal truths for an impossibility of any shared truths among different discourses, cultures, or language groups. For Bakhtin, truth needs a multitude of bearers. A single mind cannot contain the truth; one voice cannot express it. Thus, Bakhtin's view of human diversity implies radical connection among various discourses, or various cultures.

> A culture discovers itself deeper and fuller only through the eyes of another culture (but it does so not in all fullness, because other cultures will come along, they will see and understand even more). Meaning unveils its depths while meeting and touching another alien meaning: as if a *dialogue* began between

them, a dialogue that overcomes isolation and lopsidedness of these meanings, these cultures.[12]

Postmodernism could be changed toward greater dialogicality without abandoning its suspicion of metanarratives. Viewing different cultures, groups, discourses as interconnected, perpetually redefining, and co-authoring each other does not cancel the general stance against metanarratives. The difference itself may be perceived as a form of connection. Postmodern suspicion toward metanarratives can still allow for one universal, the dialogue.

Dialogue in its Bakhtinian sense is a universal, but is not a project. It does not imply any particular goal, which would be characteristic of a grand narrative. It would be hard to argue that such a non-teleological ideal as dialogue may lead to Auschwitz. For Bakhtin meaning is born at the point of touching of different consciousnesses. He does not share the postmodernist assumption that if only one leaves the marginalized cultural groups alone, they will somehow define themselves from within and develop authentic identities. He thinks that lack of relations between people is as big an evil as the presence of domineering relations between them. He argues for the multiplicity of connection, which may go beyond the current postmodern thought but does not in any way negate the general thrust of the postmodern argument.

Critical theory's philosophical component should also be reworked. In Bakhtin's world, dialogue is the end and everything else is the means. It is possible to rework from this position one's understanding of oppression and justice. I cannot lay out a dialogical theory of justice in any detail here. My aim is simply to show that the notions of dialogue and polyphony are not hostile to the agenda of liberatory theories and, on the contrary, may enrich them.

Bakhtin's insistence that dialogue is the end in itself is not easy to accept. It raises many questions. Does the emphasis on the process condemn us to perpetual inaction? How do justice and the struggle for justice fit into this ontological concept of dialogue? To answer these questions, I want to first emphasize that the concept of dialogue Bakhtin initiated does not call for giving up actions, political actions for justice in particular. Primacy of dialogue does not negate the value of justice. However, justice becomes very important but is still one of many means toward dialogue. The dialogical definition of the good life is not based on social justice. I propose justice for dialogue, not dialogue for justice.

This is not a play on words. The history of the revolutionary movements of this century makes it obvious that revolutionaries never quite know what to do with justice when they get the power to establish it (regardless of how questionable their understanding of justice was in the first place). Their definitions of the good life were sorely lacking positive content. For me, the rhetoric of justice loses any credibility without reference to what is to come after justice is achieved. For instance, the prejudice reduction, one of the main aims of multicultural education, will greatly benefit from a discussion of what is to replace prejudice. Is it going to be intergroup engagement and a productive dialogue, a mutual distancing, or detached, formalized, and legally defined relations? Prejudice reduction is a very important precondition to human flourishing, but it does not constitute this human flourishing. The notion of dialogue is constitutive to the flourishing of humans (to the concept of a good life). A similar argument could be made for other agenda items for multicultural education.

The last thing I want to do is buy into a conservative argument that any struggle for social justice leads to radical extremism and ultimately, to bloodshed. Yet every struggle for social justice governed by a *single-voiced* theory did. The problem is not in narratives of liberation but in metanarratives of all sorts. As long as the polyphony is preserved in the discourse of justice, we are safe from "progress" that is uncontroversial and thus totalizing. In this respect, I should agree with Margonis when he states: "As a directive to government policy, the socialist conception of work is a limited ideal articulating the basics that governments should ensure; one need not take this conception of freedom to be an all-encompassing portrait of the good life."[13] However, it is far from clear what the relations are between the socialist conception of work and other competing views of social justice and other elements of the "good life" theory. Why and how is it limited?

Bakhtin's concept of polyphony provides just such a theory of mutual limitations. A socialist concept of social justice must be addressed to another, opposite theory such as the ideology of economic liberalization. Only two or more mutually contradicting and yet truly addressed to each other theories can constitute what Bakhtin calls the polyphonic truth. Unfortunately, it is out of the question for Margonis to include people who strongly disagree with the socialist concept of work in the dialogue about justice. In another example, he provides examples of truths that are "not difficult to discern. One such truth is that capitalism in the United States requires, as Marx argued, millions of unemployment workers to keep wages from going too high; thus capitalism ensures poverty."[14] I have no problem with such a truth itself; in fact, I tend to agree with it. It is what is not being said that is bothering me. From the dialogical point of view, such a truth cannot be stated while ignoring the existence of the ideology of a free market, that argues a very different point about the relations between the capitalism and human well-being. Polyphony allows for disagreement, but it forbids ignoring the opponent:

> For a word (and, consequently, for a human being) there is nothing more terrible than a *lack of response*. Even a word that is known to be false is not absolutely false, and always presupposes an instance that will understand and justify it, even if in the form "anyone *in my position* would have lied, too."[15]

The two philosophical chairs of multicultural education should and will remain separate and distinctive. Even if the revisions I propose actually take place, the two philosophical traditions will not agree with each other. Even a "dialogized" version of postmodernism will not satisfy critical theorists for the lack of the ultimate goal—removal of oppression. Critical theory (even more open to doubt and more attentive to the means of attaining its goals) will never become a truly postmodern type of thinking. The difference between the two traditions will and must remain.

In this chapter, we deal with the two philosophical traditions that have never considered each other beyond redemption. All we need is a more engaging mode of disagreement. At the heart of multicultural education is the dialogue about justice and dangers of metanarratives. We must replace the weak ambivalence of doubt and hesitation with a strong ambivalence of polyphony. One can imagine a multicultural education that conveys to students the fundamental contradiction of multiculturalism between the struggle for justice and an impossibility of a universal notion of justice. The message can be simplified, as Margonis rightly argues, but the simplification should only go as far as this last double-voiced contradiction. The multicultural theory should never be reduced to a single-voiced statement. Margonis is concerned that such a message may turn paralyzing rather than encouraging. I do not see why this must be so.

First, the differences between actions and words are exaggerated. As Bakhtin suggested, "A human act is a potential text and can be understood (as a human act and not a physical action) only in the dialogic context of its time (as a rejoinder, as a semantic position, as a system of motives)."[16] If an action can also be understood as a text, there are different degrees of dialogicality to such action/text. The point is not to move people to act but to increase the dialogicality of their actions.

Second, from my point of view, people are hesitant to act when they are uncomfortable with simple messages of both the Right and the Left. When I am told that a certain political program is just, fair to all, and will not bring about any negative consequences, I get nervous and feel like I am talking to a salesperson who promises to give something for nothing. The strong ambivalence requires courage and honesty. If you tell your audience that the justice may come at heavy cost, people will be more inclined to act than if you tell them that the journey you urge them to undertake has no cost. We can reduce the cost, but we neither can have it for free, nor can we afford to forgo the journey.

NOTES

[1] Sonia Nieto, Affirming Diversity. The Sociopolitical Context of Multicultural Education (New York: Longman, 1996), 307.

[2] David Sacks and Peter Thiel, *The Diversity Myth: "Multiculturalism" and the Politics of Intolerance at Stanford* (Oakland, CA: The Independent Institute, 1995).

[3] Sacks and Thiel, *The Diversity Myth*, 30.

[4] Sacks and Thiel, *The Diversity Myth*, 31.

[5] Sacks and Thiel, *The Diversity Myth*, 32.

[6] Peter McLaren, "White Terror and Oppositional Agency: Towards a Critical Multiculturalism," *Multicultural Education, Critical Pedagogy, and the Politics of Difference* (Albany: State University of New York Press, 1995), 35-45.

[7] Frank Margonis, "Theories of Conviction: The Return of Marxist Theorizing." *Educational Theory* 48, 1 (1998): 85-102.

[8] Margonis, "Theories of Conviction," 94.

[9] Sonia Nieto, "From Brown Heroes and Holidays to Assimilationist Agendas: Reconsidering the Critiques of Multicultural Education, " *Multicultural Education, Critical Pedagogy, and the Politics of Difference* (Albany: State University of New York Press, 1995), 41.

[10] Richard Rorty, *Contingency, Irony, and Solidarity* (Cambridge: Cambridge University Press, 1992).

[11] Mikhail Bakhtin, *Problems of Dostoevsky's Poetics* (Minneapolis: University of Minnesota Press, 1984), 69.

[12] Mikhail Bakhtin, *Problemy Poetiki Dostoevskogo* (Moscow: Iskusstvo, 1986), 354.

[13] Margonis, "Theories of Conviction," 98.

[14] Margonis, "Theories of Conviction," 101.

[15] Mikhail Bakhtin, *Speech Genres and Other Late Essays* (Austin: University of Texas Press, 1986), 127.

[16] Bakhtin, *Speech Genres*, 107.

CHAPTER 15.
DIALOGUE WITH EVIL

The assumption that I borrowed from Bakhtin is that dialogue is the end, and everything else is a means. In other words, Bakhtin seemed to reject any absolutes with the exception of dialogical relation. I thought and still do now, that this is a great idea, and that dialogue as a relation can effectively describe something very central to human existence. Among other things, I suggested that education must foster a student's ability to hear a multitude of human voices and maintain internal dialogue. To do this, one must develop an ability not only to attend to the other in dialogue but also to maintain and strengthen the other's argument. To maintain an ability of moral judgment, one has to keep one's enemy very much alive, both as a viable partner of dialogue and as an internal voice within.

Barbara Thayer-Bacon raised a question about a possibility and desirability of dialogue with evil:

> So we need to maintain and strengthen skinheads, because they have some truth to them, and we will learn more about ourselves and gain greater meaning, by dialoging with skin-heads, then by showing them false? [...] I would say, yes, you need to talk to the skinheads, but I would not say you need to strengthen their positions, there are many [other] people we can talk to gain greater understanding. The problem with the skinheads that makes them so dangerous is their unwillingness to recognize the need to dialogue. So what do you do with that?[1]

In other words, she asked how far I am willing to go with dialogue and whether some intrinsic limitations appear when dealing with not just another interlocutor but with people we perceive to be evil. The question leads to several related questions: Should one attempt to enter dialogue with evil? If yes, on what terms and for what purpose? Can one have a dialogue with evil without compromising one's moral self? How can dialogue be possible if the evil side does not want to enter it? This ultimately poses a question to the concept of the relational pedagogy: What sort of relation should and can an educator have with evil?

It is not my intention to explore the concept of evil in great detail just because this chapter covers a relatively narrow issue of a relating to evil. To sketch out a general framework, I will use Andrew Delbanco's *The Death of Satan*.[2] He starts out with two opposite concepts of evil, Manichean and Augustinian. Manichean idea is an embodied, focused evil, the evil of a specific person, a mythical being such as Satan or of specific groups of people. St. Augustine introduced an idea of evil as privation, as absence of the divine. Delbanco offers historical analysis of cultural representations of evil throughout much of American history and remains a supporter of the Augustinian concept. He paints a broad picture of different incarnations of Satan marching through American history. The conclusion is quite compelling. Every time the Manichean concept of evil takes hold in America, its culture turns xenophobic and paranoid.

For the purposes of this book, I will accept the Augustinian concept, with one correction: evil is privation but not of the divine presence. Evil is ultimate monologue or absence of dialogical relation: "[T]he crusader who construes evil as malignant, external thing—a thing alien to himself—is by far worst kind of barbarian. The struggle of the twentieth century was to keep this proficient hater from seizing the world."[3] To put it simply, one becomes evil when one takes someone else to be completely evil beyond relation. In other words, when one shuts down a possibility of communication with those whom one considers evil, at this moment one becomes evil. Evil is absence of relation, an inability or unwillingness to relate to another human being. Evil is objectifying the other, taking an utterly monological stance toward the other. This, I believe, is an elemental cell of evil that proliferates into a multitude of cancerous cells of hatred, prejudice, indifference, and violence.

What should my relation to evil be if I do not want to become evil myself? A simple answer, which has been my assumption for some time, is that one needs to attempt a dialogue with evil. However, complications of such a position are great, and I will try to resolve at least some of them.

Explaining Hitler by Ron Rosenbaum[4] began as a book about Hitler, but then turned into a book about Hitler explainers. I find it fascinating, because it suggests how different strategies of dealing with evil turn out. One thing Rosenbaum makes clear at the beginning of his book is this: "the search for Hitler, the search to find coherence in the fragmentary surviving evidence, frequently led to a kind of searching *self*-examination, a reassessment of world history *and* of personal history."[5] This may sound like a platitude in our day and age, when subjectivity of all knowledge is widely acknowledged and recognized. However, it is different when you think of Hitler. A temptation to cast away evil is so great; it may blind us to the fact that our relationships with evil are so intricately tied to our relations to ourselves. The further one goes into the book, meeting all the heroes of Rosenbaum's book one by one, the greater is the temptation to never go near Hitler and the likes of him. Thus, the fear of evil sets in. Indeed, one lesson of Rosenbaum's account is abundantly clear— researching Hitler is a dangerous enterprise; our fear is well grounded.

One sad illustration of this danger is the story of an English historian David Irving. Irving began as a Hitler's biographer and then turned into a Hitler's defender and, subsequently, into a Holocaust denier (conditional denier but still a denier). His research curiosity brought him inside of what he calls "the Magic Circle" of surviving former Hitler confidants. "Once inside that Magic Circle, he encountered—he became a living example of— the continuing power of Hitler's spell."[6] One can imagine how Irving was trying to get close to the understandably frightened and unforthcoming world of Hitler's secretaries and adjutants. To gain their confidence, he had to like those people; in order to like them, he had to share their love for the Führer. Then come the explanations, how it is "to find twenty-five people of education, all of whom privately spoke well of him."[7] With a touch of disbelief, Rosenbaum reports Irving's findings that Hitler was well loved by children and dogs. He wonders how Irving's judgment became so blurred.

This story makes so much sense. In an effort to understand, to have a dialogue with someone, you must make certain compromises, and then more compromises, and finally you become much like the one you are trying to explain. This is one of the points clearly in support of Thayer-Bacon's doubts. Does not dialogue imply some sort of empathy with the other party? Is not empathy with evil equal to endorsement of evil?

Before I answer this question, let us consider alternatives. A very different story Ron Rosenbaum tells us is one of Claude Lanzman, the author of a well-regarded Holocaust documentary, *Shoah*. This is an example of another particular strategy in dealing with evil. Again, with some uneasiness Rosenbaum shows how dangerous an attempt to deal with evil may be. In his view, Lanzman becomes just as morally corrupt as Irving. He illustrates this point with a detailed account of a public attack Lanzman undertook against a Holocaust survivor who failed to understand Lanzman's film. A few other personal details portray Lanzman as an imposing, authoritarian, uncaring individual. However, his strategy in dealing with evil is enforcing a ban against any explanation. Lanzman strongly believes that explaining evil is forgiving. "And if you start to explain and to answer the question of Why," he says," *you are led, whether you want it or not, to justification.* The question as such shows its own obscenity: Why are the Jews being killed? Because there is no answer to the question of why."[8] Lanzman's maxim is "There is no why here" — "Hier ist keine warum." Curiously, he borrows this phrase from a Holocaust survivor quoting an SS guard who explained to prisoners the rules of life at a concentration camp. Lanzman chooses the words of his worst enemy to describe (or, rather, prescribe) a strategy of dealing with the evil of the Holocaust.

This problem of whether understanding is forgiving is central for Rosenbaum himself, and he never resolves it. Nevertheless, he comments that from his point of view "Lanzman leaps from epistemological inadequacy of explanation to condemning the *moral* inadequacy of those who try to explain."[9] I am not sure if such an objection is convincing. However unpleasant Lanzman's manners are, he makes a valid point. One cannot keep one's epistemology and ethics separate. To make an assumption that such an ultimate evil as the Holocaust can be explained in a sense that certain causes can be attributed to it is to take a degree of responsibility off the perpetrator.

Having said all this, I do not endorse Lanzman's solution, simply because he does not have one. Making a valid criticism of a particular epistemology does not yet make a positive epistemology. If we are to apply Lanzman's own charge to his own method, it becomes clear that *refusal* to understand, just like an effort to understand, has its own moral implications. Keeping far apart from evil makes it mysterious, inexplicable, and thus all-powerful. Okay, there is no why there, but how can I live with that? What can one possibly do to avoid another Holocaust? Moreover, not only the ethical and moral positions of Lanzman are questionable. His avoidance of evil surely affected his own moral self if we believe Rosenbaum's story. Lanzman's position is just as corrupt as Irving's, although they have chosen opposite strategies of dealing with evil. If you get too close, you may get attached to it. If you stay too far away, you do not really know it, and you may miss a moment when it becomes you.

I choose another story from Rosenbaum's book to illustrate what I would call a dialogical stance toward evil, a stance that avoids the dangers of proximity. Rosenbaum himself is quite uneasy about the strange story that he calls "A Frankenstein story: about a frightening creation that escaped from its creator. The creator is George Steiner, one of the foremost men of letters in the English-speaking world. His creation: a fictive character called "A.H." who is transparently Adolf Hitler."[10] Steiner's novel *the Portage to San Cristobal of A.H.* sparked intense controversy. What Steiner, essentially, did was to bring Hitler back to life using literary imagination. When he saw his creation for the first time on a stage, he was simply scared: "Until then, his Hitler was just the barest of initials on a page. Now, suddenly, "A.H." was a charismatic, full-bodied, full-blooded figure bestriding the stage, mesmerizing an audience with words of self-justification Steiner put in his mouth."[11] Steiner neither tried to explain Hitler nor avoided an explanation. He did something entirely different; he entered into a dialogue with Hitler.

Rosenbaum repeatedly laments that it seems to be impossible to explain Hitler, no matter what the approaches of doing so (there are many more attempts of explanation described in his book than I mentioned). "How do you explain a person anyway?" asks Emil Fackenheim, one of Rosenbaum's interlocutors. Unfortunately, he does not further pursue this question that seems to be of high importance to me. Yet explaining someone is not the same as understanding. One cannot possibly explain another, and one cannot understand with the help of explanation. Understanding of another human being is only possible as a process of dialogue. Steiner's Hitler had to explain himself. The problem is that he explained himself too well.

I will again use writings of Bakhtin, who, unlike Rosenbaum, was very much interested in the question of human inexplicability. He wrote that certain aspects of human beings always escape explanation. While Rosenbaum thinks that only "larger than life" historical figures, like Jesus and Hitler, may not be fully explainable,[12] for Bakhtin, no one is fully explainable. Moreover, he places this part of us that is unpredictable and unexplainable at the very core of human existence. Whatever is not definable is exactly what defines us.

> A man never coincides with himself. One cannot apply to him the formula of identity A=A. In Dostoevsky's artistic thinking, the genuine life of the personality takes place at the point of non-coincidence between a man and himself, at his point of departure beyond the limits of all that he is as a material being, a being that can be spied on, defined, predicted apart from its own will, "at second hand." The genuine life of the personality is made available only through a dialogic penetration of that personality, during which it freely and reciprocally reveals itself.
>
> The truth about a man in the mouths of others, not directed to him dialogically and therefore a *secondhand* truth, becomes a *lie* degrading and deadening him, if it touches upon his "holy of holies," that is, "the man in man."[13]

Bakhtin contrasts two Russian writers to emphasize the point. He describes Gogol's *Overcoat* as a description of a clerk. It is a vivid, detailed, and convincing description. However, Dostoevsky's hero Devushkin is a clerk who read the *Overcoat,* who had recognized himself and is outraged. "He felt himself to be hopelessly predetermined and finished off, as if he were already quite dead, yet at the same time he sensed the falseness of such an approach."[14] Such objectifying approach is not only morally deficient, but also unproductive. "*In a human being,*" writes Bakhtin, "*there is always something that only he himself can reveal, in a free act of self-consciousness and discourse, something that does not submit to an externalizing secondhand definition.*"[15]

If we are accessible to each other only through the sphere of the dialogical, then this is the only way to confront evil. And as I have already argued, to avoid dealing with evil is to invite it in. I must point out though that dialogue is not empathy and does not imply love or sympathy. What it does imply though is giving the other a full voice, it is taking one's opponent very seriously. Dostoevsky could serve as an example in this respect. In his novels, evil thoughts are shown from inside and spoken through the full voice of their bearers. His villains are extremely articulated, willing to engage into conversations, and do not seem to be evil to themselves. The voice of Dostoevsky is not absent from his novel, but it is given the same rights of presence as those of his heroes. He, just like Steiner, was not afraid.

What happens in our lives though is that we do not take our opponents seriously, justifying it by the fact that they do not want to talk to us. Thayer-Bacon was quite right that skinheads are not interested in dialogue, and this is why they are so dangerous. And even if they did want to talk to us, racists are normally not half as educated and articulated as university professors. They simply cannot sustain the level of dialogue we find interesting. From their point of view, we are not interested in dialogue with them. Therefore, instead of using our imagination to construct a stronger version of them, we walk away. Yet I contend that it is very easy to win an argument with an intellectually weak opponent, and the value of such victory is low. It is easy to argue with dead Hitler but immeasurably more difficult to argue with the live one. We must treat Hitler in a discourse that, according to Bakhtin, "is organized as a discourse about *someone actually present,* someone who hears him (the author) and *is capable of answering him.*"[16] For our moral victories to count we should struggle with the strongest version of evil possible, even if for that we have to invent it or to bring it back from the dead.

I understand that this is a very hard step to take. For a victim of oppression, it is hard if not impossible to enter a dialogue with an oppressor. An African American may have no desire to talk to a white supremacist. A hate crime victim may not be able to enter the inner world of his or her torturer. I would not insist that a Holocaust survivor engage in a dialogue with the Nazis. Some wounds are too deep to heal, and some gaps are too wide to bridge. In many circumstances, one's survival is more important than the sort of battle with evil through dialogue for which I argue. Nevertheless, history shows that the oppressed often become oppressors, and that real victims of evil sometimes become perpetrators of it. The hard truth is that being a victim does not reduce chances of becoming a victimizer. For an individual, it may not always be feasible to seek dialogical confrontations with evil. For whole groups of people it is a necessity.

But why bother? Why imagine, reanimate, and impersonate our enemies if we are not even talking to real people? Skinheads are not going to change if I talk to an imagined, stronger, more intellectual skinhead. My answer would be that in our relations with evil, the most important victory is an internal one. There are times when one has to fight physically or politically with evil without regard for a dialogical confrontation. However, any such victory is only superficial and does not last. In a very real sense, one cannot physically eliminate evil; one has to learn to confront it within. Maybe because so few people are willing to do what Steiner did, namely, to resurrect Hitler in order to confront him—maybe because of that there is still what Rosenbaum calls "the continuing power of the Hitler spell."[17] Amidst all the attention brought by the controversy surrounding Steiner's novel, he does not hear answers to what his Hitler had to say. In a certain sense, World War II is not over, since very few people have let Nazis state their case and have truly responded to them.

Sometimes I think about my grandfather whom I never met, because he perished in snowfields around Leningrad in the winter of 1944. What would he and countless others who defeated Nazism want of me? I do not think he wanted me become like him. Rather, he wanted me not to become like his enemy. For a war to make any sense there needs to be a continuation of dialogue with evil, a dialogue that would prevent it from returning. When in the early eighties, just before the Perestroika, Soviet society was gradually moving toward some sort of fascism, I almost failed him. It happened because as a nation we did not then come to terms with the fact of the kinship we have with our epic enemy, the German Nazism.

The same applies to many aspects of American history. A political battle against segregation is over, but the whole war is hardly won, because racism was never really heard, and therefore still exists in the minds and hearts of millions. A battle for women's reproductive rights is almost over, yet a true dialogue between the sides never existed. I am writing this in the aftermath of the September 11 attacks and can only imagine future confrontations that I hope will be more successful in destroying evil than in creating it. Right now, very few people are interested in hearing the terrorists' case; the logic of staying away from evil creates more evil.

Violence or direct political coercion directed to evil, no matter how justified, is senseless unless one sees a connection between the external evil and one's own psyche. The connection between one's psyche and one's perception of evil has been discussed extensively in psychoanalytic literature. Carl Jung stated this idea with great precision: "Anything that disappears from your psychological inventory is apt to turn up in the guise of a hostile neighbor, who will inevitably arouse your anger and make you aggressive."[18] This is why we take challenge of evil one step further, when we create it in our imagination, this is when we really confront evil. Evil is like us and it is us.

Elisabeth Young-Bruehl explicates this general idea with detail and precision in her *The Anatomy of Prejudices*.[19] She offers her critique of pure overgeneralization of prejudices. There is no one kind of prejudice, as there is no "prejudiced personality." Instead, a number of prejudices associate each with its own character type. Hysterics, obsessionals, and narcissists each produces their own particular kind of evil. What is important for me here is the realization that the same sorts of experiences that form one or the other type of prejudice are common to everyone else. In other words, we all have elements of prejudice within our psyche. When I say "evil is like us," I do not mean that people who we perceive as undoubtedly evil share with us many common human qualities. Rather, I want to emphasize that we all possess many of the qualities that make them monsters. The similarity is not in our humanity but in our monstrosity. One of the main reasons we are afraid to deal with evil is precisely this: in a fierce racist's personality we recognize our own little demons of hysterical desire. In an anti-Semite, we read our own obsessions. A sexist resonates with our own narcissistic side.

Dialogue with evil is possible only if it has an inner component, directed to one's own self. In order to address the other fully as Thou, one has to have a way of connecting the other with resources of one's inner self. For imagined Hitler to come across as truly alive, Steiner had to explore his own inner Hitler. This may strike one as too grand of an example. Yet consider a teacher who cannot understand his student's aggression mainly because he does not understand his own aggression. In order for me to create a racist, for example, as a partner in dialogue, I need to draw on my own resources, so that he comes out convincingly strong. The only way to do it is to find a racist within me, in my subconsciously motivated actions, my dreams, my anxieties. This may strike one as a dangerous game to play; yet I maintain, all the other strategies of dealing with evil are more dangerous.

This works the other way as well. One cannot deal with one's own inner problems unless somebody else is involved as a partner in dialogue. To simplify greatly, one cannot recognize one's own prejudice unless some other person with a more profound case of the same prejudice is involved. I will argue that prejudices spread and strengthen when their most outspoken bearers are marginalized and pushed outside the main public discourse.

If I may generalize broadly, the problem with psychoanalysis is in its assumption that the subconscious is ultimately beyond reach. With id, we cannot have anything resembling dialogue. I am not implying that what Freud has come to call the subconscious is identical to evil. Rather, our relations with evil and our ability to deal with evil in others and in ourselves are intricately connected to mysterious processes inside of our psyche. Many theorists of psychoanalysis seem to agree with the suggestions that while we may understand what our subconscious tells us, there is no way of direct communication with it. Id, like a skinhead, does not listen. All we can do is to work around it, trying to accommodate our conscious mind to the powerful and uncontrollable drives of id. If this is true, my project of dialogue with evil may become impossible. I want to propose that the only effective way of dealing with evil is a dialogical encounter with it. Such an encounter is impossible without sustaining an inner dialogue within the self, which looks questionable in light of psychoanalytic assumptions.

Yet no one denies that one can change relations with one's psyche. The whole thrust of psychoanalysis is toward therapy, toward changing the hidden psychic structures. The strategy that analysts use is not unlike what I propose we use while talking to evil that does not want to talk to us. Just as we can use our imagination to create an opponent, we can create a representation of our subconscious within the limits of our conscious self. The Id can have its ambassador in the ego. The point is, we probably cannot do each of the two processes in isolation. We cannot get through to the other, without accessing our subconscious; yet we also cannot access our subconscious without entering into dialogue with the other. The only thing I want to suggest is that dialogue with mean others may be in many cases more important for our psyche than dialogue with a nice, understanding therapist.

As with many other issues, bringing the problem of evil into the educational realm makes it more visible. At a conference roundtable, a minority colleague said that she has no desire to talk to racists, and sees no point to it. "Would you still want us to talk to their children?" Charles Bingham, who sat at the same table, replied. While children are not immune to evil, it seems impossible to shut them out of the classroom conversation. This would jeopardize the entire educational enterprise. An educator that wants to reduce the amount of evil in the world must learn to engage into dialogical relations with what she or he perceives to be evil in students. At the same time, an important educational aim is to introduce students to the world of dialogical relations with other people, not excluding those who the students perceive to be evil.

NOTES

[1] Barbara Thayer-Bacon, private correspondence to the author, May 1998.

[2] Andrew Delbanco, *The Death of Satan: How Americans Have Lost the Sense of Evil* (New York: Farrar, Straus and Giroux, 1995).

[3] Delbanco, *The Death of Satan*, 183.

[4] Ron Rosenbaum, *Explaining Hitler: The Search for Origins of His Evil* (NewYork: Random House, 1998).

[5] Rosenbaum, *Explaining Hitler*, 93.

[6] Rosenbaum, *Explaining Hitler*, 227.

[7] Rosenbaum, *Explaining Hitler*, 229.

[8] Rosenbaum, *Explaining Hitler*, 260.

[9] Rosenbaum, *Explaining Hitler*, 260.

[10] Rosenbaum, *Explaining Hitler*, 300.

[11] Rosenbaum, *Explaining Hitler*, 301.

[12] Rosenbaum, *Explaining Hitler*, xxiv.

[13] Mikhail Bakhtin, *Problems of Dostoevsky's Poetics* (Minneapolis: University of Minnesota Press, 1984), 59

[14] Bakhtin, *Problems of Dostoevsky's Poetics*, 58.

[15] Bakhtin, *Problems of Dostoevsky's Poetics*, 58.

[16] Bakhtin, *Problems of Dostoevsky's Poetics*, 63.

[17] Rosenbaum, *Explaining Hitler*, 227.

[18] *Jung on Evil*. Selected and introduced by Murray Stein (Princeton, NJ: Princeton University Press, 1996), 179.

[19] Elisabeth Young-Bruehl, *The Anatomy of Prejudices* (Cambridge, MA: Harvard University Press, 1996).

RELATION AND PRAXIS:
A CONCLUSION

Pedagogy of relation claims that what we do in education is less important than the sort of relations we develop. This does not mean devaluing action. The set of practices associated with education include teaching, management, educational policy making, and reforming. Paying attention to the relational side of education does not mean that these practices become less important or should be pursued less actively. Human relations are distinctly different from behavior, but they are definitely of the world of praxis. Praxis here is the totality of human practices understood in connection with many layers of human relations. In other words, praxis is actions plus relations. What I advocate is the positive contextuality of action. Handing out a detention slip, calling a parent, introducing a new policy, or pushing for a reform—all these actions will take different meaning and will produce different effects in different relational contexts. No action is good or bad, effective or futile, ethical or unethical without taking into consideration the relational dimension.

One can clearly see the danger of relativization here. Who gets to interpret the relational component of a decision? Can we establish reasonable guidelines to such interpretations? How can individuals be held accountable? How do we avoid overwhelming subjectivity in decision-making? These are all valid concerns, and it would be very audacious of me to imagine that this book alleviates them. Yet what we have now is mostly behavioral conventions—certain behaviors will result in certain consequences and results for all parties involved. Such conventions may be crude, my opponents will admit, but they are effective in most cases. However, the fact that we do not yet have adequate language to describe relations does not mean that such a language is impossible to develop in principle. Of course, any description invites simplification. The new relational conventions that would guide education will also be crude. Nevertheless, in the educational realm, even crude tools of relational analysis will prove to be much more useful than the most sophisticated behavioral controls. This has to do with the specifics of educational sphere I tried to outline.

Relativism obliterates responsibility, because all actions are deemed to be equally valid. Contrary to that, relationism extends responsibility to new territory; one has to answer not only for what one did but also for what one's actions actually meant to specific others in a specific situation. Such practices involve dialogical engagement, which ensures that any action is born of dialogue with others.

BIBLIOGRAPHY

Alston, Kal. "So Give Me Love, Love, Love, Love, Crazy Love: Teachers, Sex, and Transference?" *Philosophy of Education 1998* (http://w3.ed.uiuc.edu/EPS/PES-Yearbook/1998/alston.html).

Bakhtin, Mikhail. *Problems of Dostoevsky's Poetics.* Minneapolis: University of Minnesota Press, 1984.

———. *Problemy poetiki Dostoevskogo.* Moscow: Sovetskii Pisatel', 1963.

———. *Speech Genres and Other Late Essays.* Austin: University of Texas Press, 1986.

Baliasnaya, Liudmila, ed. *Vospitatel'nye sistemy sovremennoy shkoly: Opyt, poiski, perspektivy [Educational Systems in Contemporary Schooling: Experiences, Explorations, Perspectives].* Moscow: Russian Educational Academy, Institute for Educational Theory and Pedagogy, 1995.

Bandura, Albert. *Social Foundations of Thought and Actions: A Social-Cognitive Theory.* Englewood Cliffs, NJ: Prentice-Hall, 1986.

Beck, Clive. "Difference, Authority and the Teacher-Student Relationship." *Philosophy of Education 1994* (http://www.ed.uiuc.edu/EPS/PES-Yearbook/94_docs/BECK.HTM).

Becker, Gary S. *Human Capital: A Theoretical and Empirical Analysis, with Special Reference to Education.* Chicago: The University of Chicago Press, 1993.

Biesta, Gert. "Education/Communication: The Two Faces of Communicative Pedagogy." *Philosophy of Education 1995* (http://www.ed.uiuc.edu/eps/pes-yearbook/95_docs/biesta.html).

Bowles, Samuel, and Herbert Gintis. "The Problem with Human Capital Theory—A Marxian Critique." *The American Economic Review,* 65, 2, May 1975: 74-82.

Brower, Jeffrey E. "Medieval Theories of Relations." *Stanford Encyclopedia of Philosophy* (http://plato.stanford.edu/entries/relations-medieval/), 2000.

Buber, Martin. *Between Man and Man.* London: Kegan Paul, 1947.

———. *I and Thou.* New York: Collier Books, 1987.
———. *The Knowledge of Man.* Atlantic Highlands, NJ: Humanities Press International, 1988.
Buchman, Margaret, and Robert Floden. "Coherence, the Rebel Angel." *Educational Researcher* 21 (1992): 4-9.
Burbules, Nicholas, and Suzanne Rice. "Dialogue Across Differences: Continuing the Conversation." *Harvard Educational Review* 61, 4 (1991): 401-402.
Chernov, Vladimir I. *Analiz philosophskikh poniatii [Analysis of Philosophical Categories].* Moscow: Nauka, 1966.
Child Labor. Wage and Hour Division of U.S. Department of Labor (http://www.dol.gov/dol/esa/public/youth/cltour1.htm).
Clinton, William. "The State of the Union." *New York Times*, 28 January 2000.
Cusick, Philip. *Inside High School: The Student's World.* New York: Holt, Rinehart and Winston, 1973.
Damon, William. *Greater Expectations: Overcoming the Culture of Indulgence in America's Homes and Schools.* New York: Free Press, 1995.
Delbanco, Andrew. *The Death of Satan: How Americans Have Lost the Sense of Evil.* New York: Farrar, Straus and Giroux, 1995.
Deuel, Jay. *Tai Chi Page* (http://www.utah.edu/stc/tai-chi/stories.html), 1997.
Dewey, John. *The School and Society. The Child and the Curriculum.* Chicago and London: The University of Chicago Press, 1990.
Diller, Ann. "Pluralisms for Education: An Ethics of Care Perspective." *Philosophy of Education 1992* (http://www.ed.uiuc.edu/eps/pes-yearbook/92_docs/Diller.HTM).
Ellsworth, Elizabeth. "Why Doesn't This Feel Empowering?" *Harvard Educational Review* 59 (1989): 297-324.
Emerson, Caryl. *The First Hundred Years of Mikhail Bakhtin.* Princeton, NJ: Princeton University Press, 1997.
Facts About Corporal Punishment. National Coalition to Abolish Corporal Punishment in Schools (http://www.stophitting.com/NCACPS/NCACPS_facts_about_corporal_punishment.htm#Punishment%20in%20U.S.%20Public).
Foucault, Michel. *Discipline and Punish: The Birth of the Prison.* New York: Vintage Books, 1977.
———. *The Care of the Self. The History of Sexuality*, Volume 3. New York: Vintage, 1988.
Freire, Paulo. *Pedagogy of the Oppressed.* New York: Continuum, 1993.

Friedman, Maurice S. *Martin Buber: The Life of Dialogue.* Chicago and London: The University of Chicago Press, 1976.
Gazda, George, et al. *Human Relations Development: A Manual for Educators,* Sixth Edition. Boston: Allyn and Bacon, 1999, 1973.
Giddens, Anthony. *The Transformation of Intimacy.* Stanford, CA: Stanford University Press, 1992.
Goodlad, John. *Educational Renewal: Better Teachers, Better Schools.* San Francisco: Jossey-Bass, 1994.
Goodman, Paul. *Compulsory Mis-education.* New York: Horizon Press, 1964.
Gordon, Calvin W. *The Social System of the High School.* New York: Free Press, 1957.
Harmon, Brian. "Truants' Parents May Be Charged." *The Detroit News* (http://www.detnews.com), 29 November, 1999.
Higgins, Chris. "Transference Love from the Couch to the Classroom: A Psychoanalytic Perspective on the Ethics of Teacher-Student Romance." *Philosophy of Education 1998* (http://w3.ed.uiuc.edu/EPS/PES-Yearbook/1998/higgins.html#fnB1).
Illich, Ivan. *De-Schooling Society.* New York: Harper and Row, 1971.
Indicators of School Crime and Safety 2000. National Center for Education Statistics (http://nces.ed.gov/pubs2001/2001017a.pdf).
Jackson, Philip. *Life in Classrooms.* New York: Teachers College Press, 1990.
Jung on Evil. Selected and introduced by Murray Stein. Princeton, NJ: Princeton University Press, 1996.
Kant, Immanuel. *Schriften zur Antropologie, Geschichtsphilosophie, Politik und Padagogik* (http://www-user.uni-bremen.de/~kr538/kantpaed.html).
Karakovskii, Vladimir, Liudmila Novikova, and Natalia Selivanova. *Vospitanie? Vospitanie... Vospitanie! Teoriia i praktika vospitatel'nykh sistem. [Character Education: Theory and Practice of Educational Systems].* Moscow: Novaia Shkola, 1996.
Kennedy, David. "Notes on the Philosophy of Childhood and the Politics of Subjectivity." (http://www.bu.edu/wcp/Papers/Chil/ChilKenn.htm).
Kingon, Jacqueline G. "A View from the Trenches," *The New York Times Education Life,* April 8, 2001, 37.
Kolominskii, Yurii L. *Psikhologiia vzaimootnoshenii v malykh gruppakh. [Psychology of Mutual Relations in Small Groups].* Minsk: TetraSystems, 2000.
Korotov, Viktor M. *Pedagogicheskoe trebovanie [The Educational Expectation].* Moscow: Prosveshchenie, 1966.

Kuhn, Thomas. *The Structure of Scientific Revolutions*. Third Edition. Chicago: University of Chicago Press, 1996.

Larkin, Ralph. *Suburban Youth in Cultural Crisis*. New York: Oxford University Press, 1979.

Learner-Centered Psychological Principles. American Psychological Association. 1997 (http://www.apa.org/ed/lcp2/lcp14.html).

Lightfoot, Sara L. *The Good High School: Portraits of Character and Culture*. New York: Basic Books, 1983.

Llewellyn, Grace. *The Teenage Liberation Handbook: How to Quit School and Get a Real Life and Education*. Eugene, OR: Lowry House, 1991.

Lyotard, Jean-François. *The Postmodern Condition*. Minneapolis: University of Minnesota Press, 1988.

Lyotard, Jean-François. *The Postmodern Explained*. Minneapolis: University of Minnesota Press, 1993.

Lyotard, Jean-François, and Jean-Loup Thébaud. *Just Gaming*. Minneapolis: University of Minnesota Press. 1985.

Mahaffey, Foyne. "Are We Accepting Too Much?" In *Rethinking Schools: Agenda for Change,* ed. by David Levine. New York: The New Press, 1995.

Margonis, Frank. "New Problems In Child-Centered Pedagogy." *Philosophy of Education 1992* (http://www.ed.uiuc.edu/EPS/PES-Yearbook/92_docs/Margonis.HTM).

——. "The Demise of Authenticity." *Philosophy of Education 1998* (http://www.ed.uiuc.edu/EPS/PES-yearbook/1998/margonis_2.html).

——. "Theories of Conviction: The Return of Marxist Theorizing." *Educational Theory* 48, 1 (Winter 1998): 85–102.

Martin, Jane R. *The Schoolhome: Rethinking Schools for Changing Families*. Cambridge: Harvard University Press, 1995.

Marx, Karl. *Capital*, Chicago: Encyclopedia Britannica, 1957.

——. *Die Deutsche Ideologie* (http://www.mlwerke.de/me/me03/me03_anm.htm#M1).

McLaren, Peter. "White Terror and Oppositional Agency: Towards a Critical Multiculturalism." In *Multicultural Education, Critical Pedagogy, and the Politics of Difference*. Albany: State University of New York Press, 1995, 35–45.

McLaughlin, Milbrey W., Merita A. Irby, and Juliet Langman. *Urban Sanctuaries: Neighborhood Organizations in the Lives and Futures of Inner-City Youth*. San Francisco: Jossey-Bass, 1994.

Meier, Deborah. *The Power of Their Ideas: Lessons for America from a Small School in Harlem*. Boston: Beacon Press, 1995

Microsoft Encarta Encyclopedia. ©1993-1996 Microsoft Corporation. "Child Labor."

More Education Means Higher Career Earnings. U.S. Census Bureau Statistical Brief (http://www.census.gov/apsd/www/statbrief/sb94_17.pdf), 1994.

Nieto, Sonia. "From Brown Heroes and Holidays to Assimilationist Agendas: Reconsidering the Critiques of Multicultural Education." In *Multicultural Education, Critical Pedagogy, and the Politics of Difference.* Albany: State University of New York Press, 1995.

———. *Affirming Diversity. The Sociopolitical Context of Multicultural Education.* New York: Longman, 1996.

No Child Left Behind, Executive summary. U.S. Department of Education (http://www.ed.gov/inits/nclb/part2.html).

Noddings, Nel. *Caring: A Feminine Approach to Ethics and Moral Education.* Berkeley, CA: University of California Press, 1986.

———. "Must We Motivate?" In Nicholas G. Burbules and David T. Hansen, eds., *Teaching and Its Predicaments.* Boulder, CO: Westview Press, 1997.

Novikova, Liudmila. I. *Pedagogika detskogo kollektiva. Voprosy teorii. [The Pedagogy of the Children's Collective: Theoretical Issues].* Moscow: Znanie, 1978.

Nussbaum, Martha C. *Love's Knowledge.* New York: Oxford University Press, 1990.

O'Keefe, Lisa, and Damon Krane. "The Free Student Press Project," paper delivered at 1999 Conference of the Institute for Democracy in Education, Athens, Ohio, 10/02/1999.

Oliver, Harold H. *A Relational Metaphysics.* The Hague: Martinus Nijhoff Publishers, 1981.

Paley, Vivan G. *The Boy Who Would Be a Helicopter.* Cambridge, MA: Harvard University Press, 1991.

Physicians Work the Longest Weeks. U.S. Department of Labor, Bureau of Labor Statistics (http://www.bls.gov/opub/ted/1998/dec/wk4/art03.htm), 1998.

Polanyi, Michael. *The Tacit Dimension.* Gloucester, MA: Peter Smith, 1983.

Poplin, Mary, and Joseph Weeres, Eds. *Voices from the Inside: A Report on Schooling Inside the Classroom. Part One: Naming the Problem.* Claremont, CA: The Institute for Education in Transformation at the Claremont Graduate School, 1992.

Power, F. Clark, Ann Higgins, and Lawrence Kohlberg. *Lawrence Kohlberg's Approach to Moral Education.* New York: Columbia University Press, 1989.
President's & Secretary's Priorities. U.S. Department of Education, (http://www.ed.gov/inits.html). Retrieved January, 2001, no longer on line.
Putnam, Robert D. *Making Democracy Work.* Princeton, NJ: Princeton University Press, 1993.
Ravitch, Diane. *Left Back: A Century of Failed School Reforms.* New York: Simon & Schuster, 2000.
Remnick, David. "The Exile Returns," *The New Yorker,* Feb. 14, 1994.
Rorty, Richard. *Contingency, Irony, and Solidarity.* Cambridge: Cambridge University Press, 1992.
Rose, Mike. *Lives on the Boundary.* London: Penguin, 1989.
Rosenbaum, Ron. *Explaining Hitler: The Search for Origins of His Evil.* New York: Random House, 1998.
Sachkov, Yurii V. "Sluchainost' formoobrazuyushchaya [Shaping Chance]." In *Samoorganizatsiya i Nauka: Opyt filosofskogo rassmotreniya [Self-Organization and Science: An Attempt of Philosophical analysis].* Moscow: Russian Academy of Sciences, Philosophy Institute, 1994.
Sacks, David, and Peter Thiel. *The Diversity Myth: "Multiculturalism" and the Politics of Intolerance at Stanford.* Oakland, CA: The Independent Institute, 1995.
Savage, Dan. "Fear the Geek: Littleton's Silver Lining." *Stranger* 8, 33, May 5–12, 1999.
Selected Employment Indicators. Bureau of Labor Statistics (http://stats.bls.gov/webapps/legacy/cpsatab4.htm).
Selivanova, Natalia, ed. *Vospitatel'naia sistema shkoly: problemy i poiski [School-wide Educational System: Issues and Research].* Moscow: Znanie, 1989.
Sidorkin, Alexander M. *Razvitie vospitatel'noi sistemy shkoly kak zakonomernyi protses. [The Development of School System: Driving Forces and Contradictions].* Candidate of Educational Sciences Dissertation. Moscow: Research Institute for Theory and History of Education, 1990.
——. *Posobie dlia nachinaiushchikh robespierov [Beginner revolutionary's guide].* Moscow: Znanie, 1990.
——. "The Communard Movement in Russia." *East-West Education,* 16, Fall 1995, 2: 148–159.

———. *Beyond Discourse: Education, the Self, and Dialogue*. Albany, NY: SUNY Press, 1999.
Slavin, Robert E. *Educational Psychology*, Fifth Edition. Boston: Allyn and Bacon, 1997.
Statistical Abstract of the United States, 1999 Edition. U.S. Census Bureau (http://www.census.gov/prod/99pubs/99statab/sec04.pdf).
Stipek, Deborah. *Motivation to Learn*. Second Edition, Boston: Allyn and Bacon, 1988, 1993.
Tanabe, Clifton. "Social Power and Education," *Philosophy of Education 1998* (http://www.ed.uiuc.edu/EPS/PES-Yearbook/1998/tanabe.html).
Totten, Samuel. *Cooperative Learning: A Guide to Research*. New York: Garland, 1991.
Uemov, Avenir. *Veshchi, svoistva i otnosheniia [Things, Qualities, and Relations]*. Moscow: Izdatelstvo Akademii Nauk SSSR, 1963.
Universal Declaration of Human Rights. U.N. Office of the High Commissioner for Human Rights (http://www.unhchr.ch/udhr/lang/eng.htm).
Violence and Discipline Problems in U.S. Public Schools: 1996-97. National Center for Education Statistics (http://nces.ed.gov/pubs98/violence/98030005.html).
Walzer, Michael. *Spheres of Justice: A Defense of Pluralism and Equality*. New York: Basic Books, 1983.
Westbrook, Robert. *John Dewey and American Democracy*. Ithaca and London: Cornell University Press, 1992.
Who Is Minding the Kids? Bureau of the Census Statistical Brief (http://www.census.gov/apsd/www/statbrief/sb94_5.pdf).
Willis, Paul E. *Learning to Labor: How Working Class Kids Get Working Class Jobs*. New York: Columbia University Press, 1981, 1977.
Wolf, Shelby A., Hilda Borki, Rebekah L Elliott, and Monette C. McIver. "'That Dog Won't Hunt!': Exemplary School Change Efforts Within the Kentucky Reform," in *American Educational Research Journal*. Summer 2000, 37, 2, 349-393.
Workplace Violence, 1992-96. U.S. Department of Justice, Bureau of Justice Statistics (http://www.ojp.usdoj.gov/bjs/pub/pdf/wv96.pdf).
Young-Bruehl, Elisabeth. *The Anatomy of Prejudices*. Cambridge, MA: Harvard University Press, 1996.

INDEX

A

Absurdity of school life, 12, 124, 125
Accountability, 4, 36, 58, 81, 131, 132
Action as text, 182
Alston, Kal, 107, 108, 110, 111, 115
Ambiguity, 158
Ambivalence, 174, 182
Aristotle, 93
Athena, 108, 109, 110, 114
Athenaic relation, 6, 109, 110, 111, 112, 113, 114, 125, 147
    Definition, 109
Auschwitz, 171, 176, 180
Authority
    And control, 53, 69, 140
    And exclusion, 22, 54, 55, 57, 58, 59, 69, 70
    And violence, 62
    Crisis of, 5, 53, 54, 55, 56, 57, 58, 60, 62, 73, 79, 87, 134
    Definition, 142
    Dialogical, 148, 149, 153
    In teaching, 139
    Monological, 145, 151
    Polyphonic, 146–47
    Traditional, 57

B

Bakhtin, Mikhail, 6, 91, 92, 98, 102, 145–150, 156–173, 178–185, 189, 190, 195
Bandura, Albert, 25
Becker, Gary, 26, 40
Behaviorism, 81, 82
Behaviorist, 81
Being
    And becoming, 42
Biesta, Gert, 86, 90
Bingham, Charles, 194
Bowles, Samuel, 27, 40
Brower, Jeffrey, 93, 102, 199
Buber, Martin, 85, 89–93, 102, 105, 115, 140–145, 148, 150, 162
Buchman, Margret, 158, 161
Bukharin, Nikolai, 176
Bullying, 64–68, 104, 105
Burbules, Nicholas, 25, 139, 150
Bush, George W., 36, 37, 41, 58

C

Capitalism, 32, 37–39, 55, 61, 69, 177, 181, 182
Care, 43, 63, 86, 97
Chernov, Vladimir, 93
Childhood, 42–48, 52
    And schooling, 44
Clinton, William, 35, 36, 41, 58
Coherence, 97, 154, 158, 186
    And consistency, 158
Collective, the, 117–120
Communard movement, 118, 119, 126, 204
Communism, 4, 38, 119, 155, 156
Connectedness, 158, 171
Conservatism, 56–60, 74, 174, 175, 181
Consistency, 152–154
    And exclusion, 155

And racism, 155
  Moral, 153, 155, 156
Constructivism, 82, 83
Core activity, 122, 124, 129, 130
  And relational field, 124
Corporal punishment, 54, 56, 57, 70, 71, 80
Critical theory, 85, 173–182
Cruelty, 54, 60, 127, 128, 155
Cusick, Philip, 66, 75

D

Damon, William, 56, 75, 153–157, 161
Delbanco, Andrew, 186, 195
Derrida, Jacques, 142, 176
Desire, 51, 106, 109–111
Dewey, John, 15, 21–25, 29, 35, 41, 51, 62, 70, 71, 75, 86
Dialogicality, 147, 159, 180, 182
Dialogue
  And changing self, 143
  And culture, 180
  And justice, 180
  And power, 142
  And relation. *See* Relation and dialogue
  As an absolute, 169
  Internal, 147, 157, 185, 192
  Internalized, 98
  Limits of, 185
Differend, 164, 167, 168, 179
Dionysus, 111
Diversity, 153, 158, 162–166, 170, 171, 178, 179, 184, 203, 204
Dostoevsky, Fedor M., 145– 150, 156, 158, 161, 172, 178, 184, 195, 199
Double message, 153, 154, 157, 159

E

Economy of relation, 104, 106

Education
  And evolution, 44
  And violence, 62
  As an academic discipline, 49
  As division of labor, 15
  As liberation, 35, 36
  As production, 14
  Compulsory, 34, 39, 42, 44, 48, 53, 63
  Definition, 12, 23
  Limits of, 24, 49, 51, 79
  Metanarrative of, 38, 51
Educational reform, 83, 84, 86, 126, 128, 129, 130, 132
Educational theory, 2, 3, 6, 7, 14, 21, 35, 50, 52, 53, 79, 81, 83–87, 91, 92, 99, 111, 117, 139, 156
  And practiee, 84
  Paradigm crisis, 84
Ellsworth, Elizabeth, 139, 150
Emancipation, 35, 37, 39, 51
Emerson, Caryl, 154, 164, 168, 172
Enlightenment, 35, 37, 51, 97, 164, 166
Epistemology, 97, 98, 99, 188
  And ethics, 157, 188
  Relational, 97
  Subject-object, 98
Eros, 106–111, 114, 125
Erotic capital, 112, 113
Erotic relation, 6, 109, 110,–113, 125, 147
  Definition, 109
Evil
  As monologue, 186
  Manichean and Augustinian concepts, 186
Existence
  Half-existence, 44, 47, 48, 51
  Human, 43, 44–48, 88, 92, 170, 176, 179, 185, 189
  In schools, 47

Institutionalized, 45, 46
Existentialism, 50, 125
Extracurricular activities, 105, 113, 133
Extra-economic coercion, 39, 55, 70

F

Fackenheim, Emil, 189
Family
  And relationships, 81
  As an institution, 57, 60, 79
Feminism, 85, 86
Floden, Robert, 158, 161
Foucault, Michel, 44, 48, 52, 55, 61, 68, 69, 72, 75, 80, 142, 176
Freire, Paulo, 35, 40
Freud, Sigmund, 107, 108, 150, 193
Furstenberg
  Frank, 154

G

Giddens, Anthony, 79, 80, 89, 108, 115
Gilligan, Carol, 85, 86
Gintis, Herbert, 27, 40
Gogol, Nikolai, 190
Good school, 73, 81, 84, 112, 113, 119–125, 129–133
  And effective school, 131
Goodlad, John, 84, 130, 134, 136
Goodman, Paul, 37, 41
Gorbachev, Mikhail, 176

H

Habermas, Jurgen, 86, 165, 168, 169, 179
Hegel, G. W. F., 3, 22, 168
Heidegger, Martin, 91
Higgins, Chris, 107, 108, 110, 111, 114, 115, 126
Hitler, Adolf, 186–192, 195, 204
Holocaust, 177, 187, 188, 191

Homo Lentus, 48
Human being
  Definition, 44
Human Capital Theory, 26–29, 35
Human existence
  Questionability, 46
Hybrid school, 6, 134, 135

I

Illich, Ivan, 37, 41
Imbalanced relation, 140, 142, 145
Incommensurability, 164, 167, 179
Integrity, 15–153, 156
Interhuman, the, 6, 79, 86, 92, 162
Irving, David, 187, 188
I-Thou, 92, 93, 140–145

J

Jackson, Philip, 69, 75
Jung, Carl, 192, 195, 201
Justice, 4, 34, 46, 110, 122, 166, 174–183

K

Kant, Immanuel, 35, 37, 40, 150
Karakovskii, Vladimir, 113, 121, 126
Khrushchev, Nikita, 176
Kilpatrick, William H., 15
Knowledge
  As a skill, 100
  Consumption of, 19
  Limits of, 151
  Polyphonic, 99
  Production of, 19
Kohlberg, Lawrence, 117, 126
Kuhn, Thomas, 85, 89

L

Labor
  Child labor, 34, 35

Labor power, 18, 28–35
  Value of, 28–32
Language game, 149, 164–171, 179
Language of conviction, 176, 177
Lanzman, Claude, 187, 188
Learning
  And Learning activity, 18
  As core activity, 133
  As doing, 122
  As forced labor, 37
  As labor, 3–35, 38, 113
  As production, 5, 13, 14, 15, 23
  Motivation, 6, 13, 17, 22, 24, 25, 59, 70, 79, 81, 82, 87, 127
  Motivation and ability, 59
  Motivation and relations, 87
Learning activity, 18–23, 26–34, 37–39, 53, 71, 79, 128
  And adult labor, 19
  Definition, 23
Lenin, Vladimir, 176
Leontiev, Alexei, 15, 122
Levinas, Emmanuel, 91
Liberalism, 35, 36, 166, 175, 178
Liberatory narrative, 175
Little Green People experiment, 12, 13, 15, 54
Local consensus, 165, 166
Lyotard, Jean-François, 142, 163–172, 176

M

Mahaffey, Foyne, 65, 75
Makarenko, Anton S., 117
Mao Tse-tung, 176
Marcuse, Herbert, 108
Margonis, Frank, 86, 87, 90, 97, 102, 140, 150, 175, 177, 181, 182, 184
Martin, Jane R., 33, 40, 85
Marx, Karl, 18, 19, 24, 25, 28, 29, 30, 31, 40, 150, 181

Marxism, 15, 24, 26, 28, 34, 37, 70, 130, 176, 177, 178, 184, 202
Material interest, 127
McLaren, Peter, 173, 175, 177, 184
McLaughlin, Milbrey W, 117, 126, 134, 136
Metanarrative, 53, 167, 171, 174, 176, 177, 180, 181, 182
Modernity, 3, 163, 165, 166, 167, 169, 171, 179
Monologism, 164, 165, 167
Moral judgment, 157, 185
Multicultural education, 173–182
Multiculturalism, 173–177, 182
  Critique of, 174
Mutuality, 6, 92, 93, 106, 108, 140, 142–148

N

Nazis, 191
Noddings, Nel, 20, 21, 25, 43, 52, 85, 86, 88, 90
Novikova, Liudmila I., 119–122, 126
Nussbaum, Martha, 49–52

O

Oliver, Harold, 91, 102
Ontology, 86, 88, 91, 92, 140
  Relational, 86, 93, 97, 140, 141

P

Paley, Vivan G., 146, 147, 148, 150
Pashkov, Alexander, 122
Pedagogy of behavior, 85
Pedagogy of relation
  And schools, 124
  Assumptions, 80, 86, 87
Peer relationship, 118
Philosphere, 123, 126
Polanyi, Michael., 100, 102

Polyphony, 6, 98, 145, 146, 151, 153, 156, 158, 159, 164, 168–170, 173, 180–182
  Internal, 157
  Moral, 153
Postmodern
  Definition, 164
Postmodernism, 162, 163, 173, 174, 178–182
  And Bakhtin, 164
Postmodernity, 3, 162
Power
  And authority, 142
  Definition, 142
Power asymmetry, 92, 139, 140
Praxis, 197
Progressive education, 20, 29, 32, 58, 59, 82, 117
  Conservative critique, 58
Progressives, 15, 21, 58, 59, 80, 135
Psychoanalysis, 192, 193
Pure relationship, 80, 108, 127
Putnam, Robert D., 136

R

Racism, 56, 154, 155, 192
Rationalism, 164
Rationality, 103, 166, 169
Ravitch, Diane, 56, 58, 59, 61, 87, 90
Relation
  And action, 85, 99, 197
  And activity, interdependence, 70, 124
  And dialogue, 92–93
  And difference, 162
  And existence, 94, 145
  And reality, 95
  And relativism, 94
  And things, 95
  And thinking, 95
  As the aim of education, 88
  Definition, 94
  In classroom, 99, 146
  Location of, 94
Relational dynamics, 110
Relational field
  And core activity, 124
  And reform, 129
  Definition, 122–23
Relational paradigm, 91
Relational transformation, 125
  Two models, 111
Relationship
  Unequal, 43
Relativism, 174, 178, 179
Rodgers, Carl, 140, 144
Rorty, Richard, 178, 184
Rose, Mike, 86, 87, 90
Rosenbaum, Ron, 186, 187, 188, 189, 191, 195
Russia, 5, 15, 38, 52, 56, 58, 107, 117, 118–122, 126, 133, 136, 168, 176, 199, 204

S

Sacks, David, 174, 184
Savage, Dan, 68, 75
School
  As educational institution, 128, 130, 131, 133
  Deep structure, 120, 130
  Definition, 21
  Police presence, 57
  Specificity of, 27, 49, 128
  Suburban, 57, 127
  Traditional, 60, 70
  Urban, 56, 57
School reform, 4, 128, 132
Schooling
  As forced labor, 55
  Elitist, 58, 59, 121
  Existential status of, 42

Limits of, 127, 131
Mass schooling, 5, 35, 39, 44, 48, 49, 54-58, 59, 60, 62, 118
Self, 96, 97, 122, 143, 151, 152, 153, 167, 193
  Definition, 97
  Moral, 157, 186, 188
  Postmodern, 153
  Relational conncept of, 96
Selivanova, Natalia, 121, 126
Simple humanity, 141, 143
Sizer, Theodor, 84
Slavery, 39, 45, 177, 178
Slavin, Robert E, 89
Soviet education, 56, 117, 119, 155, 156
Stalin, Iosif, 176
Steiner, George, 188, 189, 190, 191, 192
Student-teacher relationship, 81, 107, 108, 140
Systems approach, 120, 121, 129, 130

T

Teacher
  As author, 147
Thayer-Bacon, Barbara, 97, 102, 185, 190, 195
Thiel, Peter, 174, 184, 204
Tito, Iosip-Broz, 176
Trotsky, Leo, 176
Truth
  Absolute, 165, 169
  As dialogue, 98
  Dialogical, 159
  Polyphonic, 98, 158, 168, 169, 181
  Universal, 153, 164, 165, 166, 178
Truth claims, 165, 177

U

Uemov, Avenir, 93, 102
Useless things, in education, 5, 12–18, 23, 44, 53, 79, 132
Use-value, 24, 26
Utopia, 51, 58, 62, 127, 155
  And cruelty, 155
Utopias, 51

V

Value
  And utility, 28
Value, economic, 5, 18, 19, 22, 23, 26, 28–35, 39
Violence
  And education, 62
  Domestic, 57, 60
  Extent of, in schools, 64
  Indirect, 62
  Intrinsic and extrinsic, 63
  Legitimate, 57
  Peer, 63–74, 79
  Rational and irrational, 64–65, 105
  Systemic, 70
Vouchers, 58
Vygotsky, Lev, 15, 25, 122

W

Walzer, Michael, 25, 166, 167, 172
Wastebasket Economy, 13, 17, 18, 22, 39, 42, 46, 62, 71
Westbrook, Robert, 35, 41
Willis, Paul E., 40

Y

Young-Bruehl, Elisabeth, 192, 195